A Pennine Journey

Books by A. Wainwright

A PICTORIAL GUIDE
   TO THE LAKELAND FELLS:
   Book One: The Eastern Fells
   Book Two: The Far Eastern Fells
   Book Three: The Central Fells
   Book Four: The Southern Fells
   Book Five: The Northern Fells
   Book Six: The North-western Fells
   Book Seven: The Western Fells
FELLWANDERER
PENNINE WAY COMPANION
WALKS IN LIMESTONE COUNTRY
WALKS ON THE HOWGILL FELLS
A COAST TO COAST WALK
   (St Bees Head to Robin Hood's Bay)
A LAKELAND SKETCHBOOK
A SECOND LAKELAND SKETCHBOOK
A THIRD LAKELAND SKETCHBOOK
A FOURTH LAKELAND SKETCHBOOK
A FIFTH LAKELAND SKETCHBOOK
THE OUTLYING FELLS OF LAKELAND
SCOTTISH MOUNTAIN DRAWINGS:
   Volume One: The Northern Highlands
   Volume Two: The North-western Highlands
   Volume Three: The Western Highlands
   Volume Four: The Central Highlands
   Volume Five: The Eastern Highlands
   Volume Six: The Islands
WESTMORLAND HERITAGE
   (*limited edition; out of print*)
A DALES SKETCHBOOK
A SECOND DALES SKETCHBOOK
KENDAL IN THE NINETEENTH CENTURY
A FURNESS SKETCHBOOK
A SECOND FURNESS SKETCHBOOK
THREE WESTMORLAND RIVERS
A LUNE SKETCHBOOK
FELLWALKING WITH WAINWRIGHT
   (with photographs by Derry Brabbs)
WAINWRIGHT ON THE PENNINE WAY
   (with photographs by Derry Brabbs)

A PENNINE JOURNEY

A Story of a Long Walk in 1938

A. Wainwright

Michael Joseph

LONDON

First published in Great Britain by
Michael Joseph Limited
27 Wrights Lane, London W8
1986

British Library Cataloguing in Publication Data

Wainwright, A.
A Pennine journey.
1. Walking—England—Pennine
Chain   2. Pennine Chain (England)—
Description and travel
I. Title
796.5'22'09428   DA670.P4

ISBN 0-7181-2730-7

Typeset in Perpetua
by Wilmaset, Birkenhead, Wirral
Printed and bound in Great Britain by
Billings & Sons, Worcester

And all I have writ is writ,
Whether it be blest or curst.
O remember the little that's good
And forgive and forget the worst.

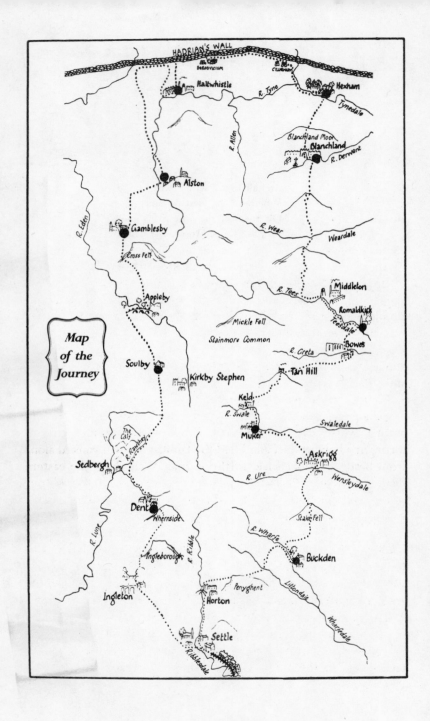

Map
of the
Journey

A PENNINE JOURNEY—FOREWORD

IN September 1938, events were moving to a crisis. Fear and apprehension prevailed throughout the country. War seemed imminent. News and conversations became concentrated on the single topic of a forthcoming conflict with Hitler: the press and our simple wireless sets gave us no respite, no peace of mind. The talk was of air raid shelters, fire drill, civil defence—and Hitler's screaming threats gave a frightening emphasis to our anxieties about the future. Everybody felt sick, upset, nervous. Nobody smiled any more.

There seemed no escape from the atmosphere of gloom and despondency, at home and at work and in the streets; things were getting worse day by day. But I was fortunate in having a fortnight's holiday due, and I fled the familiar scene. I walked alone from Settle in Ribblesdale to the Roman Wall along the eastern flank of the Pennines, returning down the west side. In the solitude of the wild Pennine hills, I found peace. On these desolate moors, war seemed incongruous. The larks sang their hearts out, the sheep grazed in perfect contentment, the sun shone on a tranquil landscape. During the whole journey, I never met another walker. Other people were preoccupied with preparations for war and I was a truant. I had the Pennines to myself, and they provided the comfort and reassurance I badly needed.

The spurious peace of Munich happened when I was midway on my travels and the cloud of apprehension lifted immediately. Like everyone else at the time, I blessed Mr Chamberlain. But the feeling of euphoria did not last long. I returned to official pronouncements about evacuations, barrage balloons, blackout restrictions, local defence volunteers, and so on ad infinitum.

In an atmosphere of acute urban depression, I found solace in memories of my escape to the hills, and I spent every free evening for several months going back there in spirit by recounting my experiences of the journey on paper. I wrote a book of my travels, not for others to see but to transport my thoughts to that blissful interlude of freedom. Three other people in the office read it and pronounced it good, or so they said. Then I put it away in a drawer where it lay forgotten until quite recently when I was reminded of it while writing *Wainwright on the Pennine Way* and mentioned it in the narrative. My publisher asked to see it. I dug it out of hiding and brushed off the dust.

This book is the story of my walk to the Roman Wall in 1938. Not a word has been changed, not a word omitted or inserted. It is printed exactly as I penned it, nearly fifty years ago.

AWainwright

THE FIRST CHAPTER

ONCE upon a time, in days of long ago, Alexander the Great complained bitterly that there were no worlds left for him to conquer. His triumphant armies had swept across a continent. Victory had followed victory; his record was one of brilliant success. Nations bowed before him in submission; there was no other so powerful. There was no country that did not acknowledge his dominion. There was no territory that was not his. . . . There were no worlds left for him to conquer. . . . Twenty-two centuries have passed since then.

In September 1938, Adolf Hitler made known to the same world his intention of further enlarging his boundaries. So often had he done it; the process was so ridiculously easy. Victory had followed victory; his record was one of brilliant success. He was acclaimed wherever he went; there was no other so powerful. He had brought greatness to his country. . . . But there were other worlds to conquer. His legions were massed on the border, ready to march.

Well now, what Adolf Hitler said and did in September 1938 gave me and many others disquieting pains in the stomach. He frightened us. He made us feel sick. For he couldn't enlarge his boundaries without trampling on our friends. Friendship, openly professed, involves many responsibilities and obligations, no less in international politics than in our individual associations, and we were being made to realise it. All that had gone to build up British prestige was at stake. And unless our good name was to be shattered for ever, we should have to help our friends and resist the invader. That, and the most uncomfortable thought that there was logic in many of Adolf's arguments, and reason in his demands, is what made us feel out-of-sorts. The funny thing was, these people weren't our friends at all; it had simply been convenient to say they were. If we'd met one of them in the street, we shouldn't have known him from Adam. Friendship springs from contact: it cannot be formed in any other way.

These, then, were days of Crisis. The newspaper headings appeared in larger and larger and blacker and blacker type; their effect was to stun you so that you read on in a state of torpor, which in turn gave way to extreme nervous debility; you couldn't get things in proper perspective at all with those screaming headlines searing into your brain. Special editions were rushed from the press; yelling newsboys dashed along in relays; the placards fascinated. Same with the wireless: you didn't want to listen; you were weary of hearing the same things time after time, but you couldn't resist. Something might have happened. Anything might have happened. You wanted badly to go to a quiet room, or out on a hillside, and forget for a while. But you couldn't. You turned on the news, and sat waiting, with an inside quaking and empty. Your colleagues, your acquaintances, people you hadn't spoken to before, all had lots to say about the problem. You were as afflicted as the rest. You had your own views; your own solutions.

So it went on, day after day, the suspense growing rapidly more acute. Words and phrases which had formerly lingered in the background of our thoughts, or been absent altogether, assumed a sudden and terrible urgency. We heard them, read them, repeated them, till we were nearly driven demented. They scared us. Fortifications, dugouts, plebiscites, armaments, bomb-proof shelters, decontamination squads, conscription, incendiary bombs, air raid precautions. . . .

I left Settle just after noon on Sunday 24 September.

Settle is a gateway to the hills.

The approach from the south is through a wide, shallow valley where the Ribble makes its way leisurely to the sea. It moves slowly, apparently too much enjoying its tranquil surroundings to be in any hurry to get to its destination; or maybe its obvious reluctance is due to the knowledge that it is heading for annihilation, that it is free only while there are singing birds to accompany the music of its waters, trees to cast a cool shade, hills to guard and protect it. When these are left behind, when the birds are silent, the factory sirens sound a death-knell. And perhaps by this time it is ready to die, for a high chimney cannot replace a tree, nor can a huge warehouse compensate for the absence of a hill. Be that as it may, the river proceeds like an unwilling boy to school: it deviates from a direct course on the slightest excuse. It prefers to loop, twist and curve, and often almost doubles back in its tracks, so that you may walk miles along its banks and find yourself after all not very far from where you started. On the map, it is a curling snake. And it is a snake that needs no occult power to keep a beholder entranced; it is itself a charmer.

Ribblesdale is lovely. A walker in this Arcadia will find himself captured by the spirit of the river. He too will digress; he will turn aside from the path often and find his recompense not in the miles he has travelled, but in the succession of exquisite pictures that glade and meadow, dell and woodland have presented; pictures, these, that he will afterwards often see with closed eyes. Ribblesdale's rewards are for those who explore.

And if, now and again, during a stroll by the river, the glance is raised, there is always ancient Pendle looking down, watching silently. He may be smiling, as indeed he usually is, for he is a benevolent old fellow; he may be frowning, and then take care, for he is not only the guardian of the valley, but controller of the weather also. Certainly he will be jealous if he is ignored completely, but they are few who, loving Ribblesdale, do not love Pendle also; who do not love to ride with the wind on his broad shoulders, wrestle with him and feel his mighty strength, pull themselves up by the hairs of his shaggy chest, and then having attained his full height, feel themselves grown in stature, too. Pendle Hill was my first climb, when a boy. I don't know how old I was at the time, but I remember how thrilled I was when I breasted the last steep slope and found myself at the shattered column of stones on the summit. How proud I was of my achievement, how curiously happy to be standing there, far above all else! But Pendle frightened me, too, with his roughness, his loneliness, his sprawling immensity. I must have been very young. Since then I have learned to love the old hill. And he has been wondrous kind to me.

Settle has attractions enough, with its Folly, its Shambles, its old-world courtyards, narrow streets and alleyways, but it cannot be appreciated properly until you are clear of the houses. Then you see the hills in whose frame it is set; hills most wonderfully green, with great patches of white where the limestone breaks through. If you see this picture in brilliant sunshine, as I did, then your memory of it will be one of diamonds glittering in a setting of purest emerald. At one time, Settle was an important halting place for coaches passing between York and Lancaster. These days are long past. The little town, normally quiet and peaceful, is tortured now by the noisy line of traffic which tears its way from the industrial towns of west Yorkshire to the Lancashire coast and the Lake District. At weekends, Settle is unbearable.

North of the town, the valley narrows. Here is none of the pastoral beauty of mid-Ribblesdale. The river is confined in a rocky trough, and flows rapidly. It frets and fumes at the obstacles in its way; the boulders in its waters throw up screens of white spray. Here the Ribble is young, and it displays the energy, the eagerness, the petulance of youth. There is music, too, in its movements hereabouts; but the symphony fades away when the wide meadows are reached.

But if upper Ribblesdale lacks trees and rich grass, it has, in full compensation, the hills. The hills come crowding into the valley soon after Settle is left behind. The lower slopes of Penyghent and Cam Fell thrust in on the right, and on the left, all the way to Ribbleshead, the huge buttresses of Ingleborough make an impressive wall. Green and white are the colours of this part of Ribblesdale. There are no greener hills than those of limestone country; the grass is soft and velvety, and cropped close by sheep. And you are left in no doubt that this really is limestone country. Wherever you wander, there are the gleaming white patches studding the fellsides, like drifts of snow that have defied the sun;

occasionally, the sparkling terraces are bared to the bright sky for considerable distances, and then you have ropes of pearls to delight your eyes.

If I say I was in a big hurry on this first day of my walk, I stand condemned, for the true walker is never in a hurry. Yet I particularly wanted to get to Buckden that night, and Wharfedale was two valleys away. You reckon distances in valleys, not in miles, when crossing high country; at least, I always do. Buckden is about sixteen miles from Settle, but simple division by four does not give the time it will take to walk from one place to the other. Three miles an hour is hard travelling when the way is rough and mostly up and down, and my own average is between two and two and a half.

Langcliffe, a mile out of Settle, is the first of an attractive series of villages in this upper valley. It lies almost in the shadow of a great quarry carved out of the white core of the hills, and the giant walls seem to overhang in a most threatening manner. At Langcliffe, too, is a picturesque Hall, situated amongst the trees south of the village. Out of the heart of the cluster of cottages, an artery shoots away over the fells to Malham Tarn and Kilnsey, and in its higher part affords a splendid panorama. Unfortunately, this route has been discovered by motorists, and improved for them, so it is no longer a way for walkers. The best thing the motorists have done for the walkers is this: they have driven them into the high places, 'where the tracks of men are dim and far apart'. For this, we should be grateful.

The sun was hot on my back as I left Langcliffe, and indeed, shone brilliantly all day. My shadow was my sole companion throughout the journey, and before many days had passed I acquired quite an affection for it. So long as I was travelling north, it was there before me, responsive to my every movement, and even, I remember, to my occasional sighs. We got along famously. I sung to it, confided in it, cursed it ever so gently. But it proved a fine-weather friend. When the skies were black, it deserted me.

The village of Stainforth, which I had not visited before, made a most pleasing picture, and might have tempted me to halt there awhile. But on turning the corner, I came across the bicycles. Not a dozen, but hundreds, lining the road on both sides of the tearoom, from which issued bedlam. I can't understand why cyclists are so noisy, but they invariably are. A pity, because there is much to admire in them. They have the right idea, but until they can resist the craving to herd together, I fear they will never experience the greatest enjoyment from the open air. To appreciate anything in its full significance, whether it be a book or a picture, a musical composition or a rolling landscape, we must be in harmony with it from the start; the senses must be attuned to it. To appreciate the meaning of a kindly gesture or a quiet smile, we must first of all understand perfectly; the heart must be in sympathy. If the appeal be to the senses, then we may share the experience with others; if it be to the emotions, we are best alone. A discordant note in a quiet place is sacrilege: the hills have a message for the soul, but we shall not hear it if we are one of many. There are times for companionship, times for solitude. It is tragic to be solitary on a dance-floor; equally tragic to be in a crowd on a hilltop.

I went on. The road climbs a little out of Stainforth, and on the crest of Sherwood Brow Penyghent comes grandly into view ahead, looking at its very best from this angle. There is no denying Penyghent's claim to be ranked as a mountain. It is rough, stony, almost precipitous on its south and west faces, and it sticks up out of the surrounding moors like a huge stranded whale on a beach. It dominates the scene. Let your gaze wander where it will in this part of the valley, unfailingly it will come to rest on Penyghent's lofty summit.

Between Stainforth and Helwith Bridge, the Ribble and the railway run alongside below on the left of the road, and there are some lovely glimpses of the river, here looking quite unrecognisable to one familiar with it only in its middle and lower reaches. Its waters are brown, except where white splashes indicate the presence of rocks in the stream, and they flow rapidly between narrow banks, heading unknowingly for a thirty-foot plunge at Stainforth Foss. This is the Ribble's only waterfall between source and sea.

I reached grey Horton-in-Ribblesdale at two o'clock. Not unexpectedly, I was feeling tired. I am always ready for a drink and a rest after the first six miles of a walk; then the next ten are easy. I lingered in Horton an hour. It is a pleasant place, and must have been even more attractive when the main highway was a lane. It has three bridges, and the guidebooks agree that there are three inns, though I have never been able to find more than two.

Horton is the Mecca of potholers: the surrounding fells are honeycombed with caverns and potholes and underground passages, and it is easy to imagine the adventures they offer to those bold enough to explore their inky recesses. For my part, I prefer to stay up above, where I can look about me, but I have nothing but admiration for those enthusiasts who find their keenest delight in this hazardous pursuit beneath the hills. I have heard potholers described as cranks. They aren't. They have discovered a fairyland, a world within a world, that is utterly beyond their critics' imaginations. Think of it. We spend our whole lives crawling about on the surface of the earth; here a new and thrilling excursion is offered us, a fascinating journey into the sunless depths below the surface. Adventures such as this make men boys again; the enthusiasm of youth returns. What a grand thing enthusiasm is! How glorious to be alive when your blood is afire!

I digress too much, but let me commit to print a query I have often pondered. I wrote above of enthusiasm, of men recapturing the wild joys of boyhood. I've wondered many a time: have the ladies the same capacity for enthusiasm? Not for climbing or potholing necessarily. For anything. Have they, too, somewhere within them a slumbering spark which can on occasion burst into a burning, brilliant flame and retain its intensity and heat against the cold waters of judgment and reason? For enthusiasm is just like that. Where enthusiasm and judgment conflict, judgment is always the loser. Enthusiasm grips a man's imagination, drives him on and on, and the hardships and discomforts of his way are nought. Enthusiasm feeds on itself. The enthusiast tingles with life and, while he yet lives, dwells with the gods.

Despite all that has been written to the contrary, I think that women are the practical sex. They do as their judgments dictate; they are not creatures of imagination. I have not yet witnessed genuine enthusiasm in one of them; often I have seen a pretence of

it, but the divine spark was missing. Conventions deny them the
liberty to indulge in the higher flights. Maybe their imaginations do
soar sometimes, but are kept in leash and hidden. Yet I doubt it,
for there are no secret enthusiasms. The man burns; the woman
throws the cold water over him. Let's leave it at that, and kindly
ascribe mixed metaphors also to enthusiasm.

For the ordinary visitor, Horton's chief attraction will be the
church, and few who behold this ancient structure will dispute its
claim to have a history going back 700 years. Grey it has always
been; now it is shabby, too, and I should imagine the interior to be
very very dusty. But you can tell by the way it rears its old head
above the cottage roofs that it has lost none of its pride. Its solid
tower stands four-square to the winds that tear up the dale; it
looks, as it must be, strong and sturdy, and incredibly old.
Someday, perhaps, it will be pulled down, and give way to a
streamlined edifice, and from that day Horton will look all wrong.
The church as it is now achieves a perfect harmony with its
moorland surroundings. Every stone in it is part of the picture.

I turned along the lane by the vicarage towards Penyghent. For
nearly two miles the lane climbs steadily between walls, but it is a
joyous walk. If I tried to describe a 'green road', my pen would
falter sadly. A green road in a limestone country! Such is nectar to
the eager walker. Up and up they go, these green roads, shooting
like arrows from the vale, pointing the way to the tops. Sometimes
they are confined within white walls, sometimes they are free to
the clean winds and the rain. Who made them is a matter for
conjecture; a few undoubtedly date from the Roman occupation,
but most simply link up the dales in most direct fashion. Now they
have fallen into disuse; they are nothing more than shepherds'
tracks. They are carpeted with the most exhilarating, springy turf,
starred with the tiniest of fellside flowers, bedecked with the
greenest of green mosses and plants. Here the walker joins the
sheep in Elysium.

Half an hour's glorious tramping brought me to the end of the
walls, with Penyghent soaring up on the right and before me a
wide brown expanse of rolling moorland. During the climb from
Horton, I had been conscious of a growing sense of keen

anticipation; I was becoming attuned to the violent contrast between my present surroundings and those where the demands of the body compel me to live. I began to appreciate the magnitude of the joyful task I had set myself and all that would be involved in its fulfilment. And when I came to the end of those walls and saw before me that which I sought, I threw off my pack and exulted mightily.

I was free. For months I had been in chains, body, mind and soul. So complete a bondage was new to me; my body is a prisoner always save for a few days each year, but my mind and soul are seldom captive. Yet latterly they too had seemed fettered; they had been in the grip of a fearsome monster we called Crisis.

Well, I was away from it all. How sweet was the realisation, not until this moment fully comprehended!

I was a free man on the hills again.

Before I continued, I turned for a last look at Ribblesdale, which I should not see again for many a day. The view was pleasing, but I left it with no regrets and went on across the moor. My way took me alongside the deep chasm of Hull Pot, which gains in impressiveness because, like most of the miracles wrought by water and erosion in this wonderland of limestone, it is entirely unexpected. Hull Pot is a gaping cavity in a level, grassy moorland. Its vertical walls are gleaming white where the sun shines upon them, but they descend into black shadow, and out of the murky gloom below there comes the murmur of subterranean waters.

The streams are a feature of this remarkable district. You may be following one as it flows along, behaving very much like any other stream, and then suddenly stand rooted in your tracks in disbelief. It is gone, vanished completely. Here it is, splashing merrily downhill; there, it has disappeared. If this is your first experience of the kind, you are distinctly shocked. There is no hole into which the waters plunge; the stream simply dries up before your eyes. Or again, you may be striding down a hillside or across a field in the valley when, wonder of wonders, a broad rapidly flowing stream rises out of the very ground at your feet, and goes splashing and gurgling on its way to the parent Ribble. But its birth is a profound mystery.

I stood awhile at Hull Pot, which is really quite big, measuring
180 feet in length by 45 wide, and watched two potholers essaying a
descent at its farthest corner, in the only place where the walls do
not fall absolutely sheer. They had little lanterns affixed to the fronts
of their hats, after the fashion of coalminers of a generation ago.
Their progress, however, was slow in the extreme, and at length I
turned away in the direction of Littondale.

I have not mentioned that I was suffering from the discomforts of
mild influenza, and its attendant abomination, a running nose. A
running nose, at the best of times, is hardly a pleasing subject to
introduce into a story, and a writer who makes so bold places his
name in jeopardy. Where, in the world's fiction, do we read of a nose
being wiped? In a novel, such reference is definitely suicidal. Imagine
Our Hero with a streaming nose and a sodden handkerchief in his
hand. It won't bear thinking about. Or, worse still, the Fair Lady.
Think of them, the poor dears, on the last page of the book, yearning
so terribly for the lingering kiss that shall plight their troth, but it is
impossible; it is denied them. They cannot. . . .

This is crude stuff, in all conscience, but the fact is that my
disability was destined to loom large before my adventures were
over. My trouble was that after the first two days I had nothing
wherewith to wipe; and three-quarters of the blasphemous utter-
ances which enlivened the later stages of my march could be directly
attributed to this deficiency.

What I started to say was that when I stopped at Hull Pot my
head began to ache, partly because of my ailment and partly because
of the sun which beat down mercilessly on the shadeless moor.
When, however, I resumed my walk, the ache vanished. Throughout
the afternoon until sundown, this phenomenon repeated itself. If I
stopped for a moment, there came a painful pounding in my temples
which disappeared instantly when I started moving again. It per-
plexed me. If I halted to strike a match, there it was; throb, throb,
throb. I tried to experiment with it, by sort of half-halting to see
what happened, but there was no cheating this vicious assailant; its
attacks were repeated if I were stationary only a moment, and
gradually became more acute, so that after a while I went on in
perpetual mobilae.

The path across Foxup Moor is not always easy to follow; it winds tortuously amongst long rank grass, and there is a confusion of sheep-tracks to bewilder the traveller. The best plan is to make for the wall which comes straight down the side of Penyghent from the saddle on the skyline; when it reaches the level ground, it turns at right-angles and goes over towards Foxup. A path will be picked up at the angle of the wall and thereafter the way is plain, but you will not keep the water out of your shoes along here. There are slimy pools to negotiate and a dozen rivulets to jump across. Hill-wandering and wet feet go together; you may keep immune for a while, but before the day is spent, you squelch; water oozes through your lace-holes and when finally you come to the highroad your shoes are like leather suckers on the macadam; there is a distinct, not unpleasant, plop each time you raise your foot. If you are spending a day on the hills, the best thing to do when you set off is to walk ankle-deep through the first stream you see. Thereafter, you need not pick your way gingerly; you can fix your gaze on the far distances, stride along, and be happy. The inevitable is bound to happen sooner or later; make it happen early.

A moor often has the desolation of death about it, but it teems with life. Put your back against it, and look at the sky, and listen. Listen carefully. Out of the profound stillness comes a multitude of tiny sounds. There are marching armies in the grass, winged battalions hovering above it. I have seen some fine dramas played amongst the tangled roots of heather. Sudden slaughter, terror, love, hate and passion: all the elements of first-class drama are here presented. The actors are lilliputian; the stage may be a blade of grass, or the petal of a mountain pansy. But the events you witness are grim; the players are in earnest. Feeling runs pretty high even among crawling pinheads. Next time you have an idle day, make yourself a couch on a quiet moor, and lie down. Sleep, if you are tired. But first, for a while, listen. And learn.

Today, however, the moor was silent. Its inhabitants were drowsing in the blazing sun; a siesta was, for once, preferable to a prowl; pax was called, and vigilance relaxed.

I was walking along towards the top of the pass when quite suddenly an awful scream close at hand startled me into panic. For a moment the blood in my veins ran cold. I was alone, quite alone: I had an uninterrupted view for miles in every direction; the brilliant sunlight picked out every object on the moor in bold relief, but there was not a living thing within sight. I went on, mystified: immediately, the ghastly cry was repeated. I shivered with fright; had it been dark, I would have taken to my heels. There was murder being done.

I slipped off my rucksack, and cautiously approached the hollow where the cry came from, fearful of what I should find. Again and again, in terror now, the scream rent the stillness. Never before had I heard such a dreadful wail.

It was a rabbit, a poor miserable wretch caught in a snare. I think I laughed when I saw it: this, the creature that had caused my alarm! I could have killed it with a kick.

How pathetic its attempts to get away! As I drew near, it tugged and strained at the wire that pinioned it; several times it leaped frantically in the air, only to come crashing down on the same spot, and no less firmly held. Its contortions availed it nothing. There was no escape; its bleeding body was weary with vain effort.

I knelt down a yard away. It did not cry again, but flattened itself in the grass, paralysed with fear, the fear of death. Its eyes were dilated; I could hear its sobbing breath. There were stains of blood on the brown fur, on the ground. . . .

I wondered how long the rabbit had been there; for how many hours, days perhaps, had it regarded the cruel thread of steel that held it prisoner? At first, it would be puzzled at this unexpected check to its wild free flight, then consternation would grow as its strivings to get away proved futile. The passing hours would bring a new torture; the slow realisation that it never never would get away; there was a purpose behind its capture, and what that purpose was it did not know. The sufferings of the mind that cannot understand must be tremendous, tragic. But now, at last, the long wait was over; here was a being from whom it should flee, as every instinct urged insistently; but it could not. Here was the enemy he dreaded, come for the killing. And this Thing that held him fast, this was the enemy's trap. . . . At last, he understood. This was the end of torment; the end of existence.

I believe I spoke to the pitiful creature. At least, my thoughts were pretty strong, and if I gave them expression, as I probably did, I must have lectured it this wise: 'What a poor, brainless fool you are. You have experienced, at the cost of a battered body, the intelligence of man. Those bleeding limbs bear witness to his cleverness and ingenuity. His methods are not direct, as yours are. He schemes, studies, plans. He devised this trap for you. But he did not force you into it. You are caught, but that is entirely your own fault. Don't blame man for your plight; that wouldn't be fair. Blame your own weakness, and your failure to appreciate the subtle ways in which man works to achieve his ends. Now you understand his mastery, his greatness. You are a beast, with only instinct to guide you. Man has a brain, and it has made him supreme. He is humane, too, and kindly. He could have devised a trap that would have crushed your bones, but see, there is only this thin wire, which itself cannot hurt you. It can only hold you fast. And you have to be caught and destroyed, you know. You see, you are a pest, something that isn't wanted. I mean, something that isn't wanted by man, of course, and he is the dictator, after all. You don't know what a dictator is? Well, it would take too long to explain, but obviously it's someone who exterminates pests. . . . You are suffering, and I am going to set you free. That surprises you, doesn't it? When you get back home, sit awhile and ponder on man's supremacy.'

I put out my hand to release the rabbit, but it cringed in terror; its quivering body was completely transfixed as it waited for the expected blow to fall; those terrible eyes watched, watched, in awful fascination. Frankly, I felt rotten, ashamed. This animal was face to face with death; it had done no wrong, but for some reason it could not comprehend, it was to be murdered, and it waited, mutely. It showed no scorn or contempt for me and my kind; it could only tremble in the presence of a greater power, but in those few moments, and later when I recalled the incident, I felt sick with disgust.

I could not disengage the wire from the rabbit's body, so cut through the cord which joined the wire to a stout peg driven into the ground. When the last strand was severed, the animal was off like a flash. But not quite like a flash. The oddest thing happened. It streaked away in great bounds, but as I watched, it halted momentarily about ten yards away, turned its head and looked at me and uttered the queerest little sound. Then it was off again, and the last I saw of it was its white tail bobbing into a burrow. . . .

So somewhere on the wide moor between Horton and Foxup there lives a rabbit which has fastened to it a few inches of steel wire, an evil reminder of its contact with the machinations of the human race. If only to spite the farmer who set the trap, I hope its fetter does not impede its connubial relationships.

But I thought rabbits were silent animals. Earlier in the year I had read that a rabbit screams when pursued by a stoat, but this was my first experience of its cry, and I hope I do not hear it again. It is ghastly, blood-curdling. . . . The rabbits I used to keep when a boy never uttered a sound, and their existence was lamentably one of privation and hardship. Looking back on those days, it seems incredible that they never complained of their treatment. I cherished a childish delusion that they liked being dangled by the ears, so I went out of my way to provide this innocent amusement for them, and they dangled by the ears for hours. I fed them on a concoction of tea-leaves and bran, meal after meal, until I stank of the vile stuff. I coerced them into the hutches of neighbouring rabbits to see what happened, but the reward from this furtive enterprise was never great. And then, when the time came for them to die, they just lay down and stiffened without a moan of reproach.

This incident on the moor left me with only one regret: it did not occur to me at the time to take a photograph of the captive in the snare. I had been walking along with my camera in my hand, on the lookout for suitable subjects, and the possibility of securing a few 'scoops' had not been absent from my thoughts. This picture, for me and my cheap box-camera, would have been a scoop indeed. Conditions for a clear snap were perfect, too. I was a little sorry for my omission.

The path rises to a height of 1587 feet, and then begins the long, gradual descent to the lonely farm at Foxup, still hidden in the upper folds of Littondale. On this sloping hillside, outcrops of limestone are again prominent, white scars of great beauty and fantastic form, and the path picks its way through a natural rock-garden. Flower-bedecked boulders, mossy crannies, and crevices delicately ornamented with ferns, together combine to make exquisite pictures. More than once, as I turned corners of the track, I was confronted with delightful vistas; the combination of rock and flowering plant arranged so beautifully that I found myself wishing it were possible to dig a few square yards and transport it bodily, without disturbance, to my own back garden. I was too late in the year to see the purple mountain saxifrage which is profuse in these parts, but the clustered blossoms of this alpine against its white background must be charming to behold.

Presently, I passed a farmer coming up the path. He carried a stick, and was accompanied by a boy who had an empty sack over his shoulder. I did not need to ask his mission. This pleasant countryside was to be converted into a place of slaughter. While he had been having his dinner, his snares had been filling; now he had to ascertain the measure of his success. There was no hazard in his task; I could imagine him systematically visiting each trap, dealing his death-blows quite dispassionately, tutoring the boy in the art of destruction. He had nothing to fear; the creatures were timid and defenceless, and anyway they were pinned to the ground. They were vermin, but their bodies would sell for a few coppers. It was a profitable hobby and, besides, the walk across the moor did him good.

I watched him disappear along the path; and when I turned and went on down the hill, I fancied I heard again the scream of terror and saw once more two big brown eyes held in fascinated gaze. . . . This killing of God's creatures is a sorry business, and I cannot for the life of me see that it is less murder to kill a dumb animal than a human being. Indeed, it seems to me more criminal. The essentials of combat are absent; we have not two equally equipped adversaries, but one only with a weapon, and he the aggressor; one only has led a sinful life, yet he is the survivor.

At Foxup starts the road that winds the length of Littondale, but between here and Halton Gill, half a mile further along, it is hardly better than a rutted lane, and few motors will get so far into the dalehead. At Halton Gill, however, we resume acquaintance with macadam. But this hamlet is not nowadays the end of all things for the motorist, as it once was; an old road leading over the south shoulder of Penyghent to Stainforth has recently been improved, and provides an exit from the valley. At weekends, this moorland road is quite busy, and it is to the credit of the motorist that he prefers the open country for his Sunday trips. But can he appreciate the clean air of the moors with the stink of petrol about him? Does he see the glorious tints of the grass and heather through the steaming windows of the car? Can he hear the lonely, plaintive cry of the curlew as he rattles along? No, but tragically he often thinks he has experienced these delights and is ready to enthuse over them. Poor fellow, he has not even had a glimpse of the wonders that await him. He has come no nearer to the secrets of the high places than if he had stayed at home.

There is only one way to know a hill, and that is to put your feet on it and walk. Wander about leisurely if you wish, but better still, make the summit your objective and struggle up to it. Plunge into the bracken and heather, and wrestle with the thousand tentacles that would hold you back; splash through the streams that silver the hillside; scramble up the rocks and know the thrill that enslaves the mountaineer; sweat and pant, slip and tumble, and curse if you are so minded, and rest often. But get to the top. And if up there you find a gale so strong as to bowl you off your feet, or you are privileged to be in the nerve-centre of a thunderstorm, so much the better. Stay on the summit as long as you may, then come down. Don't tread circumspectly now, but run; run as if all the fiends of hell were loose at your heels. Run with giant strides, leap, jump, tumble and sprawl and roll, come down helter-skelter until you reach the level ground in the valley. Wash in the stream, and bathe your wounds, and clean yourself up a bit. Then seek out a royal feed and a soft bed. . . . If you have done all this, one of two things has happened to you. Either you will never want to see a hill again, in which case you may safely assume that the rot has settled in your soul so deeply that nothing will remove it; or you will hunger for the next opportunity, do it again and again, and keep young for ever.

It was half-past five when I arrived at Halton Gill, and there was an hour and a half of daylight left. I was behind time, should have been here much earlier. I was only five miles from Buckden, but Buckden was in Wharfedale and I in Littondale, and there was the formidable ridge of Horse Head Moor between. I looked up at its steep grassy slopes. My head was throbbing again, and my legs had dragged along from Foxup in weary fashion. I was sorely tempted to continue easily down the valley to the inn at Litton, and spend the night there. But this would mean going south, and I was pledged to keep north; and worse still, it would be defeat. My programme said Buckden first night, and I had in fact sent a card to a friend when I was in Horton on which I had anticipated my march and actually drawn a map which indicated positively that I would be at Buckden that night. It would be base deceit to rest my head in any other place. Horse Head Moor it would have to be.

I passed through a gate just short of the chapel and very slowly started along the track which a rickety signpost indicated, rather unexpectedly, as leading 'To Hawes'. Hawes was a long long way from here; there were deep valleys and rolling ridges between, and while there is no doubt that if you left Halton Gill to walk to Hawes, this is the way you would go, I suspect that the vast majority of people who use the track go no further than Buckden. But of the nearer attractions of Wharfedale and Langstrothdale, the signpost makes no mention. 'To Hawes' it says; nowhere else. If you are going to Hawes, very well, here is your path; if not, well, it shrugs its shoulders; it is not concerned with you.

I proceeded at a snail's pace up the green track, faithfully adhering to all its zig-zags. The more strenuous short cuts were beyond me; I was very, very tired. The sun, now fast sinking, was still hot; my rucksack had settled between my shoulder-blades and was fast becoming an irritation. My head was heavy, and my legs weak. I wanted to lie down and go to sleep. Lie down I did, a score of times, but got to my feet again and dragged myself a little further up the hill. I was in poor condition. The hills demand a high standard of fitness in a man before they admit him to their company. That first day, I had no right to be there, and they treated me with scant respect.

After struggling upwards for more than an hour, the gradient eased and I was well satisfied to be atop of the ridge, even though in that time I had travelled a distance of only half a mile from Halton Gill. A long wall runs along the highest parts of the moor, and I rested at the gate which leads through it. The view was superb: in that moment when I turned and surveyed the way I had come, my lethargy was shaken off as though I had discarded a wearisome cloak.

The sun had disappeared only a few minutes before, and Penyghent, dark and shadowy, reared up like a great purple wedge in the molten sky. There was no disputing its majesty. Around it were billowing hills ranging to the far horizons, but Penyghent itself, on this evening at least, was a mountain, a noble peak that so arrested my attention as to make me forget my tiredness and hunger, and set my heart singing again. Northwards, the dusk was settling down into Langstrothdale, and the prospect, though vast and inviting, lacked the warmth and colour of the retrospect.

I lingered awhile; I was very conscious of being utterly alone amongst the silent hills. I would recover from my exertions in a few hours, but the reward I found on that Sabbath evening will remain with me as long as I live. This was one of the unforgettable moments.

The top of the Horse Head Pass is 1900 feet above the sea. There is a possible explanation for its unusual name. A long time ago, the chapel at Halton Gill and the church at Hubberholme in Langstrothdale were served by one curate, both places being within the parish of Arncliffe. Between them is the high, lonely moor, and negotiating it to conduct services seems to have been the most onerous part of the curate's duties. He writes, in 1743: 'It is with great danger and difficulty I pass over very high mountains and large drifts of snow to the chapel.' He provided himself with a white horse to render the journey less arduous; even so, his ultimate appearance seems to have been a matter for conjecture, for we read that one of the parishioners used to watch for a glimpse of the horse coming over the pass, from a roof-top in the valley. Then, and not until then, did the bell begin to ring for the service.

I descended into Langstrothdale in fine style. The change from upward progress to downward suited my limbs admirably, and they nearly ran away with me down the hill.

It was after seven, and almost dark, when I came on to the road by the farm buildings at Ramsgill, and I swung along towards Buckden at a good pace. After a long mile, I came to Hubberholme, and although the famous church was lost in the shadows, its presence was indicated by some twenty or thirty motor-cycles and cars lining the road. Hubberholme Church on a Sunday evening in summer is a regular place of pilgrimage, and I decided there and then that if it could attract people from towns thirty miles away, it had something to offer me too, and I resolved to come back and look at it in the morning.

Another mile brought me at length into Buckden. It was pitch dark by this time, and Buckden has no street lamps. I groped my way about the cottages and along the black lanes running confusedly between them. I hoped to find somewhere a notice indicating that accommodation was provided, though I had no idea how I was to see and read it in the darkness. I was ravenously hungry; since breakfast I had had only a dry sandwich and a pot of tea. I prowled round those little houses like a scavenger. I was famished and weary; but the engulfing blackness baffled me. I could see nothing; neither notice-board nor cottages. I knew there were cottages here, and that I was amongst them, but I was as powerless to find a front door as though I had been struck blind. The place seemed as destitute of human habitation as Horse Head Moor, and far less friendly. That night was the blackest I remember.

It seems incredible now, but I floundered about those cobbled lanes, within a compass of fifty yards, for twenty minutes, and still had not found what I sought. There was not a soul about; the village was as silent as if it lay under a plague.

Then I did what I should have done in the first place. I recalled seeing a glimmer of light when I entered the village, and I groped my way back to it. It was an oil lamp, shining through drawn curtains.

Having found a window, I passed my hand along the wall until I found a door, and I knocked on it, hard. The door opened, which suggested human agency, but I could see neither the doorway nor the person who must now be standing there. I addressed the night in general, and asked for a room. A woman answered. She was sorry; a young lady was staying with her, and she had no accommodation for me. Where could I go, then? She asked, had I tried Mrs Falshaw's, higher up the lane? No; I asked if she would take me there. She was evidently surprised at this request, and said she would not, but she went back into the house to see if the young lady would do so. I was getting impatient at the delay.

After a minute, I was startled by a voice at my side. My guide had slipped out of the house unnoticed, and was waiting. Who the girl was, I shall never know. She was, like myself, only a temporary sojourner in the place, but I imagine that wherever she goes, she will take a bit of heaven with her. Her voice was lovely, and I think she must be, too. She spoke to me as we went along; at first, she seemed a little amused, and then, since I was very quiet, she grew more serious. Had I come far? Was I very tired? Yes, she was kind; and she made the last short stage of my day's march a very pleasant memory, a fitting epilogue to a chapter that had held much of quiet joy.

She led me along the rough lane, I stumbling like a blind man. I tried hard to see what she was like, but the gloom was impenetrable. Her voice came from a level midway between my elbow and my shoulder, which was just where it should be.

The short journey was soon over. She positioned me before a door, knocked for me, wished me luck, and slipped away. Since that night I have often recalled those few moments in the darkness with my unseen helper. She reminded me of someone, someone dear to me. . . . She was kinder to me than she knew.

Mrs Falshaw scrutinised me as though I were a visitor from another planet, but she finally decided to risk everything and admit me, and having made this decision, set about making me a big supper of which I was sadly in need.

The most subtle of the pleasures of a walking tour is the complete change of habit and thought, as well as surroundings; you shed the old life, and live another. Conventions and collars go hang. You belong no more to the office, but to the farm or cottage or inn where you chance to stay, and if you are wise you will slip into your new environment as inconspicuously as you can. Avoid the hotels; choose the lowly homesteads. Be one of the company; do as they do. If the family goes early to bed, be the first upstairs. If your host eats with his fingers, do you the same. If he repeats loudly after his meal, make the attempt: he'll love you as a brother, and take you into his confidence. Oh, forget the fifty weeks of routine in the year; smash down the barriers of reserve, meet these people at their own level, high or low, wherever it may be, if you really want to know them. And they are well worth the study. . . . This is more than change: it is rest, release.

The Falshaws' house is long and rambling; the ceilings are raftered. Illumination comes from oil lamps, and upstairs from candles. You are never so conscious of your freedom as when an oil lamp is placed on the table before you; there is nothing that so surely banishes the gloomy worries of that other life you have left behind.

An oil lamp induces a contented mind. To sit in its warm glow, after a hard day in the hills, with a stomach replete with good wholesome food, occasionally glancing at the map spread across your knees, sometimes watching the smoke from your cigarette curl upwards to where the shadows dance on the ceiling, often just idly dreaming, is to be utterly content and at peace. An oil lamp has power to soothe; it is friendly; it has, which electricity has not, something of romance.

After supper, I was invited into the best room. Here I was later joined by two of the Falshaws, mother and daughter, and spent an enjoyable hour listening to their chatter. I told them nothing of myself, did not influence their conversation in any way. I simply let them talk, and listened with a mighty interest. How refreshing it can be to forget your own troubles for a while; to listen to other people, living in a little world vastly different from your own, talking of their own cares and worries and aspirations!

You will not travel far in any one of the dales before you realise how completely the lives of the dalesfolk are influenced by their geographical isolation. They are not clannish, but they belong absolutely to their own valley. The currents of life flow with the river along the dale, but never over the hills and into the next. These people know their own valley, and all that is happening in it; follow the river downstream and there are towns on its banks, and they know the towns, too. Always they have the river for company; they work and play and live and die within the sound of its waters. But of the next valley they know little; it is remote; there are the high hills between. Their life is here, where they were born.

So with the Falshaws. Their concern was the closing of the village school which meant that the children had now to travel down the dale to Kettlewell; the omnibus service down the dale; the bi-weekly cinema show at Grassington, ten miles away, but again, down the dale. At Buckden, we were at the head of the dale; it was the bus terminus, the last village, the end, or the beginning, of everything. Life started to flow here, but it flowed in one direction only: down the dale.

And up the dale to Buckden had come news of a Crisis in Europe; up the dale had come ghastly rumours; from Grassington and Kettlewell had come instructions and appeals and suggestions. The dale must organise; it must protect itself from air-raids. And I fancy the people of the dale would come still closer together in the face of this new and strange threat to their beloved little patch of green earth in the folds of the hills.

I went upstairs a happy man, and was shown into a bedroom that had all the evidences of recent and regular feminine occupation. I was a privileged guest, it seemed.

I was tired, pleasantly tired. I had had a good day, and was well satisfied. New scenes, changing horizons, like pictures on a vast canvas, had refreshed a jaded mind; new experiences had been mine, and I had given little thought to the old. I had come only from Ribblesdale to Wharfedale, but I had travelled far.

I looked through the window, into the black square of night. Down the dale—yes, I could say that with the Falshaws now — down the dale, negotiations for peace were at this moment feverishly taking place, but hope was fast fading; the guns of war were being drawn into position. There were teeming populations, down the dale, in the grip of scare and near-panic. . . .

Ah, what of it? I was away from it. Tomorrow was a new day. Tomorrow I should be further into the hills. I was free.

Yes, I was free; free from that and much else. I had no jacket to hang carefully, no trousers to fold neatly.

My clothes lay scattered on the floor throughout the night, just as I had thrown them off.

THE SECOND CHAPTER

I WAS awake early, and before five o'clock was smoking my first cigarette of the day. A candlestick balanced on the edge of the bed served as an ashtray.

Smoking in bed is a messy affair, and a deplorable habit. But the last cigarette before going to sleep has a very special soothing quality, something all its own, not shared by the others in the packet. The red glow in the darkness holds your languid gaze as you reflect on the day's happenings and the morrow's promise. Maybe you are too happy to want to sleep; perhaps some event during the day is too precious to be allowed to slip away. Or tomorrow is a prospect that pleases; it may be that you plan a day in the country, a walk in a new district that you haven't yet visited; it may hold the promise of a smile, a warming glance, from a loved one. You are content, and the red glow becomes a confidant.

The first cigarette in the morning is different. You are thinking then of the new day, facing the reality and dreaming less. The red glow isn't nearly so red nor so cheerful. The room is diffused with grey light; it looks harsh and cold and disorderly; the bedclothes are disarranged, in a lump; you no longer feel snug and warm, as you did last night. You lie and watch the grey shadows take shape. You wonder what time it is. You listen for the expected rain on the window. You ask yourself if it is a shaving morning, and ten to one it is. You feel pretty grim, and your cigarette doesn't taste half so good.

Even on holiday, these morbid reflections are not altogether dispelled. The interval between wakening and breakfast is generally zero hour, with me at any rate. But breakfast alters all that. Between the porridge and the marmalade your plans are made; you have made a weather forecast for the next twelve hours; you know, for certain, where you will be at noon, at tea, at dusk, and you are eager to be off.

I stepped out of the house into sunshine. The morning air was keen; there had been a slight frost. The sun was just peeping over the high fell which clutches the village to its bosom; its ragged crest was afire. There was a slight haze; a slender veil was drawn across the quiet valley, not obscuring its loveliness, but adding to it a captivating atmosphere of mystery. I was tingling with anticipation as I strode over the cobbles to the road; before me another day, and a vast treasury where I could pick and choose and not fail to enrich myself.

I called at the post office, which, like all village post offices, is also the shop of all trades. There is just room to stand within the door, amongst the potatoes; your eyes range over an amazing variety of articles; a querulous face appears among the confectionery, and you make known your wants from the midst of dangling items of hardware which descend from the low ceiling like stalactites.

This morning I was in sentimental mood. I was prepared to be extravagant to feed my mood; the rigid economy I had rehearsed could wait a little. I wanted two boxes of chocolates; one for the girl of last night, whose memory sleep had not banished; one for the daughter of my hostess, for cleaning my shoes unasked, and being generally most obliging and friendly to one who must have seemed rather lonely.

I stood outside the post office with my purchases in my hand, wondering now how I could convey them to the proper persons and yet remain anonymous. This was a problem to which I had not given sufficient thought. It needed courage to go again to the cottage where I had first sought admittance last night, but it seemed to me this morning absolutely necessary that kindness should have its reward, so I went there and knocked. The elderly woman who came to the door I did not of course recognise, but she was quick to identify me. She was surprised that I should call again, and when I explained my mission and handed her the chocolates she was more surprised but, I was pleased to note, evidently delighted. 'But,' she said, 'wouldn't you like to give them to the young lady yourself?' I said no, and backed away: to look on the face of the girl, however lovely she was, and I had no doubts at all that she must be altogether charming, would spoil the illusion. I wanted to remember her only for her voice as she spoke to me so quietly in the darkness. I did not want to see her; I was not in the least curious to know who she was. She belonged to last night; her memory would endure into the future, but she herself had no further part to play.

I went along the lane, hurriedly now. The door of the Falshaws' house was open, and I entered softly and left the second box on the carpet near the fender, where I had found my shoes so nicely polished when I came downstairs.

Then I went down to the road, and started again on my travels.

And while we are walking the mile to Hubberholme, along the tree-lined road we tramped last night, let me remedy an important omission. I have not yet stated my plans for this holiday; I have described at length my journey thus far, to Buckden, but hinted only at my full intentions.

The Roman Wall, Hadrian's Wall, was my objective. I had no particular desire to see the Wall, and knew very little about it except that it stretched from sea to sea across the North of England, and that portions of it could still be seen on the lonely hills of Northumberland. What I had in mind was a walk which should take me by way of the Yorkshire Dales and Durham along the eastern flanks of the Pennines as far as Tynedale, from which far-away valley I planned to return along the western slopes of the range.

Above Wensleydale, all this was country new to me. I had heard often of Swaledale, Teesdale, St John's Chapel, Alston, Appleby, and a score of other well-known places, and could have plotted them fairly accurately on a map. But year after year, with persistent regularity, I had passed them by and returned to the Lake District, which in course of time became as familiar to me as the field behind my home. I came to know it so well that it irked me to read what other people, with far less experience of its delights, had to say about it. The hackneyed themes of their writings drove me to despair: I could have written a book about Lakeland that would have pushed all their efforts into total obscurity. Someday, I may.

Well now, having quite decided that this year I would see as much as I could of the Pennine country, I looked about for an objective in the North, a point on which my travels should focus, a place to attain and turn back from. I wanted to go north, and keep on going north as long as I could, but I had to remember that every step I took in that direction must of necessity be reversed later. I did not want, however, to start out without a plan, because without a programme I find myself cursed by indecision. I didn't want simply to go north until I was tired of going north, and turn in my tracks and come back. This might have happened in a field, in the middle of a moor, in a village street, anywhere. No, I must fix a point somewhere in the north, and attain it whatever happened, otherwise there would be no feeling of anticipation to spur me on, no sense of satisfaction to my homeward march. I must attempt something definite, and do it, or my walk back would be unpalatable indeed.

So, in an inspired moment, I remembered the Roman Wall: a dim memory from my geography lessons of twenty years ago fluttered into my mind in an idle moment, and I gripped it with both hands. I got a copy of Collingwood's *Handbook to the Roman Wall*: it solved my problem and unexpectedly fascinated me so much that I read it twice. So my destination was fixed as Borcovicium, a Roman camp on the Wall, amongst the hills of Northumberland. To that spot I would direct my steps; from there, and from no other place, I would return south.

Much that I have just written is at direct variance with the accepted tradition of walkers which upholds that a person who loves walking will walk anywhere, just as his fancy pleases; he will refuse to be a slave to any programme, and will follow any byway that tempts his mood. I never do that; I couldn't. I'd rather stay at home than ramble aimlessly. I must have an objective, otherwise I derive no pleasure from walking. It doesn't matter in the least what the objective is: it may be the pillar box at the end of the road, a cricket match a few miles away, a signpost on a moorland track. It must be something to aim at. The most natural objective, to me, is a cairn of stones on the summit of a hill. Whatever it may be, it is decided upon before I move a step, and having decided upon it, nothing on earth can persuade me from it. If only I had been as resolute in my pursuit of the objectives that have appealed in other phases of life. For success comes only from first deciding on your target, and refusing to be tempted from it; from attaining it in spite of all the hardships and tribulations on the way.

With the clustered buildings of Hubberholme in sight, the Wharfe swings back to the side of the road, and few people will pass along here without pausing to sit awhile on the low wall. The river, brown as copper, flows at your feet; here, although fresh from the hills, it is a surprisingly large infant, and judging from the wide pebbly beach on the far side, it often finds its bed too small and seeks to enlarge it. From the trees on the opposite shore, the tiny tower of the church peeps timidly at you; it knows for certain that your next move will be to cross the bridge towards it, and it beseeches you to approach with respect, for although it is very very old, it is yet well-known and loved. And you are a stranger. You may not know its proud history, and treat it with scant courtesy; and it would never forgive such wanton thoughtlessness. A passing glance, no more, would hurt its pride. It deserves much more attention than that. It thrives on the affection of those who linger, and come back.

Hubberholme Bridge is lovely, and a place to dream away an idle hour. At its far end, a wicket gate gives entrance to the little graveyard, and the church is before you, its tower most beautifully framed between two dark, well-trimmed yews. The exterior of the church is picturesque and charming enough, but its chief attractions are within. The interior walls and pillars of bare stone give a rare impression of solidity and strength in contrast to the delicate colourings of the windows and ornamentations, and an unusual medieval touch is added by the oak rood-loft, which bears inscribed the date: 'Anno Dom MVCLVIII'.

Hubberholme is delightful. I was loth to forsake its charms on that bright autumn morning for the bleak hills which jealously guard it, and most people who call there with a scheduled timetable will leave it finding there is leeway to be made up. Autumn must be the best time of the year to visit this valley. I could not imagine a prettier picture than that which surrounded me as I climbed out of it. The pastures by the river were still vivid green where the hay had lain, but all else was alight with glorious yellows and browns. The hillsides were splashed with gold where the bracken lay dying; the trees far up on their slopes were feathery touches of bronze.

The old lane from Hubberholme to Cray gives a fine view across an amphitheatre of flat meadows into the throat of Wharfedale. Buckden, perched on the hillside like a Tibetan monastery, is the centre of the picture, but the dominant feature is Buckden Pike, which stands sentinel over the dale. High along its shoulder runs a motor-road which leads to Bishopdale. Higher still is the old green road, a track beloved of walkers who are joyfully entering or reluctantly quitting this fairest of Yorkshire's valleys. This green road, in common with others of its kind, shows a sublime disregard for gradients, but it was engineered, one cannot help thinking, by men who had a great love for spacious views and the fresh winds of the open fells.

Cray should be amongst the loveliest of Wharfedale's hamlets, yet it is not, and it is difficult to decide just why it falls short of the high standard you have come to expect. It lacks nothing of natural beauty. There are milky-white cascades, a whole series of them, which even the road as it cuts through them cannot rob of loveliness. There are noble oaks and sycamores and beeches in the woods below, while the rowans add a touch of scarlet to the scene. There are limestone cliffs in the background of rolling fells.

Yet the place has an air of desolation; it chills where Hubberholme charms. There are but few buildings now; an inn, a farmhouse, a cottage, a barn or two, and it gives the impression that it has fallen from grace, that once there were many more. And the stolid soul who has turned the banks of the lively stream into poultry-runs deserves a reward of addled eggs for his enterprise; he has contributed nothing at all to the attractions of the hamlet. A slimy, hen-infested enclosure does not invite a picnic, in Wharfedale as elsewhere, and though most visitors to Cray will stop to look at the cascades, they will not tarry long.

The last buildings in the dale are at Cray. Beyond, the road rises steeply for a mile to the top of Kidstones Pass, and along this route there are many manifestations of limestone, seen and unseen. I stood in a field by the highway and could hear a tumult of rushing waters beneath my feet, but of a stream there was no outward sign. Away on the right, a waterfall tumbles over a white cliff, yet though the ground sloped towards me, my eyes searched in vain for the beck which reason demanded should be there. But before the mile was completed, the limestone was behind me, and had given place to millstone grit. There are long cliffs of it, grey and forbidding even in sunlight, on Kidstones Fell on the left, while on the right it can be seen cropping through the ground at intervals on the two-mile climb to the summit of Buckden Pike.

When the last steep corner was breasted, a scene of complete desolation was unfolded. In vivid contrast to the well-wooded valley from which I had ascended, the rough wilderness of Kidstones appeared rugged and inhospitable. There were no habitations, no trees within sight, nothing to relieve the bleakness of the rolling moorlands. The pass is a shallow scoop in the hills; the hard blue road runs through it for a mile, then plunges down the far side into Bishopdale.

Near the highest part of the road, there is a signpost. It stands where a wide, grassy lane runs northwards from the road, up and up to the skyline, there to disappear over the top. This green track is a walkers' way par excellence. The signpost says: 'Bainbridge'. Wisely, it omits the distance, for once you are on the way, you lose count of the miles; your measure is the succession of glorious panoramas which greet you, one after another, as you go with the wind across the wild uplands.

Oh, how can I put into words the joys of a walk over country such as this; the scenes that delight the eyes, the blessed peace of mind, the sheer exuberance which fills your soul as you tread the firm turf? This is something to be lived, not read about. On these breezy heights, a transformation is wondrously wrought within you. Your thoughts are simple, in tune with your surroundings; the complicated problems you brought with you from the town are smoothed away. Up here, you are near to your Creator; you are conscious of the infinite; you gain new perspectives; thoughts run in new strange channels; there are stirrings in your soul which are quite beyond the power of my pen to describe. Something happens to you in the silent places which never could in the towns, and it is a good thing to sit awhile in a quiet spot and meditate. The hills have a power to soothe and heal which is their very own. No man ever sat alone on the top of a hill and planned a murder or a robbery, and no man ever came down from the hills without feeling in some way refreshed, and the better for his experience.

It makes me sad to reflect that there are people who have no urge to visit the high lonely places; who have no desire to be rid of the noise and tumult for a while. It is distressing to see the crowds of young people thronging the streets and dance halls and cinemas; they go through life without seeing the best it has to offer. There are young men of my acquaintance who have never climbed Pendle, yet they see it every day of their lives; who cannot remember having seen heather on a moor. Worse still, they cannot be persuaded to go, and I refuse to believe that I am a poor advocate. The herding instinct is growing, as if one's own company was boredom complete, and to be avoided at all costs. Young people are almost fearful of being alone, which I can readily appreciate if some of their observations are indicative of their state of mind. They are boys and girls at school, men and women when they leave. The best part of life, youth, is skipped over. It is natural for a girl to mature early, but a boy should not become a man until he is no longer physically capable of doing what he did when a boy. And when, at any age, he can no longer indulge in boyish enthusiasms, he is ready for the grave.

I am past thirty now, and I used to think of persons of thirty-odd as being awfully old, but I find that my capacity to enjoy a boyish adventure grows even keener as the years pass. I am not a day older in spirit than I was twenty years ago. When I can no longer find any interest in a map or a book of travel, nor derive any pleasure from a winding path, nor wish to sit on a fence and watch the trains go by, then life should come to an end. When memories fail to thrill, what can the future hold?

The track over Stake Pass was made by the Romans; and since the warrior legions marched over it, its invitation has been extended to all. From end to end, it is seven miles. Twice in recent months I have been along it, and not met a soul. I commend it to you. It is a green ribbon between purple and brown moors; for most of the way it is enclosed by low, tumbledown walls, which neither confine you nor restrict your views. Once you are through the little stony gorge at the Kidstones end, where the track is cut out of the living rock, you walk on grass for mile after mile, and all the time you are on the top of the earth, above all else in sight, near to heaven. The sky is your neighbour, and it is vast.

Walking on this delightful path is joy unbounded. It is level, so level that you could measure off cricket pitch after cricket pitch and need no roller; it is springy, so that your steps are elastic and prodigious; it is plain to follow, so that your eyes need not be fixed on it, but may search the distant horizons. Plain to follow, yes; it is before you all the way; it never hesitates, but sweeps on and on towards the trench of Wensleydale ahead. Its highest point is 1832 feet above sea level.

In the heart of the moors the track branches into two. Bifurcates is the better word, but it seems out of place to apply such a word to so simple a track. The left branch descends at once towards Raydale; the right branch, which is rather less distinct, continues along the tops and finally drops you plumb into Bainbridge. The right branch is the logical continuation of our path, and is a far better finish than the other, but on this occasion I went down the hill to Raydale to get a glimpse of Semer Water.

When I was in Bainbridge earlier in the year, the man at whose cottage I stayed had said that Semer Water was as lovely as Windermere, a ridiculous assertion that made me sulk for the rest of the evening. Semer Water I had not seen, Windermere I knew well; and though I consider Windermere to lack the beauty of the other lakes in that district, I resent its comparison with any other lake which another part of the country has to offer. There is nothing outside Lakeland which is like Lakeland.

However, Semer Water was again at hand, so I made a detour

to see it. . . . It is a flooded field. It is unique only because it is the one sheet of water the Yorkshire Dales can show.

Raydale, though, in whose bosom it lies cradled, is quite pretty. The head of this little valley is deep in the wild fells, but there are woodlands where the sparkling rills make their last ecstatic leaps down the hillsides, and green meadows come right against rough uncultivated ground. There are the quiet hamlets of Marsett, Stalling Busk and Countersett, and for a background a range of high fells which ends abruptly at Countersett Crag.

Bainbridge stands guard at the entrance to Raydale, and here the little valley loses its identity and merges into Wensleydale. There is a Roman camp here with a notable museum, and a workhouse, so that Bainbridge attracts both rich and idle poor. The village itself is interesting; there is a spacious village green with cottages lining its four sides, and in the middle the old stocks. The Bain flows behind the houses over a succession of weirs, and if you stand on the bridge at dusk and look down into the water, watch for the bats flitting about the arches and buttresses.

I called in the post office for a drink, and while I was there the local policeman rode up on his bicycle, dismounted, and entered the shop. The postmaster questioned him eagerly: was there any further news? No, the policeman had nothing new to offer; things looked very black, it was a bad job, there was nothing to do but wait and see what happened; aye, a bad job. Not until Hitler was mentioned, did I sense they were talking about the new war. I had completely forgotten about it.

From Bainbridge I went on to Askrigg, a much bigger village a mile along the valley, and there I had some tea.

Wensleydale is disappointing; writers have been too kind to it. I have seen it described as the comely matron of the Yorkshire Dales, but surely a comely matron has more appeal for a tired traveller than this. Wide and attractive the valley certainly is, and so far the resemblance may hold good, but it has not the comforting charm of its alleged prototype. I believe I could enjoy the company of a comely matron, but here the likeness collapses altogether for I found little in Wensleydale to tempt me to stay. By comparison, its neighbouring dales are ravishing beauties to whom one finds it difficult to say farewell. Wensleydale lacks the element of surprise; it sets all its stall out before your eyes as you descend into it, and keeps nothing in reserve. There are no hidden corners, nothing to keep anticipation alive. For mile after mile the scene scarcely changes; it is pleasant enough and unutterably serene, but there is no feature to arrest attention. The valley is too broad, the hills which bound it lack individuality. One longs for a harsh, discordant note amongst the graceful lines that compose the picture, but the unexpected never happens in Wensleydale.

The people of the valley are friendly, likeable folk who are themselves well content to live where they do: more than any other dalesfolk, they are proud of their dale, and are made happy by telling an outsider of its delights. They are willing to share their good fortune, and welcome visitors. They are so ready to enthuse over their surroundings that it hurts to have to tell them there are lovelier places. But if you do make such an observation, let it be general: don't for instance say that personally you find Swaledale or Wharfedale lovelier. Better still to say nothing at all, but listen to their eulogies and wonder if you have come there blindfold.

There is an air of quiet prosperity about Wensleydale; the meadows are lush and the cattle fat. The houses are trim, clean, well kept, and the people look happy and well satisfied with their lot. As I walked along Askrigg's busy High Street, I was very conscious that I was the only one in rags.

One delightful characteristic which the dalespeople share is their obvious unwillingness to incur a visitor's displeasure by overcharging him for his meal or his night's lodging. When the time comes for a settlement of the amount owing, it finds them shy and confused as though this were the moment they had been dreading. As often as not during my journey, I was asked to pay what I thought would be reasonable. This is jolly, when the pocket is light and one knows that penury faces the return from holiday. Possibly in my case, their reluctance was sponsored by my unkempt appearance, although I strove hard to speak and conduct myself like a gentleman, and met with a fair measure of success.

It was half-past four when I left Askrigg, and the first mile of the road which climbs steeply out of the village in the direction of

Swaledale taxed my tired limbs sorely, so that I stopped to look back more often than the view deserved. I was not exhausted, as I had been yesterday, but my legs took to the uphills rebelliously. My cold was no better, and my last clean handkerchief had been in commission since noon; unless there was a sudden improvement, the future, as regards necessary attention to my weeping nose, was gloomy indeed, and much too distressing a prospect to think about philosophically. On previous occasions, I have been without handkerchiefs when handkerchiefs were demanded and bits torn off my shirt have served, for on my walks, as alas at other times, I wear very old shirts. But this time I had hardly started on my journey, and I could see that before it was finished ten days hence, I should have to exercise considerable ingenuity to keep up the supply without stripping myself naked.

A long mile out of Askrigg, the road suddenly shoots out of its confining walls, and the climb is over. Across the common the way lies now, and its route is made clear by the stout ten-foot poles which stick out of the ground by the roadside at intervals of fifty yards. Those guide-posts are enthralling; your eyes pick them out, one after another until you have the series complete; away in the far distance, they seem no bigger than matches. When the moor is under snow, they serve to indicate the course of the road and then, I fancy, they will fascinate.

The road attains a height of 1633 feet, and as I started to descend on the other side, the scene changed rapidly. Wensleydale had been lost to sight for some time, and for half an hour I had been traversing a wide grassy moorland. Now, abruptly, in front of me the road was sloping downhill into a new valley, and my pace quickened with interest.

Only glimpses could be seen, as yet, of what lay ahead, but they were sufficient to send me eagerly forward. Almost immediately, the road bifurcated, and as I was bound for Muker I kept to the left branch. The surface of the road had changed as completely as the character of the countryside, and where before I kept to the grass verge to avoid the hard smooth macadam, here I was slipping and sliding downhill on a loose pebbly surface. The right branch disappeared at once, and I never saw it again. Actually, it keeps along the edge of the moor for some distance, while my own road was taking me rapidly down into the valley, through a rocky boulder-strewn gorge with a most impressive wall of crags above on the right.

Swaledale was in front now, unfolding a little more of its beauty with every step I took.

It was dusk when I came down to the floor of the valley, and the distant views were blurred, but I could see copse and woodland, rich meadow and pleasant pasture wonderfully blended in the shades of soaring hill and ragged peak, and my heart warmed at the sight. This was infinitely better than Wensleydale. I left till tomorrow a comparison with Wharfedale.

Muker church beckoned me along the last half-mile, and a girl who passed me outside the village bid me good evening in so cheerful a voice and with so lovely a smile that I pressed on in eagerness to see what sort of a place this was to give me such a welcome.

Muker, as I stood in the deepening twilight on the bridge leading into it, struck me as being one of the oddest places I had ever seen. I cannot say it was out of place, for Swaledale abounds with surprises, but it seemed to me first of all that I had walked into the Tyrol, for here was a flowery Alpine village, a jumble of ill-assorted houses alongside a rushing mountain stream, a charming picture, almost a fantasy. Then, since there were no snow-capped peaks to complete the illusion, I began to regard it as a typical seaside fishing village, for the rough street which runs by the stream is a promenade where young and old lean against the railings and look down into the swirling waters. But a seaside village it cannot be, for there are open fells around it and these are typically Pennine. No, it is Muker in Swaledale, and there is not another place like it.

I went on over the bridge, and never passed from the sublime to the ridiculous more rapidly or more completely. I knocked on the door of the first cottage, and it was opened by a woman who was wearing false teeth which were palpably new and untrained. She couldn't take me in, I realised quite quickly, but I stood there transfixed, gaping at her unlovely mouth. At first, I thought she

had put her teeth in back to front accidentally, but no, they were
so plain to see, and there seemed to be half a dozen clattering
rows of them. Then I wondered if they were upside down, for
they wobbled in startling fashion. No, they were in all right, but
most assuredly they did not fit. When she laughed, as she did
once heartily for a reason I cannot recall, the top set remained
clenched to the lower, and her laugh came from an aperture
which suddenly appeared above both. The effect was ghastly. She
had no shame.

I passed shuddering from her sight, walked up the little cobbled street by the church, and tried again at the first door I came
to. I knocked loudly, and an inquiring head looked out of the
next door up the street. In many of the older cottages, structural
alterations have taken place, and quite often you find that two
cottages have been made into one by removing the dividing inner
wall or putting a doorway into it, while the exterior remains
unaltered. So it was here, a dwelling with two front doors. I
always feel taken aback when I knock at one door and am
answered from another, yet this is clearly an occasion for a
surprised laugh and a show of good humour as you foolishly pace
the distance between. My own feeling is one of chagrin.

Mrs Harker was quite willing to provide bed and breakfast
and, what seemed more important just then, make me a supper.
Two ladies were staying there for the night; they had motored
from London that day without any pre-determined plans, and as
I settled down for my meal they went out to inform their
husbands by telephone of their destination.

After supper, I placed the visitors' book on the table by the oil
lamp and looked through it, and then at the pictures in the
family album. The old photographs were surprisingly good, and
often extremely funny, but it was absorbing to trace a youthful
face through the years into old age, as could be done quite easily,
so complete was the record and so changeless the expression. I
could pick out, say, a young girl, turn a page or two and see her
again, a little older and accompanied now by a frightfully
starched young man; go on a bit and see them again, this time
with a child; and later, surrounded with children. Then I could

follow the progress of the children until they too became espoused and bore offspring. Old photographs should never be destroyed.

Later, I was invited into the next room to talk to Mr Harker, and I was glad to get into the cosier atmosphere of the kitchen, for I was feeling chilled.

My host, with whose features I had been made familiar during my inspection of the photograph album, proved to be most interesting, and I came right out of my shell and spent an enjoyable hour in his company. He was, like most dalesmen, shrewd and stolid and unexcitable; he made decisions slowly and with great forethought, and he could draw on a vast fund of experience. He sat in his nook by the fire and uttered his pronouncements like a judge on the bench, and they were full of wisdom and commonsense. This is the type of man, not the type who draws a princely salary on the strength of examination qualifications, in whose company I feel a duffer. His descriptions of life in the dale were full of colour; he talked of the changes that had taken place during his lifetime in the customs of the village, and told how most things had not changed in the least: for example there had not been a new dwelling erected in Muker since he was a baby. He had been born in this house, and his wife in the next cottage, and I couldn't help thinking how lovely their romance must have been.

Then he went on to express his views on the Crisis, and summed up the position so clearly that I was astonished at his ready grasp of the essential factors of the problem. It seemed incongruous that a tiny place like Muker, so hidden away and lonely, should concern itself with air-raid precautions, but he assured me that there was a lively interest in the subject amongst the villagers, and they were rapidly preparing themselves for any eventuality that might arise. In fact, it was a source of perpetual amazement to me during my journey, to find that in every hamlet, however remote, there was a very real awareness of the gravity of the international situation and the latest developments were eagerly followed and discussed. I saw countless notices pinned on barn-doors and trees, calling for volunteers and announcing local meetings to decide what measures should be taken to ensure the protection of the property of the parish. It all seemed so wildly unnecessary, so extravagant. But the job was tackled whole-heartedly.

About ten o'clock, the two other visitors returned in some consternation, after a two-hour vigil in the telephone box. Their efforts to get a call through to London had all failed; they had tried a score of times, but the operator had told them at last it was useless; every line to London was busy, and had been constantly occupied all the evening.

They came out of the darkness like ghosts; their entrance startled the three of us round the fire. We could see at once that they were upset and shocked; and their obvious concern was not alone for their own problem. As they told of their hopeless wait, a fear which had grown upon them gradually while they had been outside in the street seemed to communicate itself suddenly to the Harkers and myself. 'Something terrible is happening tonight, something terrible. What can it be?'

This was a moment of drama. The scene is impressed indelibly on my mind: the two women standing by the door in uncertainty, their faces white and drawn; Mrs Harker in the middle of the room, looking at them speechlessly, struck with sudden fear; the old man staring at me most oddly. The firelight and the lamp cast black dancing shadows on the walls and low ceiling; for the first time I heard a clock ticking loudly in a dim corner. Something is happening, something is happening. I felt strangely cold, uneasy. Nobody spoke, nobody needed to speak; our thoughts were alike, and they were fearful, apprehensive. The night was quiet, as it is before a thunderstorm. . . .

We were five people in a little cottage amongst the hills, miles from anywhere, and the other four I had not seen until a short time ago, but a common anxiety established a bond between us; an important development had taken place, we knew, and we all sensed that it was for the worst; whatever it may be, we were all concerned in it; there was escape for none. As for myself, I felt I was again face to face with the ogre from which I was fleeing.

Harker turned in his chair at length and switched on the wireless. We watched his movements. We waited in dread and suspense. . . . A thin voice came out of the black night, grew into the familiar tones of the announcer. Herr Hitler had been speaking today in Berlin. His mind was quite made up. The territory on which he had set his heart should be his; if it was not handed over to him by the first day of October, his troops would march over the border and acquire it by force. The people of the territory were preparing an armed resistance and calling on their allies. For the first time in history, a murderer was announcing his intentions beforehand, and fixing a date for his bloodshed: such are the mathematics of modern slaughter. On October the first, the war would commence.

October the first. Today was September the twenty-sixth.

We had four days to live.

THE THIRD CHAPTER

T HE SKY was grey and overcast when I peeped out of my
bedroom window early next morning; the roofs of the
nearby cottages were wet.

It was barely six o'clock, and I could hear no sounds about the
house. I took my maps from my rucksack, climbed back into bed
with them, and lit the candle.

Give me a map to look at, and I am content. Give me a map of
country I know, and I am comforted: I live my travels over again;
step by step, I recall the journeys I have made; half-forgotten
incidents spring vividly to mind, and again I can suffer and rejoice
at experiences which are once more made very real. Old maps
are old friends, understood only by the man with whom they
have travelled the miles. Nobody could read my maps as I do.
Lend a book to a friend and he can enjoy it and miss nothing of
its story: lend him a map, and he cannot even begin to read the
tale it has to tell. For maps are personal things which books are
not. The appeal of an old map is to the memory; an old map
spread across my knees closes my eyes. The older, the more
tattered it is, the greater my affection for it. I recall our adventures together in storm and sunshine; an occasion, perhaps, when
it slipped from my pocket and I searched my tracks anxiously, as
for a lost companion, until it was found; an occasion, perhaps,
when the mist was thick and instinct and the map urged different
ways, and I followed the map and came to safe ground again. Ah
yes, maps are grand companions. I have thrown books away, but
never a map.

Give me a map of country I do not know, even of country I shall never know, and it has the power to thrill and excite me. No book has such an appeal to the imagination. A new map means new routes to plan, and ever so carefully, for the ground is strange and regard must be given to contours and watersheds and passes. My map becomes not a square of coloured linen, but a picture of the country itself. That blue daub becomes a glittering lake fringed with pine woods; the black specks a clustered village set amongst rich meadows in a corner of the valley; the faint red lines a steep mountain face soaring majestically into the heavens. My route is planned to the last detail, altered again and again; it is an ambitious programme, for there are no ties of home to bind me and limit the objective; expense is nothing. It is finished; it is perfect. It doesn't matter that I will never be able to do it. My pleasure has been great, yet, sadly enough, it is a pleasure shared by the very few. Map-lovers are scarce, book-lovers many, yet I think the reward of the lover of maps is far and away the greater. If it is ever my lot to be cast away on a desert island, let it be with an atlas and a one-inch map of the Lake District.

For this journey I had found it necessary to buy five maps of the Ordnance Survey. These took in the whole backbone of the Pennines from Pendle to the Cheviots, and spread out together, as they could be only with the furniture pushed up against the walls, they made a picture which gave me many evenings of joyful anticipation. Anticipation is always a big part of the holiday to me; realisation consists chiefly of the satisfaction of achieving that which I have pledged myself to achieve; then, when I am back at my own fireside, recollection begins and never ceases, so that a holiday is never completely finished and done with.

Anticipation is often more pleasurable than realisation; recollection is the sweetest of all and the most enduring. The mentality which urges you never to anticipate, never to count your chickens before they are hatched, is wrong all to blazes. Let your anticipation run riot, plan and dream of things far above your grasp, reach after them in your imagination even when reality is receding, think about them always. Plan new achievements, and set about achieving them. Failure and disappointment simply don't matter; go ahead with your dreaming, let your enthusiasm run away with you. You were made to rise and soar, and come down to earth with a bump, and rise and soar again. If you accomplish nothing else, you'll have kept the rot and the rust away. Let me warn you: it's the practical people who stay rooted on the earth, who make the money. But it's the dreamers who touch the stars. Which is the success you plan? Are you to 'play safe' for the rest of your life, or are you to adventure? You must make a choice, and make it early; and having made it, you must abide by it.

I had walked off the first map at Horton, and now, at Muker, I was near the top margin of the second. Teesdale was my objective for the third day, and as I lay in bed studying my third map, it seemed a very long way off. One geographical feature repeats itself consistently in the eighty miles of Northern Pennines. The backbone runs north and south, and this is the main range; the vertebrae are the separate hills which compose the range, and from the main vertebrae run the ribs, ridges of high moor extending eastwards. Between the ribs are the arteries, the rivers. A queer skeleton this, with ribs on one side only, for there are none on the west. But its flesh is firm and solid, and purple with heather.

Walking northwards, then, along the eastern flank of the Pennines involves continuous ascent and descent, and renders the journey doubly arduous and doubly exhilarating. On my first day, I had climbed up from Ribblesdale and dropped down into Littondale, up again and down into Wharfedale. Yesterday, up again and down into Wensleydale, up again and down into Swaledale. Today, it was to be up again to Tan Hill and down into the Greta Valley, up again and down into Teesdale. Reserved for tomorrow was the hardest day of all: up out of Teesdale and down into Weardale, up again and down to Rockhope Burn, up again and down to Blanchland and the Derwent. The ridges are fairly uniform in height, being little short of 2000 feet above the sea, so that in addition to walking twenty miles a day, I had three or four thousand feet of climbing.

This proved to be rather more than enough for me, and I finished each day either in dusk or darkness and dead-tired, for my reserves of strength are so meagre as to be almost non-existent. I was never at any time on this holiday completely physically exhausted, but on the Cumbrian hills have often been utterly played out and simply flopped in my tracks. Then I have found, as all walkers must have who confess to having been in this state, that nervous energy takes over the reins and drives me on, the limbs obeying quite mechanically. Nervous energy is, with me, a tap inexhaustible. The biggest jobs I ever tackled, whether walking or working or playing, have been completed on my nerves long after my body has given up.

When the church clock struck eight, I got up and went downstairs, and stood at the front door until breakfast was ready. The morning showed no signs of improvement; the sky was the colour of steel, but at least it was fine, and the roofs and cobbles were slowly drying, although it seemed to me they were doing so only half-heartedly as though they secretly knew they were wasting their time, that soon they would be made wet again.

I got away as soon as I could after breakfast, following the path which the Harkers had urged me to take, and which every guide-book selects as the finest thing Swaledale has to offer. There is only one way to Keld for the walker, and that is by the river. It is really a very fine walk. The Harkers said it was a pity I should have to go there for the first time on such a dull morning, but afterwards I wondered if I had not seen it at its best. For the narrow valley is wild and rugged, and sunshine can only soften and destroy the effect; but I saw it in the teeth of a wind that swept through the gorge as through a funnel, bringing with it sheets of heavy rain, so that the atmosphere of desolation was sharply accentuated, and the picture seen in a proper setting.

I was barely clear of Muker when it began to rain, and for the first time I shrouded myself in the cape I had brought with me. I crossed a few wet fields and came alongside the river. The Swale hurries along here in full flight, carving new channels when in the mood, so that its bed of pebbles is very wide and for the most part dry. I should like to come here when the river is in flood, and sit and watch the scene.

The path follows the left bank of the river closely, and for a mile you are heading right into the hills and cannot see how you are going to get out without climbing the high fells which confront you, but suddenly there is a sharp turn to the left, and your exit is clear. The first mile of the path to Keld has the character of a wild Lakeland valley; the second mile is different, and has the sylvan appeal of a Derbyshire dale. The path winds through woods and glades, and there are waterfalls in plenty if you take the trouble to look for them.

The river is left well below in its ravine as Keld is approached, and you enter this village by the back way, beside the chapel. Keld is like Buckden in Wharfedale, the last outpost in the valley, but where Buckden is cosy and comfortable, Keld is by comparison barren, and appears far less hospitable.

I give my vote to Wharfedale as Yorkshire's loveliest dale, with Swaledale second. Buckden and Hubberholme share first place as villages, but Wharfedale can show nothing like Muker.

As I left Keld behind me, patches of blue appeared in the sky, and by the time I came to the bridge where the Tan Hill road starts, the sun was shining brilliantly. From this point, it is four uphill miles to the Tan Hill Inn which stands in supreme isolation in the middle of a vast moorland. It is the highest public house in the country, and if this claim has been vainly disputed, surely none will argue that it is not the loneliest. The road to it from Keld is a strip of macadam thrown on to the rough moorland, and it passes through a scene of utter desolation. The silence grips your soul as you march along.

I had not gone far before the rain came again. The blue splashes overhead were wiped out, and a cold, clammy mist descended on the earth. I lived in this mist for four hours until I came down on the other side of the moor. I could see the width of the road, no more; there was a white wall before me and around me; my world shrank to the compass of a few yards, and those few yards were wet, sodden, soaking.

I enjoy a mist; it hides you so completely. If it is a mist on a mountain top, there is not a person in the world to witness your actions; you are as alone as the first man on earth. A mist sharpens the faculties, as those of a blind man are sharpened. You sense danger, and there is nobody to help and advise; you have to use your wits and keep alert, for you are at a disadvantage with this

baffling adversary. He has strange powers, this white monster. He
can ensnare you so easily; he tempts you from the plainest of
tracks; he makes the meekest of men adventurers. He can
transform a blade of grass into a tree, a boulder into a huge crag, a
sheep into a lion. He drops his silent veil and you enter an
enchanted land. Yes, it is good to walk in a mist now and again,
and know your own limitations, and be scared by your own
helplessness.

I should not have enjoyed this climb to the inn nearly so well
had it not been for the grass verge that borders the narrow road
throughout its length. Here I could stride along on the softest of
carpets as quickly as I pleased, for, with the hard road only a yard
away, I could not possibly go astray. No motors passed me; no
pedestrians.

One busy little fellow I came across: a furry animal in a
desperate hurry to get below ground out of the rain, but lacking
the patience to continue any one of the dozen burrows he had
started. At first, I could not give him a name. He was six inches
long, and had a stumpy tail; his body was covered with short grey
fur, except for his long snout and his feet, which were pink and
hairless. He had no sense of smell, and if he had eyes they were
blind. I knelt down within twelve inches of him, and watched him
for a quarter of an hour. Only when I touched him was he aware of
my presence; then he stopped rooting and seemed a bit startled,
but could only crouch and had no idea where to run for safety. I
drew on my limited knowledge of natural history and called him a
mole, and I left him there sticking his silly nose inquisitively into
every tiny clump of grass, scratching into the roots and turning
over thimblefuls of black earth, turning away in disgust and
starting his feeble operations a few inches away. For me, there was
the Tan Hill, a fire and a drink; but this strange little beggar, cursed
as he was with dissatisfaction at all his efforts, seemed likely to be
longer before he could rest his limbs in comfort.

I enjoyed every inch of that march to the Tan Hill. I had not so
much as a glimpse of the countryside; the sides of the road were
fringed with rushes and long rank grass, and these suggested the
wilderness which I knew there must be all around me. Steadily

uphill I went, with the white wall five yards away receding before me as I advanced, and silently creeping up behind. The grass beneath me I could see distinctly, each blade and leaf bearing its glittering jewel, but objects further away were shadowy and indistinct. I felt as though I were in a cocoon, or as though the heat of my body had melted the mist immediately around me. There is no monotony for me in such conditions; out comes my map; I note the main features of the way I have to go—a bridge, a sharp bend, a sudden steep rise—and I set myself a time in which to reach each of them. In this way, I make myself absolutely familiar with my route beforehand, and I have played the game so often and know my pace so well that I can determine my position exactly by a glance at my watch.

I left Keld at quarter to eleven, and told myself that I should be at the bridge across Stonesdale Beck at twenty past. At twenty minutes past I was completely enveloped in mist, and visibility was nil, but within two minutes I heard the murmur of running water and sure enough the low parapet of the little bridge grew into shape before my eyes. The next feature was a sharp turn to the right, three-quarters of a mile ahead; the road was fairly level along here, fifteen minutes would suffice. Fourteen minutes go by and my eyes are on my watch; on I go into the mist for a few more paces, straining my eyes for the bend which I know is now but a few yards ahead, and almost immediately the wet macadam swerves across my vision and I turn right. I can imagine only one pursuit more fascinating than map-reading, and that is map-making.

Up and up sweeps the road; the mist no longer lies heavy on the land, but is becoming mobile, drifting silently. I am nearing the top of the moor, and peer excitedly into the gloom for the signpost which I know stands at the road junction at the summit. Out of the murk it comes, a ghostly shadow, standing solitary, like a black gibbet. It thrills me to see it at last, the only landmark erected by man along the whole stretch of moor.

I welcome it as a friend.

The Tan Hill Inn stands within fifty yards of the signpost, but there was not the slightest evidence of its existence. I went slowly now until I came to a board stuck in the ground by the roadside; it read 'England's Highest Inn'. I looked intently about me: presently I could discern the dim outline of a building across the road. I crossed to it, entered the porch, and pulled my cape off. Then I went along the passage and into the big, stone-flagged kitchen.

There was instantaneous relief to the eyes, as there is when I put on my glasses after mislaying them. I could see clearly again, and the transition from blindness was so sudden as to be almost startling.

A huge fire was burning in the grate, a fire big enough to feed a factory boiler; quite the biggest blaze I have ever seen in a dwelling-house. I sat on a chair in the middle of the floor, and a small pool began to form around my shoes. I had a drink, and some bread and cheese.

Presently, the family foregathered in the kitchen for dinner. There was the innkeeper, who is, I believe, first and foremost a shepherd; a grizzled companionable old fellow who came in out of the mist and straightway wolfed a meal that would have lasted me a week, using his spoon as a shovel. There was a good-looking young man of my own age, and the young woman who had provided my refreshment. They had little to say to each other, and I wondered as I watched them how long I could survive in their lonely environment. They had little to say because they had no gossip; they had no neighbours. Themselves they knew so well; there was nothing new to discuss.

They listened eagerly to the few observations I made and, when I told them I was heading for Teesdale, were very ready with advice as to the best way to get there. The mention of Teesdale caused the young man to observe that the day before a man's body had been pulled out of the Tees at Cauldron Snout, whereupon the old fellow looked up from his dinner, and asked, with the air of a teacher addressing a class, whether the inquest would be held in Durham or Yorkshire; a question that surprised me, although I knew of the country people's likeness for testing the local knowledge of their fellows. The young man replied that it depended on which side of the river the body was pulled out, and the old man gave a grunt of agreement. I consulted my map, and found that the Tees, throughout its early course, forms the boundary between the two counties.

I spent an interesting hour in the Tan Hill Inn, and was loth to leave the blazing fire for there was no improvement outside. The young man had asked, shyly, if he might look at my map, and studied it with a childish absorption. Probably never before had he seen his home on a map, nor been able to see, as in a picture, its relation to the few other farms and villages he knew. Here he had an aeroplane's view of the countryside he lived in, and it was a revelation to him. Roads he knew in part could here be traced in full, and for the first time he followed their course to the distant places he had heard of but never visited. Not until I was pulling on my cape did he hand it back to me, half-apologetically, and the smile on his face and the new interest in his eyes made me wonder if, in this unlikely spot, I had met a kindred soul. I resolved to send the map on to him when I had finished with it and was back at home where I could buy another; but I never have. Often it's the kindnesses which are easy to perform which seem the most trouble.

I went out into the rain again and looked back when I had taken twenty paces, to find that the inn had vanished completely—and I was alone once more. I had originally intended to have the inn behind me at noon, for I had still sixteen miles to go if I was to be in Middleton that night, but it was nearly half-past one when I said goodbye to its cheerful warmth.

I swung along at a good pace for two miles until another signpost pointed out the pony-track to Bowes and Barnard Castle, and here I left the hard road behind. I was now at a lower elevation, and could see for greater distances, but the drizzle gave way to pouring rain. It is five long miles from Tan Hill to the farm buildings of Sleightholme, and the way lies across a dreary upland waste marked on the map as Bog Moss, a name which struck me, as I splashed through it, as being singularly apt.

Sleightholme, that afternoon, was too saturated to show signs of life, and I passed through the farmyard without attracting attention even from the kennel. In a pasture beyond, however, there was life, and life abundant, and in a form I particularly detest. Thirty or forty young bulls ranged the field I had to cross. I hung gloomily over the gate and surveyed them, slowly marshalling together all the facts I had learned about bulls. Bulls do not become vicious until they are three years old; a bull with a ring in its nose is not necessarily vicious, but a bull without a ring in its nose may be; a bull over three years old is not to be allowed to roam in a field where there is a public footpath; young bulls are called bullocks. My mental processes on this occasion were slow, but I arrived eventually at the conclusion that the beasts before me were bullocks under three years of age and therefore quite docile, and this conclusion was happily borne out by events, for I got to the other gate without incident—though to be sure I kept close to the wall all the way.

Talking about bulls, I am always totally unable to identify a bull by the shape of his head, as most people seem able to do, and I fear that this lamentable ignorance will one day cost me dear. If the hind parts are visible I can make a decision quickly and accurately, but if the brute is sitting down or facing me, I am lost. Too often I have been stricken with palsy upon meeting one of these animals face to face, and only by cautiously circling round for a sideways view has confidence been restored. But one of these days, it will be a bull over three years old, I feel sure, and I have not yet evolved a satisfactory plan to adopt if this circumstance arises. Run fast I cannot, and my fondest theory, that of making towards a pre-determined haven in a series of sharp zig-zags, has never been tested.

A mile beyond Sleightholme, I walked out of the mist and rain and into brilliant sunshine. Before me was a most extensive panorama, for I was still fairly high, and three miles ahead was a cluster of roofs and a prominent white building as big as a gasometer set on a gentle slope, and this could not be other than Bowes. Behind me was a murky gloom, fell-top and cloud intermingled in a streaming grey blanket.

It was now three o'clock, and I began to realise that my prospects of getting to Middleton before dark were remote. I pushed on as quickly as I could, rejoicing in the feel of the hot sun on my back.

The three miles to Bowes seemed interminable. The countryside was not particularly attractive, though I find all new ground interesting, and the big white building ahead, to which my eyes were invariably drawn, appeared to get no nearer. This building I thought must be a castle, though I could not remember hearing of Bowes

Castle before; and I was unable to confirm it because Bowes, unfortunately was just off the side edge of my map.

I passed through innumerable gates bearing neat yellow inscriptions: 'Shut the gate and use Cooper's dip'. Shut the gates I did, and always do; but I cannot foresee any circumstances in which I will find it necessary to use Cooper's dip. Even if the occasion did arise, I very much doubt whether I should insist on Cooper's, for I do not deny that the imperious command, repeated on every gate, began to annoy me. They seemed to set up a personal attack on me, and disreputable though I was, I do not for a moment concede that my condition warranted the application of any make of dip.

The road I was walking along, instead of making a direct course for Bowes, started to prevaricate in the most exasperating manner and, without a map to guide me, I began to wonder whether it did actually lead to the village, for the white building was now directly to my left over a mile away, and still the road showed no signs of turning towards it. At one point, my way led through a delightful little wood, and just beyond here I overtook a farmer with two sheep dogs. I asked him if I should get to Bowes if I kept on, and he said I would, that the road turned eventually and came into the village from the far side. Thus comforted, I asked him what the white building was, and he said it was the new air-raid shelter. I fell for it. I should have realised instantly that an air-raid shelter, if it showed above the ground at all, would not present such a square, solid target, nor be the most conspicuous thing in the landscape, but my reasoning on this day was never acute. I think the fog must have got in the wheels. He chuckled at my credulity, and then explained that it was Bowes Castle in such a gentle voice that my mortification was increased. I went on in a bit of a huff, leaving him to proceed more slowly.

From the hillside, Bowes had seemed commonplace enough in its bare surroundings, but as I crossed the Greta in the floor of the valley and climbed the hill into the village, I reversed my earlier opinion. There are some fine trees near the bridge, and lovely woodlands flank the river; there are picturesque cottages and stately residences, and the most charming gardens I ever beheld, so that the man who was leisurely sweeping the dead leaves from the shady road in the midst of this perfumed Paradise seemed to me to have the most desirable task anyone could desire.

The main street of the village runs uphill between irregular rows of cottages, and has nothing of interest to show, unless it be the Unicorn Inn, which Dickens featured in *Nicholas Nickleby*. I had tea in the cold parlour of a house by the castle. My clothes were still damp, unpleasantly so, and my feet were soaking wet. I had to contend with fits of shivering during the meal, and my teeth chattered so much that it required an effort to put anything solid into my mouth, though, once in, it was uncontrollably masticated in very thorough fashion. Generally, I felt pretty miserable during this brief halt, and was glad to be off again.

I visited the castle, there being no charge for admittance. This is a remarkable ruin, surrounded by a dry moat. I spent several minutes pirouetting in the corners of the railed enclosure before I could get the whole structure in the view-finder of my camera. Finally, I did this to my satisfaction, and it was not until later that I discovered that this and subsequent snapshots were quite wasted, for whilst on the moor I had set the camera for a time-exposure, and omitted to readjust it. From Bowes to Blanchland in Northumberland, the shutter of my camera was wide open.

It was five o'clock when I left Bowes behind, and Middleton was still ten miles away. I realised now that I was unlikely to get so far that day, for my feet were definitely beginning to mutiny, and my legs were so stiff that I was alarmed, from time to time, to hear them creak.

The weather now appeared to be quite settled, and masses of white cumuli were drifting slowly across a blue sky casting shadows across the pleasant countryside. In a lane outside Bowes, I came across a gipsy encampment, the first of many I was to see. The caravans were standing in a wide dry ditch, along which a dozen or more piebald ponies were grazing. The community had built a fire in the grass, and a few grown-ups and several children were sitting idly round the flames. One of the men called out to me, and asked the time; and before many days had passed, I learned always to have the answer to that question ready when a gipsy camp came into sight. I never saw any of these Romany folk working; always they were squatting before a fire, doing absolutely nothing at all but gaze in the embers.

What their philosophy of life is, I cannot guess, but it must be perfected at a very early age, and I imagine none but those who are whispered the secret in their cradles can ever hope to understand it. Idleness has no defence; it causes mental and moral and physical stagnation; but the men I saw in these camps were completely inactive. They were not resting from their labours, but simply lounging, killing time. It was almost pathetic to see them, for theirs were not happy faces, but the hopeless, expressionless faces of men sunk deep in melancholy. Always, as I passed, one of their number would eagerly ask the hour, as though they were men with but little longer to live; yet I cannot to this day understand the benefit they derived from knowing the time, for the questioner invariably relapsed into stupor again. They were as men without hope, waiting for the end; they were refugees, outcasts, yet neither.

Soon I came to heathery uplands where a clean wind was blowing, and my spirits rose above physical discomfort and I even managed to introduce some semblance of rhythm into my laggardly pace. The sight of heather is to me like the sound of a band to marching men; it encourages and stimulates energy. Thus far, my way had led over brown grassy moorlands, but here I first made acquaintance with a purple landscape, and as I walked into the heart of it on that tranquil evening I was as a king entering his kingdom.

Teesdale was now opening out before me. A haze clung to the valley, robbing me of details but adding greatly to the charm of the view. I descended from heather to pastureland, and then my way carried me further downhill amongst meadows and woodlands, until ahead I could see the slender spire of a church peeping from the trees. And so I entered Cotherstone in Teesdale, and pronounced it good. This place is rather larger than a village, yet a village it is, for it has a village green. It bears the air of quiet prosperity which one expects from its stately surroundings. It is austere and aloof, and very pleased with itself. Its houses are large and of good appearance, its roads neat and its hedges well-trimmed, and there is a church handsome enough to grace the finest avenue of a city. There is an older part of the village around the corner, but my first impression was that Cotherstone resembled a better-class suburb of a large and thriving town. It is a place where the residents peep through the curtains rather than stand at the door.

Mimic warfare was being waged on the village green as I crossed it; a few small boys were engaged in grisly combat with invisible weapons and, because the agents of destruction could not be seen, the grim carnage seemed all the more horrible. One little fellow dashed at me, pointed his finger with dramatic effect, and said: 'Bang! You're dead!' I am not too far from my schooldays to appreciate the significance of this disquieting observation: it behoved me to clutch my gushing side, sink to my knees, and yield up the ghost with a hollow moan. I refused, however, to satisfy the blood-lust of my youthful adversary, not because sinking to the grass would be unpleasant, in fact I was sorely tempted; but because I was so far spent that had I done so I am quite sure I would have remained prone on Cotherstone village green all night.

Cotherstone offers no welcome for the visitor. It can manage quite well, thank you, without their patronage. If one of the cottages were to exhibit an 'Apartments' sign, Cotherstone would be outraged and humiliated, its dignity lost beyond recall. There is an inn, but there were motor-cars parked outside, and this is a bad token for the walker, so I went on and out at the other end of the village.

The evening was peaceful. The fields on each side of the road were carpeted with a dense white mist, so that the trees appeared to have neither trunks nor roots, but floated like driftwood on the sea. The western sky was still rosy, but the purple cloak of night was being drawn over the face of the quiet earth, and the pleasant landscape was settling down to a serene sleep.

Two miles further I came to Romaldkirk, and as it was then quite dark and I had walked over twenty miles, I looked about for a lodging for the night. Romaldkirk is a friendly place, with two inns abutting on the village green, which slopes downhill from the main road to the church, and on a summer's evening the villagers like to

congregate on the green and exchange gossip and watch the traffic
go by. The Rose and Crown was out of the question for me; it looked
much too fine and expensive and would have scrutinised me from
head to foot, I knew; so I waded through the long grass outside its
door and made my way to the Kirk Inn, an unpretentious little
house which half turns its back to the green and the busy road, and
seems to look coyly through its lashes and over its shoulder at the
Rose and Crown, as though this noisy and blatant neighbour were a
lover. Which heaven forbid, for if a union takes place the Kirk Inn,
like many a shy sweet woman, will have to hide her quiet comforting
ways, and give the stage to an arrogant husband.

And I am sadly afraid that this union will take place before long.
The Kirk Inn is not a place of laughter and song; it is forsaken and
lonely, and neglect is eating its heart away. Tragedy broods about the
house; once, I have no doubt, it was the cosiest tavern in Teesdale,
but it has at some time received a wound it cannot forgive, for the
friends who deserted it then have not come back. It is the quietest
inn I know; the silence of its rooms can be felt. The tick of the clock
can be heard all the evening. Occasionally, a laugh or a shout drifts in
from the Rose and Crown higher up the road, but within the Kirk
Inn there is the quiet of death. I opened the door of the inn at half-
past seven. It was not opened again that evening.

The lady of the house is a widow of about forty years, a quiet,
pleasant woman. She has two daughters, one a schoolgirl, the other
eighteen or so, and of such beauty that I was staggered by the only
glimpse I had of her. The woman was almost pathetically eager to
have me stay there, and I have plenty of evidence that the few
shillings she would gain would be most welcome. The poverty of the
place had its roots in the kitchen, and spread outwards from there. I
asked for biscuits, and heard one of the girls slip out by the back door
when her mother told her to go to the shop for some, and to get also
bacon and eggs for my breakfast; in fact, the house was so quiet that,
as I sat in the front room, I could hear every word of conversation in
the kitchen, and little of it was cheerful.

I felt strangely depressed, uncomfortable. Poverty I have been
familiar with, but never have I been able to regard it complacently,
especially where women and children are the sufferers. Yet it cannot

be evil, for born of its misery are sterling qualities which those who have not known it cannot comprehend. Number amongst the brave, the legions of poor women whose lives are a constant, wearying struggle to keep up appearances, who keep their sorrows to themselves, who utter no complaint in the face of a future which offers no release but that of the grave. But do not say that they do not suffer because they are accustomed to privation, and could not appreciate better circumstances. At the same time, be sparing in your spoken sympathy, for poverty does not kill pride.

I wondered what blight lay over the house, for the clock continued to chime the half-hours to an empty bar; and before long, I sensed that the woman would be reading my thoughts, and this made me yet more uneasy.

I never discovered the secret of the Kirk Inn. To this day, I do not know why it was avoided by the villagers. I came ultimately to the conclusion that the woman had been involved in some sort of scandal, and evil tongues had built a barrage round the place. For a mischievous tongue in a small community is a murderous weapon, and village life is coloured and sweetened and made palatable by gossip.

During the evening, the woman came into the front room and switched on a wireless set I had not previously noticed. She told me that the Prime Minister was to speak. Again that queer restriction at my heart! I had tried all day not to think of the awful business that had been scheduled in a madman's diary to commence on the first of October; it had seemed incredible in broad daylight that such lunacy was possible. I could not associate Tan Hill or Cotherstone Moor with war. But now, in the quiet of the evening and in strange surroundings, it all became real again, and when I had listened to the Premier's talk and gleaned not one shred of hope from his despairing words, I was sunk deeper than ever in despondency.

I went to bed early that night, for the room was cold and I had told my hostess not to trouble about a fire, though she implored me to let her make one.

I was shown into a poorly-furnished room overlooking the road and the church. The faded paintwork and cracked plaster were in keeping with the general appearance of the house. But an eiderdown and extra blankets had been brought out and placed on the bed. That was in keeping with the character of my welcome.

I looked out through the window into the darkness, before I crept into bed. Away up the road, the Rose and Crown was a blaze of light.

THE FOURTH CHAPTER

A THREATENING SKY next morning could not rob Romald-kirk of its charm. It had been too dark last evening to appreciate its quiet beauty, but now I found that I had unknowingly spent the night in an arbour of great loveliness. I found no other place in Teesdale quite so pleasant as Romaldkirk.

I was away early, for I had a long march ahead of me. I was due in Blanchland in time for supper, and Blanchland was in Northumberland. I was still in Yorkshire, four miles short of Middleton, where I should cross the river into Durham.

The rain came before I had gone far along the road, and I uttered a particularly vile and unusual oath as I flung off my rucksack and donned my cape. My clothes were still damp from yesterday's soaking, and my shoes were stiff and fast becoming shapeless. I wanted a day of sunshine to dry myself thoroughly, for I carried not a stitch of clothing in my pack, and I regarded the low clouds up the valley with a very jaundiced eye.

My small rucksack was in fact virtually empty, and I could have managed quite well without it. I incline to the view, never before expressed, that a rucksack is not at all necessary on a walking tour. How some hikers can enjoy themselves beneath the weight of their huge, fifty-pound burdens completely passes my comprehension. I have had expeditions in the Lake District without a pack, and gone short of nothing. I take a light raincoat or a cape, always; but never a change of clothes, nor an extra shirt, nor pyjamas. The clothes I wear when I set off must suffice: if they get wet, it is unfortunate for walking in wet raiment is unpleasant, but they have never failed to get dry afterwards. Pyjamas are, of course, a nuisance at all times and have no saving grace. A pair of slippers is a comfort, and additional socks are essential, but these will slip easily into a pocket.

On this occasion my rucksack contained four maps, the one in use being carried in my pocket. I had a toothbrush and a safety razor, a bottle of Indian ink and a pen, pencils and a rubber and a few postcards. I had also a miscellany of ointments and safe and certain cures for influenza, widely different in form and actually resembling each other only in the fact that they were one and all highly recommended by the medical profession. These latter properties were of course an innovation and were introduced only because my condition warranted some attention, but not one of them succeeded in diverting my running nose into other channels. All told, the entire contents of my rucksack would weigh less than two pounds, so that I was free to square my shoulders and stride out as quickly as I pleased.

Between Romaldkirk and Middleton the scenery rapidly deteriorates. There are fewer trees, and the grass is not so green; the river still writhes in its bed after the shock of High Force, a few miles upstream, but it has lost its freshness hereabouts: industry has tainted it, given it new colours and a scum to remember it by. Industry has, in fact, made a mess of this part of Teesdale; quarries and mines and railways have carved fantastic shapes in the hillsides and added nothing to the beauty of the dale. Middleton gets a black mark for its enterprise.

I crossed the bridge into the town at half-past ten. Yorkshire, at long last, was behind me; Durham, for the first time, was beneath my feet, and I began to feel that I was getting somewhere. Two-thirds of the journey north had been completed, and the Wall was seeming very near. Today, I should not see it, nor tomorrow. I could, if I wished, get there tomorrow evening, but I preferred to come to it in early morning, not at dusk when I was tired. There is often pleasure in delaying pleasure, and in this case I was content to dwell in anticipation a little longer.

I have said little in this narrative of my reactions to the set purpose of my expedition now that it was at last being experienced after the months spent in planning it. My feelings were much as I expected them to be: my enthusiasm grew with every mile I covered. I took a lively interest in all I saw on the way, but the dominant thought that every step was taking me further north and nearer to my objective was never absent, and I revelled in marking off my progress on the map. Villages and rivers and hills which had seemed on Sunday and Monday a very long way ahead were now falling as far behind. Swaledale had been but a name when I started, but now it was a memory, and because the days were full of incident, it was already a distant memory. Tan Hill I had often heard mentioned; now I had been there. I had read much of Teesdale; here it was before me; I was seeing it for the first time. My eagerness to press on to my goal was such that I was experiencing real sorrow when each evening I could push my legs no further and was forced to halt.

Most days I ate nothing between breakfast and supper, and indeed on the rare occasions when I did stop for a midday meal, I felt that I was wasting time and was off again after a few bites. I could not rest for more than a minute without being impelled onwards by impatience. I did not walk fast; it was enough that I was moving, and moving northwards. The Wall was ahead, and still out of sight. I needed no other spur. If there had been a pot of gold awaiting me, I could not have been more eager.

Middleton is the capital of upper Teesdale, and it was the largest collection of roof tops I had yet seen. For all that, it is scarcely a town, having a population of less than 2,000, yet its inhabitants, I fear, have the minds of town-dwellers. Their homes are built in long, ugly rows, and they have cheerfully despoiled their natural surroundings so that money can be won from the earth; they have sacrificed a heritage of beauty and built a cinema.

Middleton is built on the Durham side of the river. It is the terminus of a single-track railway from Barnard Castle, but from it a mineral line runs further up the valley for two miles to a hideous lead mine, within sound of the waters of High Force, and the noise and smoke of the engine which goes to and fro along this line assail the senses as one proceeds upstream. High Force deserves a poem, but it will never be written until the mine is abandoned and overgrown, and the railway torn up.

At Newbiggin, I left the road and started to climb out of the valley. A kitten kept me company for half a mile, following close at my heels, but just as I was becoming attached to it, it left me at the last farmhouse without so much as a farewell. A dog would not have been so callous; it would have watched me go until I was out of sight, and wagged its tail whenever I looked back.

Hereabouts I walked off the top of my third map, and stowed it away and produced my fourth. I was now as far north as the top extremity of the Lake District: had I turned here and gone due west I should have passed through Penrith and found myself on the flanks of Skiddaw. I liked to compare my latitude with places on the other side of the Pennines, places I should visit on my return. It was interesting, too, to come across signposts pointing west to Kirkby Stephen, Appleby, Alston and other small towns which all had a place on my return programme. But I was never tempted to follow these roads and cut my journey short. My affection for the Roman Wall was quite unreasonably increasing from hour to hour, and a purse of sovereigns would not have deviated my steps from the direct course to it. I was a pilgrim going to Mecca.

It had not rained since I left Middleton, but as I got higher into the hills and saw my way rising over a bleak moorland and into mist I knew that once again I was to be made wet. Walking in rain is most enjoyable when you have made up your mind not to worry about keeping dry, and it is best to make this decision early. There is an invigorating quality about rain which makes you glow with exhilaration. Always turn your face to a weeping sky, not away from it, when you are in the open country, and you have a tonic which will keep you in good humour for days.

My glasses are a handicap on a wet day, though. Drops of rain cling to them until they are jewelled in every movement; the lenses become prisms of soft colours, but they no longer serve their purpose and visibility is almost totally obscured. I dare not discard them, for without their aid I am blind, and so I am compelled to make frequent pauses to wipe them. Once, in a leisure moment, I tried to fashion a pair of windscreen wipers for them with match-stems, and the device was perfect so long as

I operated them with my fingers, but I never could think of a method to make them work automatically by mechanical propulsion.

On this occasion, the mist was so dense and its lower limit so well defined that the hill appeared to be beheaded. I approached a white wall which seemed as solid and immovable as a cliff; it did not drift down to meet me, but sternly awaited. Ten yards below it, I turned and could see Teesdale and the fells beyond in extensive panorama. Then I went on, and a cold shroud dropped over me; all but the green track at my feet was blotted out. I was again in a miniature fairyland of unreal, ghostly shapes, my only companions the sheep which, unlike those around me a few minutes before, now looked big enough to saddle and gallop away on.

It is a long four miles from Teesdale over Newbiggin Common to Swinhope Head where the track crosses the watershed, and in a mist, when your eyes are taken away from you, it seems twice as far. Your feet occupy the centre of your little world, and you watch them stepping out left, right, left, right, over the wet grass, and you wonder how they keep on doing it without making a mistake. Left, right, left, right, they go, interminably. What would happen if they went left, right, left, left, right? The problem fascinates. You try it; you exert all your willpower to make them blunder, but they will not. You conclude that their actions are not controlled by your brain, after all; and you pause to wipe your glasses and look about you for the hundredth time, quite uselessly.

Swinhope Head is 1992 feet above the sea, and, as this was my highest point northwards, I sat on a stone in the shelter of the wall that joins the path at the summit, and celebrated the occasion with a damp cigarette, spreading my cape out around me until I looked for all the world like a tent with a gargoyle on the apex for ornament.

It was twenty minutes to one, and I thought of my friends hurrying home from the office for lunch. I had already been away long enough to have established a definite break with the life to which I was so accustomed. No other type of holiday could have induced such a feeling of severance from the familiar; it was change complete ... Yet I thought often, too often, of those I had left

behind. I would note the time and say to myself: 'What will
so-and-so be doing now, at this minute?' I didn't actually say 'so-
and-so', of course, but substituted a name. Usually, I would be able
to guess pretty accurately, for our habits and duties are governed
by timetables. Often, too, quite foolishly, I wondered if they were
thinking of me. They wouldn't be, I reflected sadly; I was gone for
a while from their sight and just as surely from their thoughts. Ah,
me! Pity the man of sentiment pitchforked into a hard-faced,
unsympathetic crew. Nobody but himself knows his sufferings and
disappointments.

I thought of Hitler a bit, and then went over the crest of the hill
and down the other side. The descent is much more abrupt, and
the map shows a beguiling short cut which I searched for and
found: a black track amongst the rushes. The next few minutes
until I rejoined the honest green road were altogether unpleasant; I
was soon floundering knee-deep in slimy peat. I hoisted my
flannels up to my thighs, repressing a shudder at the skinny limbs
thus revealed, and waded miserably through the morass. My shoes
collected mud as clogs do snow, and generally this was the most
unprofitable short cut I ever made. Pass it by, if you are ever in
Swinhope Head.

Out of the mist came the shadowy forms of conifers and the
vague outline of a farmhouse, a lonely dwelling in the lap of the
moors. The house was quiet, and appeared deserted, but a number
of garments were hanging in the yard to dry. It was raining, and
must have been raining here for two days at least. I thought how
grand it must be, to wash your shirt, put it outside in the pouring
rain to dry and then go to bed, and wait, wait . . . This is the simple
life. With the right companion to share your vigil, it could touch
the divine.

Half an hour later I was out of the mist, and was looking down
on a soaking, bedraggled valley. This was Weardale, quite the least
attractive dale I saw. The aspect, seen under a leaden sky, was drab
and uninviting in the extreme, like a landscape painted by an artist
afraid to use his colours. Yet Weardale has natural features which
should make it striking, and they combine well. High moors wall in
a deep, narrow valley where road and river and railway run

abreast. It is the finishing touches that are lacking. There is no suggestion of warmth and comfort, cheerful things on a wet day; there is no object in the scene that looks interesting. The grey houses are strung out along the roadside, so that the villages appear to be larger than they really are. There are no fields on the valley floor, no woodlands to wander in; there is no room for them. Instead, the fields stretch up the hillsides, each with its enclosure of stone walls; from a distance they have the appearance of a patchwork quilt, although quite lacking its colour and variety. There are cottages on the bare slopes, sometimes a cluster of them, but more often they stand solitary. Every group of houses has its chapel, and without exception the places of worship are plain, ugly buildings. There are valleys in industrial Lancashire more pleasant than Weardale.

I passed under the railway bridge and into Westgate. It was raining in earnest now, and I searched for a place where I could have a hot drink. I tramped the length of the village without success, and pulled up at the far end and joined an old man who was sheltering under a tree. He cudgelled his ancient brains to think who might provide me with a cup of tea, but either they had ceased to be of service to him or not a soul in the place kept tea, for when his final deliberations were made he pronounced emphatically that my quest could not be other than barren.

He suggested that I should go on to Stanhope, six miles away; I could be there in ten minutes, he said. This comment gave me an inkling of the frightful delusion he was under. He thought I was a motor-cyclist and had a machine parked somewhere in the village. I told him I was walking. He chuckled, touched my cape, and winked at me. I said that I had no motor-cycle in spite of the cape. I was going to Blanchland, I told him; what was the track like over the fells? Better now than it used to be, he answered; I could get a motor-bike across quite easily. I intended to walk there, I said; I hadn't a motor-bike. He winked again, and grinned. I found the old fellow interesting; here, after the many manifestations of apparent senile decay I had been pained to note in some of my acquaintances, was an actual case. I asked him if he thought I could get to Blanchland before dusk. Oh, easily; I might have to push my bike a bit, but I should be there in an hour or so. I gave it up then, told him it was a B.S.A., and left him winking and chuckling.

The climb out of the valley is steep and in spite of the rain I had perforce to walk slowly. I stopped once to look back on unlovely Weardale, and from this new viewpoint too, the scene was inexpressibly dreary. Sunshine may give it a pleasanter aspect, for admittedly this was not a good day for forming impressions. Yet I have seen Wasdale and Eskdale in pouring rain, and they are not dreary under a ceiling of clouds. Nor depressing, as Weardale is. It may be that on this particular afternoon, it was the sound of children's laughter that was lacking, and that the heavy, dull atmosphere would brighten when the schools emptied. But the sombre colours would remain.

I was soon in the mist again, but a cold, chilling breeze was now blowing from the west, refusing to let the vapours settle. Instead, the mist drifted across the road in ragged formation, throwing out long, ghostly fingers which were moist and clammy to the face on contact. Only the hollows were swathed in clinging robes of white; the open moorland carried merely a flimsy veil, torn open in places where crags broke through and thrust their black pinnacles to the heavens. Through this wilderness, the narrow road ran straight and true to the top of the ridge.

A signpost marks the highest point, Scarsike Head at 1769 feet, and from there onwards a new valley comes into view as the road starts to descend. This is Rookhope, scene of a long-ago skirmish between the decent men of Weardale and the sheep-thieves of Thirlwall, a battle which was the subject of a subsequent poem by Scott or somebody, called 'Rookhope Ryde'.

Once it must have been a place of considerable activity, for there were lead mines and smelting mills and a mineral railway threaded the winding valley. But the days of prosperity are gone from Rookhope, and only the hideous scars remain. No desolation is so complete as the desolation of abandoned dwellings, and here they are in plenty, crumbling ruins where once was bustling activity, death where there was life. I never see a ruin without wondering what the man who planned the building, and stood back and admired his finished work, would think now of his proud creation, what sadness would fill his breast. Tragedies such as this are all around us, in our own lives. We have all built our dream-castles and seen them crumble to dust, sadly if the neglect has been our own, bitterly if someone we loved and trusted has failed us. And we are never able to rebuild with quite the same enthusiasm afterwards. We have lost the inspired touch, and our later efforts are shabbier and less worthy affairs altogether.

A minor road runs the length of the valley, keeping company with Rookhope Burn, and providing the only link with Allendale. But for the presence of the road, Rookhope Head would be a wild, lonely place indeed, for the bleak moors crowd round to witness the birth of the stream, and shut out the light of day. These gloomy hills are trackless, and only the cry of the plover disturbs the silence.

I came down into the valley by the side of the disused mill, crossing the abandoned railway which runs behind it, and found myself at a signpost. This again pointed uphill, to Blanchland. I was both tired and hungry, and it seemed ages since I had left Romaldkirk, but I started on the last lap with a show of energy which was not all feigned. The name Blanchland rather intrigued me, though for no particular reason because I had never heard of it until a month ago. Perhaps it was because Blanchland was in Northumberland, and, once there, the Wall would be near. At any rate, I was anxious to see it, and I made towards it in earnest. It was five o'clock and there were two hours of daylight left: Blanchland was six miles away, beyond the high fell that confronted me.

My map suggested that I should find nothing better than a rough path between Rookhope and Blanchland, but recently a motor road has been constructed over the felltop. This was not pleasant to walk on, but the hardness of its surface was more than compensated by its colour. The road wound before me like a pink ribbon, but looked at closely, it was not pink at all, but of many hues. The chippings used are neither limestone nor granite, but of a substance like mica or quartz, remarkable for its transparency and delicate tints. I picked a handful at random from a pile by the roadside, and studied them. There were crystals of purple and turquoise and emerald and pink, and others that glittered like cut glass. Beautiful pearls, a few shillings a ton. I carried a pocketful about with me for the rest of the holiday.

I was halfway up the hill when a motor-car overtook me and stopped. The driver opened the door, thrust out an arm, and waggled a finger. It was unmistakably a beckon. That finger was a tempter without a voice. I was well-nigh spent, for I had walked all day over rough country without a bite to eat and rest and refreshment were still two hours away. And now Satan provided a carriage for me: I could journey in comfort, and be eating in fifteen minutes. But I refused, and watched his ambassador glide easily out of sight.

I should have had to be bound and gagged before I would have ridden in that car. A thousand pounds offered in cash on the spot would not have induced me to enter, and if you cannot believe this, then you must treat the whole narrative as a fable, for it contains no truer words. I was pledged to do this trip on my feet. The pledge was made only to myself, but none the less it must be honoured. If I had climbed into that car, my whole holiday would have been irretrievably ruined; I might as well have returned the next day by train without seeing the Wall at all. I should never have forgiven myself. If I had known then, when the car stopped for me, that to continue walking meant death from exhaustion on the moor, I should still have refused and gone on in my own way. This is pig-headed obstinacy, or it is heroism. Delete where inapplicable but please believe me.

I had my reward.

I reached the top of the ridge just as the sun went down. For the last half-hour I had been walking through heather, and now it was all around me, stretching as far as I could see, and giving rich colour to the rolling moorland. But it was not the heather alone that held me entranced. As the sun vanished, the sky was cleared of clouds as though a huge magic broom had swept them away; overhead, and down to the wide horizon, was a vast canopy of purest blue, a cold, brilliant blue. In all the heavens, there was not a speck to mar the wonderful colouring; I might have walked through the stratosphere and looked for the first time into infinite space. Around me, and far into the distance, the hills were etched crystal-clear, and landmarks stood out prominently, in bold relief, giving a stereoscopic effect so unusual as to be almost startling. The valleys below me were hidden in an impenetrable white mist, as if they were stuffed with cotton wool; a pure unstained white, solid and yet soft; it seemed that I could have walked from my present position right across the vale of Blanchland to the moors beyond and sink no further than ankle-deep in this white clinging mass. These, then, were the colours: blue, purple, and white; there were no others.

The evening was still; there was not a sound to disturb the tranquillity of the peaceful scene. I saw it alone; there's the pity of it. The hills should have been crowded on an evening like this. The picture will never be repeated; it will never be quite the same again. I alone was privileged, and I was a man made conscious of his soul. . . . It is of those I love that I think in moments such as this; I want them near me to share my experiences, to understand what I feel but could never express.

I looked out across Northumberland, and wondered what I should find there. Durham had disappointed; Northumberland could not do that, for it held that which I sought. But of the county itself I knew little; I had imagined it to be bleak and uninviting. Yet this first glimpse of it, under a serene evening sky, with purple slopes rising gracefully out of ethereal mist, whetted my appetite for more.

I must have presented a sorry spectacle as I came slowly down the hill into Hunstansworth, for I was very very weary and my legs were so much out of control that they acted quite independently of my wishes. My eyes still searched out the smooth places on the road, but my feet went where they willed. I could no longer recognise these quivering limbs as my own; they did not belong to me, but to someone else. Somewhere between brain and legs there was a severance; my lower half was detached and pursuing its own course, and I, wonderingly, was borne along with it. I was in that condition which most walkers experience once or twice in their lives: so utterly exhausted that if I had stopped I should certainly not have been able to resume, yet still capable of going on indefinitely. My desire for a meal, acute a short time ago, was now receding, and this is always a sign that the limit has been passed.

But in spite of bodily distress, I was quick to appreciate the beauty of my new surroundings. I was amongst trees again, great oaks and beeches and elms, and they spread a carpet of leaves for a welcome; there were pleasant pastures around me, and the scent of hay. The mist had gone; only the haze of twilight remained over the land, a gentle coverlet for a lovely sleeper.

Between Hunstansworth and Blanchland, the scenery is delightful. Two rivers join here to form the Derwent, and their meeting is a secret tryst in a bower of great beauty. And no two kindred souls coming together in this Arcadia could do other than commingle and go on together thenceforward to the end. It is a place for lovers.

Just as Wasdale owes its appeal to the hills, and Windermere to the lake, so this valley of the Derwent owes its attractiveness to the trees. They are always prominent in every view; sometimes they stand singly, more often in avenues or forming wide parklands, but they are one and all fine and lovely. They are high, so high that you cannot see the hills and, as you look up, the tracery of their topmost branches is silhouetted against the sky, far above.

I crossed the bridge out of Durham and into Northumberland. Ten minutes later, I came at last to Blanchland. And Blanchland, more than any other village I saw, deserves special mention. My walk along the valley had prepared me to expect rather a pretty place of flowery gardens and rose-covered cottages, and my map had told me that there was a church with a tower. And all these there are, but it is not these that make Blanchland spring vividly to mind when, long after, you live again your travels in retrospect.

When you set foot in Blanchland, you step into the Middle Ages; it is its strange, medieval appearance you remember it by. You feel oddly out of place as you wander through the old stone arch and enter the square courtyard which is the heart of the village. It is fantastic that you should walk into this old-world military camp with a rucksack on your back; you should gallop in on a fiery steed, bending low to avoid the arch, and pull up with a flourish amid a cloud of dust. A sports coat and flannels make you grotesque here;

clanking armour is the men's wear. Your walking-stick should be a glittering lance.

Your imagination is indeed impoverished if you can enter this picturesque village for the first time and not thrill at the spectacle it affords. Especially if you see it in the gloaming, as I saw it, in the magic moment when it is neither day nor night. For then, you cannot be quite sure that you are not dreaming, that your eyes are not bewitched. I responded magnificently. I was centuries back in history. My thoughts were a jumble of the Holy Grail and the Round Table, of St George and the Dragon, of Galahad and Lancelot and Horatio on the bridge. And Blanchland, after all, is not as old as these.

My eye flashed as I looked round the dim square. Now, damsel in distress, scream! Now, hand me my lance and lead me to the joust! Now, matador, loose the bull! I was ready for anything.

I stood there by the arch for quite a while, looking across the cobbled square at the rows of old stone cottages which enclose it. These must, in the distant past, have been barracks, but for generations they have been the homes of the villagers; they are all built exactly alike, to a pattern. I walked across to one which has been converted into a general shop, and entered it. It was almost odd to see the shopkeeper weighing potatoes on modern scales for a woman who waited; and I was still so much under the spell that if, when I asked for cigarettes, the man had smiled queerly and told me that Raleigh wasn't born yet, I should have gone without a word. The medieval atmosphere of Blanchland is something to marvel at.

The shopkeeper suggested Mrs Elliott's when I asked about accommodation, and pointed out her cottage to me. I went there, and made my wants known to the old woman who opened the door and, after due reflection, was admitted. I groped my way into a dark room where there was a big fire, and sank into a chair. There was an elderly man sitting across the fireplace whom I did not notice until my eyes were accustomed to the gloom; a rosy-cheeked, white-haired old fellow who gazed sombrely before him and said nothing at all. The woman lit an oil-lamp and made me a supper. Her speech was almost unintelligible to me; she spoke in a sing-song dialect that was quite foreign.

Reaction set in the moment I sat down. My legs were so stiff with fatigue that I could hardly drag them to the table when my meal was ready. I ached abominably. It required effort to raise my arm to eat, and even when I had got a little load of vitamins mouth-high, my hand would start to quiver and tremble like that of a man afflicted with palsy, so that I had to snap at my food and, being unused to this practice, I plastered quite a lot of it on my chin, whence it slid back with a dull plop to my plate.

After supper, I crawled back to my chair by the fire and sat there for two hours. My body gradually went numb and torpid, not by any means an unpleasant sensation. In plain truth, it walked out on me and went to sleep. My brain alone remained awake, and even that organ was drugged and stupefied. I was in a state of coma, like a tortoise in December. I felt extravagantly drowsy, yet I did not want to sleep. It was grand to be just a head without a body.

The old woman sat opposite me across the fire, pegging a rug with dexterous fingers. After a while, the smooth action of her hands began to fascinate me; there was a beautiful rhythm in her movements that acted as a silent lullaby. The husband had gone out, and the house was as quiet as a mortuary.

We had one caller. A youngish woman, a neighbour, came in with the news that the Prime Minister, the French premier, Mussolini and Hitler were to meet at Munich tomorrow. This was staggering, stupendous news: history was being made with a vengeance these days. Yet the only effect of the startling announcement on me that night was to make me feel cosier than ever.

The young woman stood by the door as she made her proclamation; then, seeing me, she came into the room to view me more closely, and being pleased with what she saw, sat beside me. She had a curious interest in me, I could see. More than that, she was attracted to me. She was all smiles. She fawned on me. She made no effort to conceal the fact that she was conquered and awaited my attentions. At last, at last, a dream come true! Sad that it should happen this particular evening. For I could only look dully at her. A man without a body cannot a-wooing go. He will get nowhere at all. Opportunity knocks only once at a man's door. Circumstances will never again be so favourable. I let her go, alone.

And so to bed, by imperceptible movements. I could not walk on both feet simultaneously, but had to get one firmly planted and drag the other alongside. This was worse than pins and needles at their very vilest. The old woman clucked and chattered in sympathy as I passed slowly from her sight. Every step on the stairs was a problem.

I got between the sheets somehow. I heard the clock strike eleven, twelve, one, two, three, and lay there unable to move a muscle and much too tired to sleep. Normally when I go to bed I turn over every twenty minutes, as regularly as if I were wound up to do it, until sleep comes. Tonight, however, the effort was far beyond my power. I could not even lift an arm to light a cigarette.

I lay there with my thoughts.

I thought for a time about the day's events. And then, very softly, the girl of my dreams came to me; as she does every evening when all is still, to tuck me in and say goodnight, or to stay with me and talk quietly in the darkness. This charming little lady is most constant; she never fails or disappoints. She is always the same sweet, sensitive creature, ever concerned about me, quick to respond to my mood, happy when I am happy, sympathetic when I am sad. I know her so well now, for many years have passed since she first came into my life. And, because she is the only one I can trust with my troubles, she understands me well, too; her words of encouragement and comfort are the only words I need to hear.

We are not always a little sad. Ah, no; we have shared very happy moments, she and I. We have been companions on many a delightful journey, and known the quiet joy of comradeship; together we have broken the bonds that would keep us to the earth and soared in wonderful flights of ecstasy. She can be coquettish, on occasion; and the merry twinkle in her sparkling eyes is never long absent. She loves to tease me, sometimes, but I do not mind, for always there is a warm embrace to follow, and the few precious words, whispered ever so softly, that never cease to thrill.

I gave her my heart long ago, and am her slave until I die. Out of my imagination she has been born, and grown with the years from immaturity to gracious womanhood. So she comes to me, ever ready to comfort, to laugh and be gay, to understand. It is the perfect communion. She alone has the power to stimulate me, to set me reaching for the stars; she is the source of all my inspiration.

She is the dearest little person in the world, and she has become the most real. For me, she lives. Her kiss is my last experience every night before I sleep, her warm tender lips the caress that closes each day.

Am I a fool, thus to dwell in dreams?

THE FIFTH CHAPTER

I WAS AWAKENED next morning by a thunderous knocking on the door, an incessant pounding that brought me back from insensibility with a thumping heart. It was broad daylight. More often than not I watch the grey light of dawn filter into my bedroom. But this time old Morpheus had hugged me like a brother, or had milady's goodnight kiss been a drug? I cannot recall ever before being so soundly asleep. My bed had been a grave. And having come suddenly back to life, I departed from it without delay.

My rest had worked wonders. I felt very fit, my strength was renewed, red blood coursed furiously along my veins. I was in a swashbuckling mood. Another day; a man revived. New adventures awaited me. There were drops of rain on the window. No matter. I gave excerpts from 'On with the Motley' as I dressed. The heart-broken laugh I omitted, or rather reserved until I was clear of the village; it gains in dramatic effect on a hilltop, there you can make it as harsh and bitter as you wish, choke yourself with sobs if you are so minded.

My legs, though, were still stiff, and when I came to encase the unlovely things in my trousers I found I could not bend my knees enough to carry out the operation smoothly, the usual rhythmic motion with which I am accustomed to entering this garment being out of the question. Call me a prude if you will, but I simply would not go down to breakfast without them. Some garments, for example a shirt, can be put on from both ends, and to keep out of the rut, occasionally I defy convention in this respect. But although

I toyed momentarily with the idea of pulling my flannels over my head, I could see, without experimenting, that the nature of their construction would prove an insuperable obstacle. I got into them eventually by fastening them erect by the side of the bed and sliding shamelessly into them.

Mrs Elliott remonstrated with me when I got downstairs for being late for breakfast. She had been knocking for ten minutes, she told me, before I answered. She asked me if I was better. I told her I was superb, and sat down to my bacon and eggs. It always is bacon and eggs, by the way. There is no alternative; you have no choice. Bed and breakfast means bed and bacon and eggs. This morning I had no difficulty in hitting the target; in fact, I was so hungry that the target met halfway whatever was coming.

In the morning light I could see the room better. It was not remarkable, except for the huge cavernous fireplace which was let into the wall of the house to a depth of three feet. On the fire, on the hob, hanging from hooks suspended from the interior of the chimney, were half a dozen kettles and pans, and there was room for many more. The old woman was never away from the fire; it was the centre of her little establishment; every excursion she made either started there or ended there. It was the depth of the fireplace that made me notice the thickness and strength of the walls of the house. These are built of large blocks of stone, and in vertical layers, so that a few layers could be stripped off and still the house would be intact. There are enough stones in the walls to build four cottages of the same size. The doorway itself, which leads directly into the front room, is deep enough to be called a passage.

Breakfast finished, and all dues and demands met, I took my departure. It was still raining slightly, but the sky was bright, as though the sun was trying to break through the thin clouds, and I did not trouble to wear my cape. Blanchland in the morning is a different place from Blanchland in the evening. It still appeals to the imagination, most vividly, but it has not the magic power to transport you back through the ages. Blanchland in the morning is twentieth century; there are the walls and towers and architecture of the past, but I was conscious as I looked at them that these were created long ago, before my time; not, as I felt last night, that they were contemporary. Other things there are, too, which heighten the contrast and destroy the illusion: petrol pumps, road signs, a modern post office. Still, Blanchland is unique and its setting is lovely. It is a place for a honeymoon.

I could afford to travel leisurely today. It was an off-day for me. Hexham was my destination and I had not more than ten miles to walk. I would be there in the early afternoon, have a look at the town, and go to the cinema in the evening.

My way led out of the valley and into a wooded ravine. Very soon the sun was shining brightly, and I was content to amble slowly along by the side of the tumbling beck. Morning is the best part of the day for walking. The air is freshest then, the earth sweetest. The flowers preen themselves after their bath of dew, and stand erect with rare self-assurance, proud of their bright clean colours. The birds are happiest in the morning, and most lively then. They dart across the path before you, wheel and soar above the trees, swoop unerringly to their nests. They chatter and chirrup and sing in unending chorus, blithely contented and gay, and so very very glad to be alive.

And you, you are at your best and freshest in the morning. You have breakfasted; your cigarettes taste good. Your sleep has revived you; your body is again at your command and not sullenly rebellious. There is the full day ahead, and it holds great promise. Yes, it is good to walk on a quiet path towards the hills early in the morning.

I climbed uphill for a couple of miles until I was beyond Pennypie House, and then I was on the open moorland once more. Here the path became indistinct, dwindling to a narrow track which crossed a maze of sheep-runs and was not easy to follow. But few people who cross Blanchland Moor will keep their eyes on the path. The panorama is magnificent. Ahead I could look over Tynedale and the Vale of Hexham to the low hills beyond, where the Wall is. So near, now! My heart gave a leap as I topped the last rise and saw before me that which I had come a-seeking. So near, now; within sight, at last.

The coast, far to my right, was obscured in a haze, but the intervening plain was clear and out of it, ten miles away, rose the great blast furnaces of the ironworks at Consett, capped by a white cloud of smoke. Blanchland now was hidden by its trees, but the valley of the Derwent, a vivid green strath between dark uplands, could be traced until it merged into the far-away haze. These views were distant, for Blanchland Moor is a wide plateau, and when you are in the middle of it, looking to the horizon, it stretches before your eyes for miles, so that the background appears as a mere fringe on the edge of the moor itself.

Yet it was not the immensity of this moor that made it dominant in the landscape I saw. It was the heather. I had not seen the glory of heather until today. It was the heather that gave the colour to the picture; a gorgeous crimson-purple, dark where the shadows chased across it, bright in the sunlight. Every slope and undulation carried its own banner of warm colour.

I wandered knee-deep through it. So long as my shadow was before me as I walked, I was going north and could not lose direction. The day was glorious. The sun was powerfully hot; it seemed incredible that October was but two days away. I lay down often, and tarried long, for Hexham had no attractions to compare with this. There was no breeze on the moor, but overhead white clouds were drifting quickly across the blue dome of heaven. I watched them come, stealing silently out of the west, squadron after squadron; witnessed their solemn procession above my head; saw them dissolve into the mist to the east. Big clouds and little clouds, there were; stately schooners in full rig, travelling in slow majesty; tiny yachts with wispy sails, speeding quickly to overtake the others, eager to make a race of it. I lay there, stretched out in the heather, and reviewed the fleet.

Clouds are the most transient of nature's creations. They come out of a clear sky, disintegrate before your eyes, vanish. You never see the same cloud twice. Every moment of its brief existence brings a change, a change of form or tint or texture; but its beauty remains constant to the end. The beauty of the clouds is there for us to see every day, if we are not too busy to look up, but if they peep at us over grimy buildings we shall not appreciate their grandeur so well. Seen from a mountain side, they have never the dull, leaden effect which often characterises their appearance when they overhang the towns; they are never grey, never shapeless, never lustreless. Best of all is to look at clouds from above. Look down on them, not up at them; climb through them to Gable's summit on a wet day, and stand there in brilliant sunshine, looking across to Scafell or Pillar, rocky islands in a sea of billowing white. You will love clouds thereafter, be they ever so bleak and forbidding. For from above, they are always white, pure white. And always very beautiful.

I continued on my way towards Hexham, very slowly, at what I call hymn-speed. I have not mentioned that I sing as I go along. I always do. Seldom loudly, more often in a murmur. I recognise few limits in my repertoire; I can treat myself to anything. I bellow in opera, warble in ballad. My choice on any particular occasion is governed by my speed, and governs my speed; my feet march in tempo. My favourite uphill song is 'Volga Boatman', which suits my movements admirably: I find I can grind out a note with every step, and each verse earns a pause, a brief halt. For slow travel, or when I am tired, hymns are best; not the noisy modern tunes, but the old ones, the softer melodies: 'Breathe on me, breath of God', 'Jesu, Lover of my Soul', 'When I survey the Wondrous Cross', 'Nearer, my God, to Thee', 'Lead, Kindly Light', and best of all, 'Abide with me'; old familiar tunes which can never lapse and be forgotten; quiet tunes and comforting words learnt in childhood, and later loved. But if I am rendering light opera, or polishing gems from musical plays, then be it known that I am in high spirits and the way is smooth. 'Toreador', from me, is something to marvel at. 'La Traviata' acquires a new significance. 'Indian Love Call' and 'Vilja' have brought tears to my eyes in many a quiet place. Favourite ballads are 'Rose of Tralee', 'Roses of Picardy', 'The End of a Perfect Day', 'Alone', 'Little White Gardenia' and 'Serenade in the Night'. For accompaniment downhill, the waltzes of Messrs Strauss never pall. Last of all are the rousing marching songs, which usually end the day, unless I am very weary, when my choice is invariably 'Lead, Kindly Light'.

At two o'clock, when I had expected to be in Hexham, I was still lingering on the slopes of Blanchland Moor amongst the black-faced sheep, reluctant to leave them behind, as I inevitably should when I went down below the heather. These black-faced sheep are fine, hardy animals. Heather is their diet by preference.

White sheep are spineless creatures, and will not eat it. A white-faced sheep on a heather moor would starve to death; a black-faced one in a grass pasture would pine to death. Bees also like heather, a fact I learned for the first time on this holiday. Coming over from Rookhope yesterday, I had been surprised to find a dozen wood hives in a hollow on the top of the hill, and I was told later that bee-keepers in the district often take their charges up the hillsides in September, and leave them among the heather for a few days. It sweetens the honey, I was informed. It sweetens the honey: I thought this a fine expression. And all my glowing appreciations of heather cannot pay better tribute. It sweetens the honey.

When I eventually came to the plantations of conifers that are creeping up the hillside, I looked back for a long time at the way I had come, at the glorious purple expanse. I should not see its like again this year; the memory of what I could see now must sustain me through the long winter.

Several hundred acres of uncultivated land on the lower slopes of the moor have been planted with firs, and the track develops into a sandy lane running between them. At present the trees are small, only a few feet high, but when they are fully grown and shade the road, this part of the walk will be even more delightful. The method of planting is so haphazard as to make one wonder how the young trees survive. No effort is made to clear the ground of the tangle of roots and coarse growth upon it; the soil is not prepared in any way. Along comes a man with a spade; he cuts a sod a foot square, no matter what is growing in it, and turns it over. He goes on two paces and does the same again, and so on until a row of upturned clods of earth are completed. Then the young trees, three or four inches high, are stuck unceremoniously in the middle of each, and left. Rain and sun do the rest. If you have ever spent half a day planting a miserable shrub in your garden, you can only marvel.

While the firs are still young, the plantations bear an artificial appearance which is not pleasing to behold; the trees stand in rows as straight as furrows, each one equidistant from its neighbours, and the whole work savours too much of mathematical exactitude. Telegraph poles and pylons may run in straight lines, but please, not living trees. If the wind may not carry the seed, then let us pretend that it has, and grow our trees in odd corners and unexpected places. To get a tape-measure on the job is awful: it is birth control, and this itself is surely the ugliest thing the mind of man ever devised. An avenue of oaks, set with geometrical precision, is disturbing to both mind and eye; you find yourself comparing the specimens, and all comparisons are distasteful; worse, you find yourself counting them as you go along. You approach them as an auditor does a set of books, and an auditor does not look for beauty.

Yet, for all that, I cannot understand the outcry which is raised against afforestation. I cannot think that the Whinlatter Pass, always quoted as an argument against the activities of the Forestry Commissioners, looks less beautiful in its new garb. It could be improved, admittedly, by the introduction of more deciduous trees, for evergreens in a mass lack variety and colour, but even as it is, the scene is quite attractive. And to ramble in a wood of firs and pines is a great pleasure. A rocky peak, seen through a foreground of pines, gains tremendously in height and majesty. No, I cannot believe that a tree ever detracts from a view.

Further along, I came across a number of women gathering blackberries in the shrubbery bordering the lane. They did not work together, nor carry on any conversation, but were so intent on their task that they did not even look round as I passed. There was no doubt that they were working in competition; and competition, in that lovely Northumbrian lane on such a glorious afternoon, seemed oddly out of place.

Competition belongs to big business, to the towns, where man is turned into a machine and grows to like it. Where competition enters into the struggle for existence, it is a sad, sad thing. It does not encourage talent, but destroys it, for true talent is never exploited simply to pile up money. Competition breeds imitation. It has banished the craftsman who was his own master and could sing at his work, and introduced the labourer who has no time to lavish care on his task but must keep ahead of his fellows at all costs. His brain is less concerned with the work of his hands than with devising methods of bettering his rivals. Competition has taken pleasure out of vocation, made it a duty, and set a time-limit. It fosters suspicion. It makes a man everlastingly conscious of his neighbours.

Gathering blackberries on a warm autumn afternoon in a fragrant hedgerow on the edge of a purple moor; is it really conceivable that there can be a more delightful occupation? Work becomes a picnic. But let others come along, and you cannot afford to go about it leisurely, looking only for the best. You enter into a race, for the field is limited, and learn to be content with second best.

So it was with these women. They were not collecting blackberries, but money. They resented the presence of others on the same mission, yet sullenly acknowledged their right to be there. Their enjoyment was gone. I have nothing else to say about competition.

Along this lane, I walked off my fourth map, and with a comfortable feeling of accomplishment got out my fifth and last. Four miles to Hexham. Buckden, Muker, Romaldkirk, Blanchland, with all their delights, were relegated to the background of my thoughts now; not forgotten, by any means, but stored away in memory. They would return with the long winter evenings. For the present, Hexham and the Wall were enough to occupy my thoughts as I walked along. Not one of these thousands of steps lacked purpose; each one brought me nearer. I had walked close on ninety miles now; before a hundred had passed underfoot I should be on the Wall, and one more ambition would be satisfied. Is it any wonder that I should stride along with a joyful heart and a ready song? Is it? Are you still incredulous that I could derive such keen pleasure from completing a mission which, after all, held an interest for nobody but myself, from which I could show no material profit and must in fact suffer a measure of hardship? Is my pen so dull and expressionless? For I walked along towards Hexham the happiest fellow in the world.

Northumberland had not ceased to surprise and delight me from the moment when first I set foot in it, or rather from the earlier moment when I stood and looked across it for the first time from a Durham hilltop. Now, on these last few miles to Tynedale, the scenery was exquisite. The road took me by vast natural parklands, along wooded ravines where danced the clearest of streams, across the golden breast of many a sloping hillside. Does it really matter that I am tired and hungry? Surely not. Discomfort is temporary; what else I experienced would last for ever.

At one point, the road narrows and plunges downhill to a stone bridge spanning a shallow gorge. This is Linnets Bridge, where the trees stand thick and high so that only occasional splashes of sunlight brighten the scene. The stream here is deep; there are dark, silent pools between the rocky walls. But see a house built in a clearing near the bridge, half-hidden from the road, with rock-gardens that come down in terraces to the edge of the water. Through the colourful flower-beds runs a rivulet from the hill behind; a gay, chuckling water-splash which assumes majesty only in death, for it tumbles into the main stream in a graceful cascade. Imagine, a waterfall in your own front garden!

I hung over the bridge and yearned for that house, so much that I am afraid I became quite oblivious to all else. I saw at last the house of my dreams; at last, I need not look inwardly to picture it; it was before my eyes. Everything as I had planned it. The house itself was unpretentious; it was an incident merely in the planning of the garden, and rose inconspicuously from a corner of it; the house belonged to the garden, and was a part of it. . . . There would be a few high rooms, and one would certainly have a huge fireplace. One room there would be that was all windows, and every window would have its own entrancing view. . . . The gardens were not laid out meticulously, and there were no featureless lawns. Instead, there were winding paths full of little delightful surprises, a shrubbery big enough to lose myself in, an orchard, rock gardens where all manner of alpines crowded in colourful ensemble. And, a waterfall!

And, since this was the house of my dreams, what more natural than I should see there the girl of my dreams? Oh, I could see her so plainly. She walked amongst the flowers, tending them here and there; she had a word for the dog romping at her side, for the birds watching reverently from above. I saw her come at length to the edge of the water and, glancing down in the still pool, catch sight of my reflection as I stood on the bridge; she welcomed me with a glad smile, and bade me join her.

I sighed a little, and went on my way. Life would be very sweet if we could dream all day long. We dream only of pleasant things, and the awakening is always a shock, but what matter? If we have glimpsed perfection, we must expect disappointment.

Now, as each chapter in this journal has been set apart to record each day's events, and on this particular day I had a very light programme, I make no apology for mentioning again, at this stage, in order to extend the chapter to the same length as the others, My Cold, which was still with me. Perhaps, though, I should apologise and approach the subject only with trepidation, for the susceptibilities of my reader may have been offended by what has gone before in this connection. Let me just say again that my nose was the biggest feature in each day's adventures, and I promise that afterwards it will find no mention in this chronicle.

My handkerchiefs were of course rendered useless long ago; for a day or two I carried them in my pocket, sodden balls which had become untouchable. Then I threw them away with loathing. My cold had developed into a chill, and after sundown I would have shivering fits which I diagnosed, at different times, as indicative of ague, pleurisy, influenza and double pneumonia. But it was my nose that caused most distress. It ran from Settle back to Settle, through Yorkshire, Durham, Northumberland, Cumberland and Westmorland, and dripped all along the Roman Wall. I used all manner of makeshifts, and made one ghastly experiment, not repeated, to clear it once and for all by adopting the method preferred by manual workers. But it never ceased to run. Something like the Boulder Dam was needed to check the flow.

I shall not mention it again, but for the remainder of this book will draw an impenetrable veil over it, as I longed to do at the time. But remember, pages hence, as I describe a wonderful panorama, perhaps, or some great emotion, that I was all the time suffering from this malady. Say to yourself, as I describe dusk on the Wall, or a view across the Vale of Eden: 'And just fancy! His nose was running all the while.' Never lose sight of the fact, for to me at any rate it continued of prime importance right to the end of the journey.

Hexham remained hidden until I was almost on top of it. During the last mile, I became increasingly eager for a glimpse of it. I could not give a logical reason for my growing excitement as I approached the town, but true it is that I walked very quickly and came to every corner of the road in expectancy. Probably it was the view across the town to the hills beyond that I wanted, for on the hills beyond was the Wall, and Hexham was little more than an hour's march away. Certainly I came to it with the same feeling an Everest climber must experience when he arrives at last in Darjeeling. The Wall belonged to tomorrow; tonight I would sleep in its shadow. Hexham, to me, meant that the culmination of my efforts was assured without a doubt. Once there, nothing could prevent me carrying out the programme as I had planned. It was so near to the Wall that if I were stricken down during the night, I could crawl the intervening distance on hands and knees in the morning. For the rest of the day I could dwell in pleasurable anticipation of the morrow. Success was within my grasp, but I preferred to dally just a little longer, secure in the knowledge that it could not evade me now; that it was mine when I cared to claim it. I felt like a youth who has fared well in an examination, and knows that the ultimate publication of the results can only be in his favour. I should camp outside the walls of Mecca tonight.

Hexham would be the first town I had seen since leaving Settle. During these five days I had been completely alone. On the Sunday I had seen a farmer and his son, and two potholers; on Monday, Tuesday and Wednesday not a soul, unless sheep have souls; today I had seen a few women picking blackberries. Apart from these, I had seen nobody at all outside the villages. Now I was approaching a town, for although Hexham has a population of only 9000 and is not a borough, it is nevertheless a town. While the houses were yet out of sight, I had evidences in plenty that I was nearing a place of some size. First of all, a footpath came into being by the side of the road, then grates began to appear in the gutters at regular intervals, white lines became frequent, there were suburban homes, then people. A young mother, radiant and smiling as all young mothers are, passed me with a perambulator, taking her baby for an airing. A group of children, just out of school, were playing in a ditch. A postman was making his afternoon deliveries.

Then Hexham came suddenly into view as I topped the last rise and saw the road plunge steeply down the other side. And Hexham looked that rarest of oddities, a lovely town. It was below me, set in a wide valley at the foot of well-wooded slopes. The smoke of a thousand chimneys drifted listlessly above the houses, merging in a faint blue haze, out of which stood up boldly the pride of Hexham, its Abbey. The town is prosperous, unless, being unfamiliar with prosperity, I cannot recognise it. I saw hundreds of new houses, and many more in course of erection amongst the trees on the hillside overlooking the valley. This verdant stretch of Tynedale has become, I fancy, a rural retreat for the businessmen of Newcastle. They have chosen well.

I descended the hill. A speed limit sign appeared at the roadside, and this, to me, was the boundary. Past here, I was in a town again, and the country was behind me. Street lamps now. A school, a garage, a row of shops. And people who looked at me with a curious interest. I felt that these men and women should know that I had walked all the way from Settle. But they would not have understood, not they; if I had told them, they would only have said, 'Why?' I was feeling pretty pleased with myself, but to appear less conspicuous I slipped my rucksack off my shoulder and carried it under my arm. A young lady was walking along the footpath ahead of me. She wore silk stockings, and her neat ankles and lovely legs were magnets for my eyes. I followed slowly behind her for quite a long way; I had sunk back to the primitive in these past days. When at length she went into a shop, I felt suddenly lost. There were crowds of people at the bus-stops, a stream of traffic along the street, noise and bustle everywhere. For the first time, I was aware that I was alone.

I wandered about aimlessly for an hour or more. The older part of the town is interesting; there are archways, ancient buildings, fragments of ruined walls, in unexpected places. And wherever you stray, there is always the tower of the old Abbey peeping at you over the rooftops. It is a most inquisitive tower, and it regards you with open suspicion. You may be lingering in some quaint corner, and then as you turn to go, you see it regarding you disapprovingly. An ancient inscription on a wall halts your steps, and as you study it, you see also, out of the corner of your eye, the stern, haughty face of the old tower. You creep away abashed, like a small boy under the frowning gaze of a policeman.

I came back to the main thoroughfare and went in a café for a meal. The girl who attended to me spoke, not unnaturally, Northumbrian, which was another language altogether to me. It was most interesting to note the gradual change of dialects as I progressed from day to day. The Falshaws of Buckden I could understand easily, for I am a Yorkshireman myself, yet their speech is far removed from that of the people of Ribblesdale. At Muker, the intonation was different, and I heard words I could not understand. At Romaldkirk, the woman of the Kirk Inn spoke quite nicely, but the dialect of the Teesdale villagers was new. Mrs Elliott at Blanchland, I could not converse with at all. She knew what I said, or meant, but her own words were well-nigh unintelligible.

Here among the folk of Hexham I found a language quite strange. The nearest approach to their tongue is Scottish. They end a sentence with a high note where mine would be low; they make you feel that they haven't finished what they intended to say, and have broken off sharply in the middle. They use words and expressions I have never heard before. All the time I was in Northumberland I never heard anyone say 'Yes'. They say 'Ah-ah' quickly, intoning it as I would say 'Maybe'; first 'Ah' low, second high and querulous. I wondered how a young woman granted favours to her young man, or accepted a proposal of marriage. The young man will implore: 'What is your answer, Dorothy, ah-ah or no?' And if Dorothy replies 'Oh David, haven't you guessed? It's ah-ah, you dear boy', well then, it seems to me, anything might happen.

The girl in the café answered 'Ah-ah' to all my requests; I asked for nothing that was not within reason. She suggested several times, until I understood properly, that I should try the Abbey Café for accommodation, and told me where it was.

So to the Abbey Café I went, and found it a high building which yet looks tiny, for it is built right alongside the Abbey. I asked the young woman if I could stay there that night; she said 'Ah-ah' and led me upstairs to a cold bedroom on the second floor overlooking the market place. The room was big, with two windows, but it looked, and proved to be, cheerless, and the coldest thing in it was the empty fireplace. It was foully furnished, and the iron bed, scantily clothed, held little prospect of comfort. My dream girl would have to do her darnedest tonight.

I stayed there half an hour, writing postcards, and then went out and along to the post office. It was six o'clock, and the sun, though still brilliant, was fast losing its warmth. I sat in the bowling green by the Abbey for a few minutes, and then walked through the delightful little park to the cinema.

I really enjoyed the show, and not least the screened advertisements which preceded the main picture. I was surprised to find that Hexham provided the best of everything: it was, in fact, without an equal as a shopping centre. I could have the best coal, the best blouses, the best furniture, the best houses, the best false teeth in the North of England. The finest craftsmen would slave assiduously to satisfy my humblest request; the accumulated experience of several thousand years was at my disposal. All estimates were free and without obligation. My orders would be delivered anywhere. Would I call round sometime and see the windows, or visit the showroom? Dammit, I will not be pressed to buy.

Two short interest films were shown, both good, and then a newsreel which brought me up against the Crisis again. I saw an old man with an umbrella dismount with difficulty from an aeroplane. He spoke to me. He had just returned from Godesberg, he said; he hoped there would be peace. But his face was grave. I began to wonder what had been happening that day in Munich, and resolved to break a vow when I got outside, and buy a newspaper. Strange, I had not given Munich a thought all day. But while I was lying on my back in the heather watching the clouds, this same old man had been pleading earnestly on my behalf. I felt a little guilty and unpatriotic.

The feature film was 'The Housemaster', and it was received quietly by the audience. Usually in a small-town cinema the audience are quick to respond to certain situations which arise in every film, and their response can only be expressed by noises emitted from the mouth. The kiss, sweetest of gestures, is made horrible to the sensitive onlooker by the wholly-disproportionate smack which accompanies it. Let there be but the merest touching of lips, and from all parts of the hall there rises a hundred different interpretations of its music. Let there be a passionate embrace, and it is as though a hundred plugs were pulled forcibly from a hundred plugholes. . . . I sit and cringe. What fools they are to mock a kiss!

After the performance, I wandered about the streets. The night was cold; a few stars glittered in a black sky. I had entertained a slight hope that some young lady might invite me for a stroll, but none approached me, and after shivering at a likely corner for some minutes, pleading silently to be importuned by any one of the many who passed, I gave it up and bought a newspaper and made my way back to the Abbey Café.

The café was in darkness. It was a lock-up shop, and business for the day was finished. I went in and groped my way up the staircase. The building was silent, deserted. There was a pale light in my room from the lamps in the market place, sufficient to enable me to find the means of illumination. A small gas bracket was fitted to the wall above the bed and I lit this, drew the curtains, and secured the door. There was no supper for me this night. Someone must have called later to lock up the shop, but I heard no sounds.

I took off my shoes and climbed into bed fully dressed. It was bitterly cold in the room, and icy tremors, recurring at frequent intervals, chased about my back until my shudders became so violent as to elicit a creaking sympathy from the bedsprings.

I read the paper for half an hour, and then undressed and turned out the light. In spite of my discomfort I was well content. I thought not of tonight, of the cold and gloomy quiet of the house. I thought of tomorrow.

I snuggled down under the blankets.

Tomorrow, the Wall.

THE SIXTH CHAPTER

I SLEPT surprisingly well, and wakened about seven o'clock. The room looked colder than ever as I surveyed it through the smoke of a cigarette, but I glimpsed blue sky between the ill-fitting curtains and my spirits rose high. Before noon I should be there, at last. Four hours more I must wait in impatience. Hadrian's Wall by this time had begun to acquire quite a new significance. I was eager to see it, not now only because it meant achievement of my aims, but because latterly my thoughts had invested it with romance; as I had come nearer to it so had my appreciation of the magnitude of the task undertaken by the Roman legions of long ago grown gradually keener. Whether I should find an imposing fortification, or a scrap of crumbling ruin, did not matter. I should see something that was as old as the Gospels, something that had withstood the ravages of time and tempest since the land was heathen. I should touch a stone that had not been moved since a long-forgotten Roman soldier placed it there, and I should think as I regarded it that there it had been in the days of Boadicea, there it had been in the days of William the Conqueror, there it had been when Royalists and Roundheads divided the land.

I knew I should be thrilled at the sight of the Wall, be it ever so disappointing in itself; its appeal was no longer to the eyes but to the imagination. But how foolish of me to be impatient, to wish the four hours fled! For nineteen centuries it had been awaiting me.

Soon I heard cheerful sounds in the shop below; the clatter of dishes, water running from a tap, quick footsteps, a woman quietly singing.

A good breakfast, and then the Wall. I lay there elated. I wished all my friends could have been in bed with me at that moment—alas, there would have been ample room—and felt as I did.

I can record honestly that on this morning I leaped out of bed, absolutely in the fashion I have often planned. I exhibited my nakedness at the window for a fleeting instant. The sun was shining on the higher part of the Abbey tower, and lo, the edifice was no longer frowning, but smiling; across the market square a newsagent's shop was decorated with placards, all of which said PEACE in big letters. Mr Chamberlain had been to Munich and seen Hitler. A peace pact had been agreed. There was not to be a war. . . . This was tremendous news. God was in His heaven.

I was a solitary figure at breakfast. I dined alone in the big room on the first floor. I occupied one table, and there were fifty empty. But the girl had made a fire for me, and I was comfortable. I thought again how splendid girls are, how wonderfully they have the knack of doing the little unexpected things that warm the heart and make life sweet. It is the little attentions which really aren't necessary that somehow make all the difference. On a holiday like this, you meet few people, but these are mostly girls; girls who slave for a few shillings a week in a cheap inn or boarding house. Their existence must be drab and monotonous, unless the evenings hold recompense, yet invariably they are cheerful, willing to be of service, anxious not to intrude. They are humble creatures, yet they have less cause for humility than many of those who sit like lords before them and command.

I made one call before I left Hexham. I left four spools of exposed film with a young lady who appeared with vermilion lips behind a chemist's counter. My photographic masterpieces existed as yet only in my mind; I was eager to see how they compared with actual impressions which could be held in the hand and carried in the pocket. I arranged with the girl that the prints should be sent to Haltwhistle by the evening bus and left at the agency there where I would collect them.

Then I was off, with wings on my feet and all up the back of my legs. The morning was superb; the sun shone brightly from a cloudless sky. I wanted to canter, to run with my knees drawn up under my chin like a spirited horse. I wanted to kiss somebody, passionately, and canter again. Ever felt like this? It's a grand feeling.

I crossed the Tyne at Warden Bridge. The river here, still thirty miles from the sea, is very broad and mature. It plays no antics, but moves slowly and austerely eastwards. The other rivers, the Wharfe, the Swale, the Tees, were pigmies compared to this. Only one other river have I seen larger, and that the Thames.

Ten minutes along a leafy by-road brought me to Warden Church, half-hidden amongst the trees, with the rooftops of the village peeping beyond. Warden stands away from the road, so draped in foliage that most strangers will pass it by without noticing it. The church, however, cannot be ignored. Its high, narrow tower has not a single feature to relieve the bare monotony of the plain walls; it looks not like a church tower at all, but a granary, and it is the colour of ripe corn, yellow, but dusted white where the sunbeams filter through the surround of trees and come to rest on the walls. Most village churches have eyes, twin dials that watch and measure your progress, but Warden Church is without, and while it seems to look down on you in surprise, its expression is blank. It is dumbfounded that you, a stranger, should have found your way to it and discovered its secret. For it is quietly ashamed that it has no clock to tick away the hours; it is destined to stand there, gaunt and silent, to the end of its days. And so to hide its distress, it has drawn the trees close around it and withdrawn from the gaze of the curious.

For two miles beyond Warden the lane writhes and twists along the valley of the North Tyne, amid scenes of great pastoral beauty. The river is below to the right, across sloping meadows; it never comes near enough for you to make acquaintance with it. It sings to you, and you must be content with its music, for you may not see it. A fringe of green bushes secures its privacy, and leaves you to guess at its loveliness. It is shy, and like all shy creatures, is happiest behind a screen.

The hedgerows along the winding lane were of luxuriant growth, and many wild flowers were still in bloom. Tall trees, with branches interlaced and stout trunks festooned with creeping

plants, cast a cool shade across my path. The air was fragrant and
sweet. Harvest was not long past, and the bushes by the wayside
still carried their wisps of hay, snatched from passing carts and
held, in spite of jealous breezes, as souvenirs of the summer that
was fast dying.

High on the opposite side of the valley, a village came into view.
My map gave me its name: Wall. Wall! Proof positive that a wall
there was, or had been. I gazed across the river at the little cluster
of houses lying there so serenely in the morning sunshine, and
pronounced a blessing on the place. Sight of it set me athrill. I
knew now that this was no dream. I was near. The very land I
stood upon had been tramped by Roman warriors. My grasp was
closing.

I went on quickly in exultation, map in hand. The road was
empty, before me and behind me; I was a marathon runner within
sight of home, and I had not a rival. Nor spectators. I was quivering
with expectancy: nobody knew or cared. The gates of Mecca were
opening before me: nobody knew or cared. I was alone. There was
not a soul in the world to witness my triumphant entry, nobody to
share my feeling of achievement. Only the sun to blaze pitilessly on
the white road, a few birds to sing overhead.

A few moments now. Around the corner, still hidden from
sight, was the Roman camp of Cilurnum, a fort on the Wall.
Cilurnum, garrison of the Second Ala of Asturians! I palpitated
with excitement. If it had been a rendezvous with She of whom I
have written, I could scarcely have been more eager.

I quickened my pace. Every bit of masonry along the roadside
was scrutinised as I tore past. All of it was old, but not old enough.
I was desperately keen: the Wall had become suddenly and
urgently of tremendous importance; it meant something to me
which it could not possibly have meant to others who had been
before me. If I had driven to it in a car, I doubt whether what I saw
that day would have interested me sufficiently to tempt me to get
out. But I had walked. I had walked from far-away Settle, a
hundred miles south. Six days I had been marching, just to live
these few moments of attainment. The weary climb out of
Littondale, the mist on Tan Hill, the soaking rain of Weardale:

these incidents and others which seemed to have happened months
ago were not detached events; they were part of the continuity;
they had all contributed in some measure to the ultimate joy which
was now mine, and my emotions would not have been the same if
they had not happened. Nobody ever came to the Wall in the same
frame of mind as mine that day. Around eleven o'clock on the
morning of September the thirtieth, I really lived. I shed everything
that thirty years had clothed me with: restraint and staidness
vanished into the sparkling air. I was alive, alert, eager; I was a little
boy awakening on Christmas morning. The sun was shining. Life
was good. Existence at last had a meaning.

I came to the Wall as I knew I would, half-running.

The lane from Warden emerges on a road which runs like the
string of a bow from Newcastle to the Cumberland border. This
highway, which dates back to the Rebellion of 1745, is known
locally as the Military Road. It is at once the most remarkable road
in the North of England and the most romantic. The man who
planned it was the finest road engineer of his time, and the greatest
vandal in history. He tore down the Wall for a distance of twenty
miles, and built his road on its foundations. His name was General
Wade, and there is nowhere a statue to his memory.

At the precise moment when I arrived at the junction of the
lane and the road, I was standing on the Wall. I could not see it.
Had I ripped up a few inches of macadam, I should have disclosed
the stones on which the Wall had been erected. Until a decade ago,
when the road had a gravel surface a thunderstorm was enough to
wash the bare stones clear. Now only an earthquake could do it.

I turned down to the right towards Chollerford and the river,
and in three minutes had entered the gates which give access to the
ruins of Cilurnum, and was knocking loudly at the door of the
caretaker's lodge: It was eleven o'clock on the most glorious
morning of all time, and the wretch was still abed. A bottle of milk
and a newspaper were on the doorstep. There is a charge for
admission to the sacred field behind the house and I believe the
business prospers, for Cilurnum, now called Chesters, is the most
accessible of the Roman camps and the most visited. In addition to
the camp, which is second only to Borcovicium in the extent of its

excavations, there is a museum which contains practically the whole of the Roman inscriptions and sculptures unearthed along the length of the Wall.

I passed through the wicket-gate in the fence which keeps the little dogs out of the enclosure, for little dogs, though not lacking imagination, can only be expected to show their customary disrespect for masonry, ancient or modern. And good heavens, here of all places we must have no profanity.

Cilurnum is five and a half acres in extent, and rectangular in shape, with rounded corners like a playing-card. Not all its area has been excavated, but the principal buildings and gateways have been revealed. The Wall came out of the sunset to abut on the west rampart, and on the east side ran down to the river, across it, and beyond over many miles of low hills to the sea. The crumbling walls of the fort are now between three and six feet in height; the paved floors are grass-grown. There is an inexpressible sadness about the place, as there is about all things from which the glory has departed. . . .

But for me it was rebuilt. I sat on a tree-stump, and surveyed the ruins. And as I watched they rose again to their full stature; out of the grass of the field sprang the ramparts of the fort, and it was reared before me in all its majesty, an impregnable citadel of white stone. On either side of the fort stretched the Wall to the horizons, fifteen feet high and half as thick, an unscaleable obstacle of great solidity and strength. Along its broad top paced the sentries, solitary figures who paused often to look over the parapet to the north. Always they looked to the north; somewhere in that direction lay the savage marauders whom they had cause to fear. But it was at the gateways that there was most activity. A road ran behind the Wall, linking Cilurnum with Procolitia on the west and Hunnum on the east, each five miles distant. This road passed through the middle of the fort, entering and leaving it at gateways where there were armed guards stationed. There was bustle and shouting: evidently the garrison was being reinforced, for I saw a cohort of infantrymen come marching up the hill from the river, preceded by a centurion. Best of all, to see the cavalry ride up the slope in a cloud of dust: this was a picture which made my heart leap within me.

This was not imagination. It was all real; it happened as I sat and watched. I remained unseen beneath the shade of the trees, but I was in dread lest I should be observed and taken before the Governor. For what excuse had I to offer?

I slipped away at length and walked down to the river, where a bridge carried the Wall to the far bank. It was pleasant here, in a shallow ravine with the fort out of sight, and I lay down on the grass awhile to reflect on what I had seen, and to wonder who on earth I was and why I should be at Cilurnum on this sunny morning when the garrison was being changed.

When I retraced my footsteps, the camp was in ruins again.

I went back to the lodge, where the newspaper and milk had not been disturbed, and out into the road. On a tree opposite the gate a notice was pinned, calling for ARP volunteers. I could then doubt no longer that I was back in the twentieth century.

From Cilurnum, I turned west. After almost a week with the sun on the back of my neck, it was a change to have it on my cheek. From this point too, until I was once more in Settle, I should be walking into the wind and the weather.

I started on the nine miles to Borcovicium with a will. I kept to the hard road; even if there had been an alternative, I should still have kept to the road, for so long as I walked on the macadam I was, for the most part, walking on the Wall itself. And it is no hardship to walk on a road such as this. From Cilurnum it makes a beeline for the top of the hill to the west, and from thence proceeds along the height of land for many miles, absolutely in a straight line. It cuts the country in twain like a knife an apple, and as ruthlessly. Nowhere does it deviate an inch from its course. You can see it before you all the way, mile after mile of it. And since you are high, it seems to lead directly to the sky on the front horizon. This is grand country. The panoramas are more wide and expansive than any I remember seeing. You are on the only ridge between Cross Fell and the Cheviots, and these alone restrict your view. The air is fresh, clean, invigorating. There are no towns, no chimneys, no dirt: you are traversing a wild upland where even a farmhouse is enough of a rarity to hold your attention. West from Chollerford, there is not even a wayside inn for twelve miles. But the feature of it all is the magnificent skyscape. The countryside is below eye-level; you must look down to see it, so that you are made doubly conscious of the vastness of the sky. It is a huge canvas; the land is a mere strip of brown along the bottom; all the rest is blue sky and white cloud.

But if the road is straight, it is far from monotonous. If you are Wall-hungry, as I was, every yard of the way has interest. Along here, you will find the merest scraps of Wall, but the Vallum and the Ditch are at their finest.

What is the Vallum? The Vallum is a ditch with a difference. It is a trench seventy miles long, thirty feet wide and seven feet deep. But measurements alone cannot describe it; you must descend into it and walk along it. It accompanies the Wall right along from the North Sea to the Solway Firth, and is always to the south side of it. But it was there before the Wall was conceived; Agricola was sweating blood in it while Hadrian was in his cradle. It was never intended as a fortification, for it seldom occupies a strategic position; in places, it runs through shallow valleys which would have been death-traps for soldiers stationed in it. The explanation generally accepted for its existence is that it was flung across the country after the Romans had overrun the northern counties to mark the boundary of Roman rule; it was a frontier. Where it is still well preserved, as at Limestone Bank, it is a most impressive spectacle, and even where it is filled in and grass-grown, its course is plainly marked, running dead straight east and west as far as the eye can see.

After the Vallum came the forts, seventeen in all, built at intervals of about four miles along the north side of the Vallum. Connecting them, and stretching from coast to coast, was the Military Way, a road which is now by far the least conspicuous part of the fortifications.

Then came Hadrian in 121 AD on a tour of inspection, with his lieutenant, Aulus Platorious Nepos. Imagine the scene. He comes hurtling up Watling Street in his chariot, cursing like a trooper at the lumpy road, and stops rooted in amazement when he comes to the Vallum. He sends for the Clerk of Works, one Lollius Urbicus, who was later to conduct a punitive expedition in Scotland.

'What's this?' demands Hadrian, pointing with a trembling finger at the great ditch. 'It's a Vallum, sire,' replies Lollius, touching his forelock respectfully. 'Who the 'ell done it?' shouts Hadrian in his broken English, huge veins swelling in his temples. 'Agricola, sire,' is the ready answer. Hadrian turns to Aulus in fuming disgust: 'You know my opinion of Ag. This is typical of him. Now what earthly good is it?' Lollius intervenes: 'If I may say so, sire, I never did see much reason in it. Shall I fill it up?' Lollius was the first of the yes-men. Hadrian tugs at his great moustaches and reflects. 'Build a wall,' he says brusquely at last, and climbs back into his chariot. Lollius springs forward to give him a leg up.

And so the Great Wall came into being. Work proceeded simultaneously at different points across the country; each fort would be responsible for building a portion and linking up with its neighbours. Quarries were excavated behind the line of the Wall to provide the stones, which were of a uniform size, measuring on the face about eleven by seven inches, as much as one man could carry. Inscriptions carved on the uncut walls of the quarries and on blocks used for the Wall have been invaluable in enabling the work to be dated and the builders named with accuracy. An example of this can be seen on a cliff at Coombe Crag, where has been carved an inscription which translated means: 'A Vexillation of the Second legion were, in the consulship of Flaxius Aper and Albinus Maximus, employed here to hew stone.' I wonder what the thoughts were of the quarryman who carved this message? Was he passing idle moments, as a boy at school initialling his desk with a penknife? I cannot think so: I prefer to think that this man knew he was building for the ages to come; knew that the monumental task on which he and his fellows were engaged would be the subject of interest and admiration for countless centuries to come, and was determined that no doubt should arise in the future and credit for the work be misplaced. He would do it with pride.

The Wall when finally completed crossed the country from sea to sea, a distance of over seventy miles, forming an unbroken barrier to the invaders from the north. There was not a breach or loophole anywhere. Unlike the Vallum, the Wall ran along the crests of the hills, often on the brink of precipices, always where it could be most easily defended. Its original height was probably about fifteen feet, and in addition the north face was extended to form a parapet, behind which the sentries who paced the Wall would be secure. At intervals of a mile along the Wall, milecastles were built abutting on it; these were twenty yards square and served as temporary quarters for the sentries. Between the milecastles, two turrets, placed equidistant, rose from the top of the Wall, small towers which were used as look-out posts. There is evidence that the turrets and milecastles were always occupied, and it has been computed that the Wall had a permanent garrison of four thousand men. The site of every milecastle and turret has been located. Some of them are still remarkably well preserved, but traces of most have entirely disappeared, so that the wayfarer may pass over them unknowing.

As an additional obstacle to attack, a Ditch was dug a few yards north of the Wall, almost throughout its length, and may still be seen. Where the Wall is naturally unassailable, as for instance where it runs along the brink of a cliff, the Ditch was unnecessary and is therefore absent.

The plan of the fortifications is everywhere constant. Most northerly is the Ditch. Then the Wall, with its milecastles and turrets. Then the forts, all of which abut on the Wall, linked to each other by the Military Way. Then, most southerly, the Vallum, in disgrace, and filled in at regular intervals to make easy passage to the Wall from the quarries.

The Wall was overthrown by barbarians eighty years after completion when the Roman troops were called away to conduct a campaign in the south. It was subsequently rebuilt in the third century in the reign of Septuricus Severus, and so extensive were the repairs that, until a century ago, Sep was credited by tradition as being the actual builder of the Wall. Recent excavations have, however, proved beyond doubt that the Wall existed in the time of Hadrian.

The fortifications are situated across a tract of country which is everywhere lonely and often wild and desolate. The central portion is hilly, and here the hills swell gradually from the south to break suddenly in cliffs which face the north. There are twenty separate summits and without exception this feature recurs in each of them. Between the summits are gaps or depressions, often considerable in depth, so that from afar, the effect is that of rolling waves breaking on a beach. The Wall falters nowhere. It crosses every summit and gap in the most direct fashion, in places climbing slopes so steep that you must pull yourself up with your hands as you follow it. It is in the central portion that the Wall is best seen; here it can be climbed and its top patrolled for miles. Here, too, only the bleating sheep and screaming curlew disturb the silence. Elsewhere, however, and particularly near the extremities, the Wall has vanished; it proved too handy a quarry for farmbuilders of not so long ago and it is not unusual to see buildings in the vicinity largely constructed of stones taken from the Wall.

Walking the Wall from coast to coast must be a fascinating way of spending a holiday. Regarded simply as a walking expedition, the journey would hold full measure of pleasant experiences, for the country to be traversed is wild and free, and the air a tonic. But nobody ever walked the Wall without being conscious of its great significance or without being thrilled by the sight of its ruinous majesty. Here is something that grips the imagination till it squeals; something that transports a beholder right out of the present and back to the dim past. You can hear the legions marching, marching. Spend a few hours on the Wall, alone, and it is a shock to come once again to the habitations of twentieth-century man. It is important that you should be alone.

My narrative has run ahead of me, for I am still plodding up the rise from Cilurnum. The last hamlet by the roadside is Walwick, a place of flowers, and very soon after it is left behind the road runs out of the trees and soars up to the top of Limestone Bank. Here, for the first time, the Vallum and the Ditch came into sight. The road runs like an arrow across open country, and is hereabouts not actually on the foundations of the Wall but parallel with it and fifty yards south. The Vallum, also an arrow for straightness, cuts through the fields alongside the road. The Ditch is the third straight parallel line, running to the skyline in the pastures north of the road. The Ditch, of course, always gives the clue to the location of the Wall, for it was never more than a few yards away. The

Vallum is not a reliable guide; it is always to the south, but may be a hundred yards or a mile distant.

Halfway up the hill, a portion of the Wall appears in the field to the right, in fine condition, with the facing stones as clean and white as though new. I rejoiced exceedingly at the sight, for this was my first glimpse of the Wall, and I lost no time in going across to it. The masonry of the Wall is unmistakeable; wherever it is seen the beholder is not left to doubt and wonder; recognition is instant. Here, below Limestone Bank, there is an unbroken stretch fifty yards in length and five feet in height, standing in the middle of a wide sheep-pasture, isolated. The broad top is overgrown with briars and hawthorns, so that you realise that the Wall is not constructed solidly of stones throughout its depth. The core, in fact, is composed of rubble and earth rammed down hard, but still retaining enough fertility to provide for the structure, when its usefulness was finished, an ornamentation of green growth.

I climbed the Wall to look for the Ditch, which I knew must be on the other side. It was there, surely enough. Not now a ditch, but a shady dell where young trees and bushes of gorse grow side by side and rabbits scuttle away into the ferns at your approach. I sat down awhile in the shadow of the Wall. It was a quiet, peaceful spot; a place for a picnic. Once it had resounded with the clatter of stones, the noise of toiling men. But that was long ago, long ago. Strange, that the same sun which shone this afternoon should have shone also then! There must have been many afternoons just as this while the work was in preparation. . . .

It was not only possible, but highly probable, that a Roman soldier had sat on the shady patch of grass where I was sitting, in much the same easy attitude. He wouldn't have smoked a cigarette, as I was doing, and he would have had a better shave, but would his mood of reflection be essentially different? What would his thoughts be? He would consider the glory of the day and the grandeur of the distant prospect, this is certain, for no man could sit there and not be aware of them; appreciation of natural beauty has not been brought by advancement in culture and learning. He would contemplate the half-finished Wall, measure its increase in height since last he rested there, forecast the day of its completion and imagine it as it would be then. He would think of his family, rather sadly, for they were across the seas and he was a stranger in a hostile land. He would wonder what they were doing at that moment, each one of them, and wish that he could go back for a time and be amongst them. He would not be unhappy. No man inspired with idealism is really unhappy in the gloomiest of circumstances. It is only when ideals are shattered that the man of dreams begins to suffer.

Could this Roman soldier have come back and sat with me, and viewed the remains of his labours, I do not doubt that he would have been a very disappointed man. His wall had stood in defiance of storm and tempest for nineteen hundred years, and only the ravages of man had broken its defences. Yet, no matter how, it was now a crumbling ruin. And he had thought he was building for eternity. We all have a feeling akin to this, I think; we all feel we are building for all time. We each of us feel, too, that we are in some way immortal; we know that our friends and neighbours must die when the time comes, but ourselves? It seems unbelievable that the lives we live must come to an end; all our experiences have been of life, not of death. It seems ridiculous that our work, to which we have devoted years of conscientious and painstaking service, should ever be forgotten. Yet it is. And we are not all builders of walls. These Roman legions were fortunate; their handiwork has lived long, where ours will die with us.

After a while, I continued across the field to the top of Limestone Bank which commanded on that autumn afternoon a magnificent view. Northwards, the wooded valley of the North Tyne could be traced to the far-away Cheviots, a bright green ribbon amongst brown moorlands; ahead was a vast tableland, with the metalled road leading through it, on and on, unswerving, to the jagged line of low black hills where lay the camp of Borcovicium and the limit of my journey; to the left and below was the pleasant valley of the South Tyne with the Pennines towering beyond.

But Limestone Bank would be a remarkable place without the view. Here, by some geological freak or cataclysm of nature, a thick strata of solid basaltic rock runs through the ground. Here is the Vallum at its very best. It comes into sight out of a little plantation and for a hundred yards or so is right alongside the road. I glanced over the parapet of the low wall at the roadside and was looking down into it. Not for the first time that day, my heart leaped out of its socket. The sight of the Vallum was tremendously impressive. The trench is deeper here than elsewhere, and the walls steeper; there is little vegetation to hide its black, gleaming nakedness. And black it is; shades of green and blue there are in the rock, but black is its colour, and it has the hardness and durability of marble. Huge lumps of basalt lie strewn in chaos; they line the brink, some have rolled down into the bottom of the trench. A few white, bleached tree-stumps give the place an atmosphere of death.

I descended into it, and the road was out of sight. I saw it now as its makers had left it, and marvelled at their industry. The task had been accomplished with primitive instruments. The diggers had nothing better than staves and wedges to work with yet they managed to get eight feet down into the earth through this solid mass of unyielding rock, and excavate a trough twenty feet wide through it. But if explosives were absent, depend on it there would be plenty of blasting. Where wedges failed, the force of expletive would succeed. And while the makers of the Vallum accomplished their task, the diggers of the Ditch, a generation or two later, abandoned their similar enterprise, for if you visit the Ditch across the way you find that it gets halfway into the basalt and then terminates. You can actually see the wedge-holes in a huge block of stone where endeavours have been made to detach it without success. Since those days, the block has been split by frost, but it still remains for all to see, the one natural obstacle the Romans never conquered. What heart-burnings there must have been! For, having failed to break or dislodge it, the workmen went no further with the Ditch at that point.

The Vallum quite captured my imagination; I acquired a jealous affection for it which the Ditch never shared. Later, it was to give place to the Wall, but wherever I saw the Vallum, that day or the next, I greeted it with joy, and I was always on the lookout for it. Where the Wall is to be seen, it dominates the picture to such an extent as to make other features insignificant; but the Vallum is different. It is shyer, quieter, and far less obtrusive; it is not at all offended if you pass it by without comment. It is feminine; the Wall is masculine.

I cannot say how much of my description of the Vallum at Limestone Bank, or indeed of anything I saw on the journey, is fact and how much is exaggeration. I have not recorded anything that seems unreal and untrue. I have said the Vallum was tremendously impressive, and so it was, to me. But as I climbed out of it, a motorcar went past with two big, cow-like women lolling inside; they looked at it casually, without interest. It did not arouse a comment, and the car went on at a fast speed. I was enraged at their indifference to my beloved Vallum, really angry that they could pass it by without a trace of emotion. Nor is this exaggeration. We are all ready to rise quickly to the defence of those of whom we are fond; with most of us, it is only on the occasions where a loved one is slighted that we can be accused of hot temper. And these demonstrations of affection are by no means confined to things animate. I know that many people would regard the Vallum with about as much enthusiasm and interest as they would show at a trench dug along the gutter of a street to contain electric cables. Many more would stop to look and possibly be sufficiently interested to make the usual inquiries: who did it, when, and why? A few, having heard of it, would go out of their way to pay a visit. But most of these, I am afraid, would be disappointed, and ridicule it, and soon forget.

There are kindred spirits, however, who have waxed enthusiastic about the Vallum, and it is comforting to read their experiences and, more important, to be able to understand them. How very few books are really understood! If the reader is not of the same mind and in the same mood as the writer, if they have not a common interest, there cannot possibly be contact. Words themselves are a poor means of expression, for all true emotions are inarticulate. The measure of a writer's success is his ability to make clear what is unwritten, to induce his reader to read between the lines. Unless the mind of the reader is in complete sympathy with the mind of the writer, unless there is accord, it is futile to read on. Communion is never established by words alone. I have written things in this book which most people would ridicule, even though I have been in dead earnest. But I am not to be abused because of that; somewhere there must be one who will understand perfectly. It is for this person I have written. The others, if they will not come my way, can go to hell.

Old William Hutton of Birmingham traversed the Wall from end to end in 1801. This is what he says of the Vallum: 'I climbed over a stone wall to examine the wonder; measured the whole in every direction; surveyed it with delight, with surprise, was fascinated and unable to proceed; forgot I was upon a wild common, a stranger, and the evening approaching. . . . Lost in astonishment, I was not able to move at all.' This is grand stuff, better than any of mine, and I understand his feelings absolutely. But he is guilty of exaggeration, says what is obviously untrue, and thus for most readers throws the whole passage into discredit. He says he was unable to proceed and not able to move at all. I saw no signs of his petrified body, and am quite sure that he did ultimately move away of his own volition. But he was not a liar. Few people who tell lies are liars. What William suffered from was ultra-enthusiasm and a magnificent imagination. His writings were for those fortunate people who are likewise afflicted, but for no others. He was seventy-eight years of age when he made the journey.

A mile beyond Limestone Bank is the site of the camp of Procolitia. The intervening distance has no evidences of the Wall to offer for the road is again built on it, but the Vallum and the Ditch are with you all the way. Throughout the length of one field, the Ditch is in perfect condition; the grass had been newly mown when I was there, and the sides of the depression were as smooth and symmetrical as if a roller had been over them. I walked in the fields along this mile, crossing a dozen times from Vallum to Ditch and from Ditch to Vallum, anxious not to miss anything. There is no law of trespass for worshippers of the Wall. If an object looks interesting you make a beeline for it, and your course thus becomes a series of zig-zags, so that an unknowing spectator would think you demented. The farmers are used to seeing solitary figures wandering about their fields, and raise no objection; generations of walkers have behaved exactly in the same manner.

Procolitia, now known as Carrawburgh, was the first fort west of Cilurnum, and I did not need my map, therefore, to know that I had come about four miles and was halfway to Borcovicium. Procolitia has never been adequately excavated; it is overgrown, but mounds indicate the lines of the walls and ramparts. In its glory, it was garrisoned by the First Cohort of Batavians. Now it is all desolation.

Two miles further, I passed a small farmstead built on the lip of a ragged tarn. This house has the fine name of Shield on the Wall. Before me now, close at hand, was the first of the hills that stand out in a row, like giant tumuli, above the countryside. The road swings slightly south to avoid them and thus leaves the line of the Wall, which now in turn goes straight ahead to the first summit, free and unhampered. This, if you intend to walk the Wall and have only one day to spare, is the place to start. This is where the excitement commences, and before dusk your senses will be half-paralysed with it. This is where that portion of the Wall which is spared to the twentieth century, begins. Make a note of the name, Shield on the Wall, and go sometime, will you? I'd love to take you, and put you on the Wall facing westwards, and see you started on your way up the hill. There I must leave you, for you must do this walk alone. But I could be waiting at Borcovicium, just to wave as you come marching past, still on the Wall. And I could race you to Thirlwall, and be waiting there to lead you to a supper. I shouldn't talk at all, or intrude ever; I should be well content to watch you on that homeward march in the dusk.

Because the road swings away to the south at Shield-on-the-Wall, it turns away from the line of the fortifications and thus crosses the Vallum, which had been plodding along patiently at my left hand ever since Cilurnum and now kept determinedly on in direct fashion, following the direction of the Wall. At the point where the road crosses the Vallum, there is naturally a pronounced dip, and I could stand in the bottom of this depression and look right along the bed of the trench. I sat on the parapet of the little bridge there and revised my plans. It was after three o'clock; I was hours behind schedule, and had only now come to the Wall proper; I had at least twelve miles further to go before I could find accommodation and most of this over rough ground; there were less than four hours of daylight left. These were the facts which impelled me further along the road, the most direct course, instead of making a detour across pastures to the summit ahead. I was reluctant to let the triumvirate of Ditch, Wall and Vallum go out of sight, for by keeping to the road they were all to the north and temporarily out of sight. I felt like a deserter as I went on along the macadam, but I must confess that my decision was rendered easier because the fields I would otherwise have crossed were dotted with black beasts which were not cows, though certainly bovine.

I went on at a good speed for two miles, and then decided to strike up the easy slopes to Borcovicium, now not more than twenty minutes away. I turned up a slimy lane for a few hundred yards and came to a gate which bore a crude notice: 'Beware of the Bull'.

I allowed myself to be frustrated and went back to the road, maintaining my good speed, and put another three-quarters of a mile behind me. By this time I was beginning to tire of the hard surface, and the sound of my footsteps was becoming an irritant. I prefer not to hear myself walk.

Beyond a farmhouse called Beggarbog the road has been widened for parking, and a big yellow road-sign announces that nearby are the remains of Borcovicium, known now as House-steads. There was one big car parked there, so that I was not to be the only visitor, and I was pleased to think that others beside myself had an interest in things Roman; I felt a warm glow of affection for them, whoever they might be.

I passed through the wicket-gate, and a request to keep to the path told me also that this must be a fairly frequented spot. The owners of the car were returning from the camp, two young fellows who stared at me superciliously when I proferred a timorous greeting and passed me without response. . . . It's strange how little irrelevant things flash into the mind when the whole body is keyed up for some major enterprise. I was terribly eager to get to the camp and the Wall, almost to the point of frothing at the mouth, yet I distinctly remember thinking when those two youths came into view that had there been another of us we could have sung 'Sweet Adeline'. Yet, reflecting on it, I fancy they would have disapproved. There's a big gulf, even yet, between those who have a car and those who enjoy their outings.

Soon I crossed the Vallum again and climbed steeply up the slope beyond. The field was overrun with young black bullocks but, with one or two frisky exceptions, they were docile enough; with their curly topknots and big dark eyes and soft muzzles, they looked almost pretty. I made my way to the farmhouse which is adjacent to the site of the camp, as all visitors must do, for an admission fee must be paid.

The farmer-cum-caretaker was standing in the small kitchen as I approached, surrounded by the trinkets of his dual profession: guidebooks, eggs, mineral waters, milk, postcards, chocolates. I bought a bottle of ginger beer against all the dictates of past experience, and regretted it afterwards, for it dilated my shrunken stomach into a bladder, and, although I fought hard and bitterly against this distressing effect, it made me repeat all over Borcovicium.

I talked with the farmer for several minutes. He was a powerful man, as tall as I and twice as broad; his eyes were blue and his face red and jovial. His musical accent was delightful to hear, and his voice, strangely for a man of his size, was wonderfully soft and gentle. Of all men I have heard speak, this farmer in his lonely Northumbrian outpost is the only one with voice so pleasant in tone as to make me wish I could hear it often. He gave me an assurance about the bullocks that I was badly in need of, and granted me permission to walk along the Wall as far as I wished. He surprised me with his estimate of the number of visitors to the camp annually; never a day goes past, he said, without someone coming, and in summer people come in parties to look at the ruins. I wanted to tell him of my own journey, for it seemed fitting now that I had arrived at the very limit of my travels that I should announce the fact to the man I found there, and he would have been greatly interested, I have no doubt. But for some reason or other I refrained and bade him good afternoon and went over to the ruins.

Here I was at last at the foot of the rainbow, at the end of my quest. The foot of the rainbow! Yes, it was that, and I entered into its opalescent splendour with a singing heart.

Borcovicium is built on a pronounced slope. It has been extensively excavated, and because it is the loneliest of the forts, it is the least disturbed; the ramparts, gateways and principal buildings are all there, plainly to be seen. I passed through the South Gateway, and had there been a gate still in place to bar and bolt behind me I could not more effectively have shut myself away from the world of today.

I walked slowly through a dead city, along a main street lined with shattered walls. A profound stillness lay over the camp, a silence so intense that I could hear my heart pounding as I went along. The effect of this wholesale devastation is almost overwhelming to the mind. In a way, the scene is awful, horrible. The ages which have wrought this decay are forgotten; I felt, as I stood there, that I was the sole witness of some terrible catastrophe which had wiped out a community of which I had been a member, that but an hour had passed since it happened and I was still unnerved by the shock. There is the courtyard, the commandant's house, the main hall; all empty, deserted, without a suggestion of life; the walls are crumbled, the columns broken. It is as if an earthquake had overthrown the place, and all the inhabitants had fled in terror. Not long ago this street was a busy thoroughfare, the courtyard a tumult of voices; there was singing and shouting everywhere. Now it was silenced for ever; death had stolen in and chilled the very stones. An empire had fallen.

I came at length to the North Gate, and the supreme moment.

Never, never in all my travels have I been so overcome with apprehension. I was utterly lost amid a rush of fanciful images which laid siege to rational thought, swept in and assumed complete control. There was the din of trumpets, the sound of a marching army, and I was a trembling figure in the midst. What caprice was this, that wildest fantasy should become so real? I stood now on the very spot I had sought; this moment was the culmination of all I had striven to attain. And for me, for me alone, a scene was relived; I was taken back through the centuries and privileged to witness a thrilling pageant of history. . . . The lesson I learnt was that life's trials and troubles are nought when it holds such compensations.

The North Gate is built on the edge of the cliff. It is in direct line with the South Gate, and the sloping main street connects them. As you approach the North Gate, there is nothing to suggest the view that comes suddenly, surprisingly, before your eyes when the top is reached; the whole effect leaps into sight at once in most startling fashion. The gateway is before you, a structure of immense strength. Between the portals you see the ground drop away in front, and by advancing a few paces you can look down the steep declivity to the level plain below, and beyond to the far Cheviots across a barren and inhospitable wilderness.

But it is the Wall that makes the scene unforgettable. Here it is, at last, in all its imposing majesty. Not now in broken, pitiful scraps, but a solid, massive barrier that sweeps on and on to the distant horizons, a colossus of stone that neither cliff nor torrent can impede, a squat monster that pursues its way relentlessly and brushes all obstacles from its path.

I saw it first creeping over a hilltop a mile away to the east, and my fascinated gaze followed its sweeping course towards me. I watched it rise and fall with every undulation of the ground, a serpent riding the waves of the sea. Near at hand, it plunged down into a ravine, only to come soaring up to the North Gate in one great leap. Distance robbed it of its tremendous girth, but as it came out of the ravine towards me I saw it in its full stature. I stood spellbound at the sight. It was like a living thing: a monstrous crawling reptile that saw me from yonder summit and came sinuously in my direction. Unyielding, unrelenting, it crept to me; nothing could halt or hinder its movement or shake it from its inexorable purpose. I was hypnotised: the spectacle had the frightening intensity of a nightmare. I could only stand transfixed, waiting. I saw it slide down into the ravine, and there disappear for a moment; and then it came sweeping up at me in one great bound . . . And then, then I found that it was not a living creature at all, but a poor battered line of stones that grovelled on the earth in apology. No longer could it inspire dread in the heart of a beholder, though it could even yet command respect and veneration. But it was a shattered remnant, no more.

I must have lingered at the North Gate for a very long time. When I finally bestirred myself, I noticed for the first time that black clouds had piled up in the western sky, and hung brooding overhead. The sun had gone from the landscape and given place to drab greyness. There was oppressiveness in the air; the silence, profound before, was now an expectant hush. The rain was coming; the earth was waiting. I felt strangely chilled as I resumed my walk.

The Wall forms the north rampart of the camp. Its deterioration has been constant, so that the top is fairly level and quite exhilarating to walk upon. Generations of walkers have worn a path along it, a brown track where the rubble is exposed, firm and solid to the feet, and fringed on both sides with long grass. It is wide and ample enough to follow in comfort, but a few false steps would pitch you over the edge, so that it is well to halt if you wish to let your gaze rove around, as you will often.

A hundred paces from the gateway, the west wall of the camp branches off at right angles and runs away down the slope. I was now on the Wall proper, and could see it disappear into a dark wood a short distance ahead. I entered the gloom beneath the trees, still on the Wall, which here bores its way through the shrubbery in very obstinate fashion. The north face of the Wall was soon on the edge of a precipitous cliff to which a few pines clung; as I went along, I could look down vertical clefts between rocky buttresses to rough scree far below. A false step here would be disastrous, but it is a glorious experience to traverse the very brink on so wonderful a path. This is Cuddy's Crag, the most romantic spot on the whole length of the Wall. It is a place to bring a fire to the dullest eyes, to inflame the most prosaic mind. For the person who is already under the spell, here is the perfect Elysium. Cuddy's Crag is a place to dream of by your fireside on a wild winter's night.

Out of the trees again, a milecastle comes immediately into view, and it should be observed closely, for no finer specimen exists. Like all the milecastles, it has a gateway through the Wall itself, leading to the open country to the north. This breach makes it necessary to detour to regain the Wall at the other side, and the

time-honoured custom, as the well-worn path indicates, is to walk
round to it along the ramparts of the milecastle itself. When the
Wall is regained, it begins at once to slope downhill to the bottom
of a narrow depression, gradually at first, then so steeply that
foothold on the loose, crumbling path becomes precarious. No
sooner is this awkward descent negotiated than the way leads as
abruptly up the breast of the rise opposite. This is magnificent
travel: ridge-walking with the added attraction of an enchanting
causeway which seems as ancient as the hills themselves.

Looking back from the top of the rise, the retrospect is superb.
It is a familiar view that meets the eyes. I recalled having seen it,
scores of times, in history books at school, in books of adventure
and travel, on picture postcards. Yet now I saw it for the first time.
A scene such as this cannot be captured by the camera; it is libel to
publish a photograph of it and add the title: 'Cuddy's Crag and the
Roman Wall'. It must be seen, and I fancy I saw it at its best, under
a threatening sky. It is a savage place, and a menacing pall of black
cloud is a more fitting adornment than an expanse of blue heaven.

I went on my way, sublimely contented, wonderfully happy. We
experience few days which hold continuous delight from dawn to
dusk; our moments of ecstasy, alas, are fleeting things that come
suddenly, often unexpectedly, and slip easily from our grasp when
we would restrain them; our pleasures are transient and
temporary, and we can do nothing to delay their departure. No
will-o'-the-wisp was ever caught by being chased. . . . But here, for
me, was a day of days. I enjoyed every minute of it. There was a
surprise round every corner; each changing scene had its own
delights, so that often I lingered, loth to depart, and yet always
looking forward to see what still lay in store for me. Reluctantly,
and yet eagerly, I was turning for the first time the pages of a book
that held me enthralled and which I must soon relinquish and
might never see again.

Another half-hour brought me to Crag Lough, the smallest and
by far the prettiest of the three moorland lakes which lie north of
the Wall. Here, so late in the year, were shrubs in blossom, and
wild flowers danced amongst the reeds and rushes at the water's
edge. Dusk was falling, and a grey, diaphanous haze hung ever so

lightly over the lake. The huge cliff that carried the Wall reared up out of the water, a black citadel crowned with slender pines; away to the north were dark lonely moorlands. There was an eeriness about the scene that chilled, but it was all beautiful.

The Wall on the precipice above the lake is too broken to walk upon, but a bewitching path runs between the trees alongside the ruins, and this affords splendid downward views into the pellucid waters two hundred feet below. It is as though you are peeping from the battlements of a castle down the steep walls into the wide moat beneath. The occasional cry of a water-hen and your own footsteps are the only sounds to disturb the stillness.

I continued along the ridge for another mile or so, and then, since the light was fast fading, halted a long time to look behind me at the way I had come, before turning off at a tangent and descending through long grass down the hillside. I left the Wall very reluctantly. As a spectacle it had exceeded all my expectations, but its great appeal for me lay in its power to captivate the imagination. I have never been so elated, nor yet so profoundly moved, as on this autumn day on the Northumbrian hilltops. Had the Wall been new, or in perfect condition, I could not have loved it half so well, nor admired it more. It was old, incredibly old: therein lay its attraction. I was fortunate in having it to myself all the way, for the presence of others would introduce a discordant note and destroy the whole effect, be they ever so quiet and respectful. Marching feet along the Wall should be heard through the inventive faculty of the mind, never through the ear. Take away the loneliness of the Wall, and all its charm is gone, too.

Rain began to fall as I neared the road. I consulted my map. The white building ahead was the Twice Brewed Inn, which meant that I was still five miles away from Haltwhistle. Until now I had been aware neither of weariness nor hunger, though I had already walked twenty miles and not had a bite of food for close on twelve hours, but no sooner had I turned my back on wonderland than I was assailed by aching limbs and a keen desire to eat. I turned out my pockets as I trudged along in the rain, hoping to find a forgotten sweet or piece of chocolate, and finally unearthed five peanuts in a nest of cigarette ends, a miserable surplus from some unremembered orgy.

I came limping at length out of the darkness into the feeble glare of a street lamp, and more gleamed murkily ahead in the gloom, revealing wet, glistening pavements and streaming gutters. The yellow circles of light showed dingy houses, cheerless stone dwellings lining a narrow street. This was Haltwhistle. Grey is its colour; a drab, depressing grey, with never a splash of green to relieve the monotony. There are no gardens, no trees. The main street writhes along between rows of dull cottages, twisting and turning as if seeking escape from the ugly buildings which press onto it, and when at length it bursts free at the far end of the town, it shoots away across the fields like an animal released from a trap. Haltwhistle is ugly. Poverty lies over it like a plague. The mines are closing, one by one, but still the people linger, as they always do long after hope has fled. There is despair in their eyes, in their hearts, in the way they slouch along the dismal street. Haltwhistle is the antithesis of Hexham: one is dejected and sullen, the other gay and charming.

I walked from one end to the other without finding an inn that offered an inviting welcome. All doors were shut against the pouring rain. I loitered at the bus terminus for a time, for I had come the last few miles in growing excitement at the prospect of receiving my package of prints from Hexham. But the terminus was deserted; there was not a soul to question. Every shop was in darkness and all doors shuttered. I stood and waited, sunk in my dripping cape, watching the rain splashing on the oily, greasy patch in the road where the buses halted. But after a few minutes I gave it up and retraced my footsteps along the empty pavements. I called in at the Red Lion which advertised itself as a commercial house, but the lady of the house ejected me with a shake of her head and suggested I should try the Grey Bull. I went across the road to the Bluebell, but met with no more success. The landlord had no accommodation for me; he suggested I should try the Grey Bull.

The Grey Bull had me. This is a big, rambling hostelry standing square and solid to the street, halfway up the hill. It has no

pretensions to architectural grace, and indeed is strikingly unbeauti-
ful both within and without, but it provided me with shelter when
I had begun to despair of finding any. Prosperous days at the Grey
Bull are a memory: nowadays the place is steeped in melancholy.
Half the rooms are in darkness, and footsteps on the bare stone
corridors echo weirdly through the house. There is a continuous
murmur of voices from the kitchen, but no laughter.

I dined well in the glow of a gas-jet, at one end of the vast
dining-room on the first floor. My supper was punctuated by
frequent momentary appearances of my hostess who was most
anxious to know if all was well on the table and, particularly, if
there was a sufficiency of everything. Every minute or two she
appeared, assailed by doubts that only a personal scrutiny could
satisfy. Her first concern was for the vinegar, which she regarded
with disbelief when I produced it from behind the newspaper I was
reading: she simply could not remember having brought it. Two
minutes later, she burst in with an apology and a bowl of sugar,
both of which were unnecessary, for there was enough sugar
already on the table to give diabetes to a regiment. Then she
brought a plate of cakes, adding to the half-dozen varieties that
surrounded the milk. Followed bread and butter to replenish the
dwindling stacks at my elbow, more cakes, gallons of hot water
although the room was already clouded in steam. It was incumbent
upon me, of course, to make some comment every time she came
to me, so that I came to listen for her footsteps outside, and only
when I could hear nothing did I dare stuff my mouth. But after the
loneliness of the day it was comforting to be waited on so
assiduously, to have someone at least conscious of my presence and
to exchange a few words of chatter.

After supper, I settled down to read an abridged copy of
Collingwood's *Guide to the Wall*, which I had bought at
Housesteads. I have already said that I found this Guide fascinating
when I read it before leaving home, but now that I had seen the
Wall and become familiar with the places mentioned I found my
enthusiasm for the book rising to fever pitch. I read it again and
again, completely enslaved by the racy narrative and the really
splendid manner in which the writer had managed to convey the

atmosphere of the Wall. It became increasingly evident to me as I read, that I should have to return to it on the morrow, although it had been my intention to continue south. The Wall was calling to me out of the printed pages, an irresistible call, a challenge. I would go back in the morning, tramp the breezy heights once more. There was much that I had not seen, and wanted to see. Not far from Haltwhistle were the celebrated Nine Nicks of Thirlwall where the Wall rises and falls abruptly along a serrated ridge of whinstone before settling down on its smoother run to Carlisle; I would go there. My decision to return filled me with exultation.

Strangely, I thought little of the war that had never started. The depressing clouds of fear and apprehension had vanished in this day's sunlight. Good old Mr Chamberlain. Good old Mr Hitler: he was not a bad sort after all.

I went to bed. Again I could not sleep. The rain had brought with it a breath of winter, and I shivered miserably in the darkness beneath a sparse covering of sheets. It was a bitterly cold night. My hostess's concern for me ceased the moment I shut the bedroom door, as was only to be expected, and I took shameful advantage of this escape from her watchful eye: I got up at midnight, lit the candle, ripped every carpet from the floor and threw them across the bed. Then I carefully dressed, lit a cigarette, and climbed back into my dugout. Still I was cold. I could not control my quivering flesh. I blew on my hands, and massaged myself to bring warmth as well as I was able, for the carpets on the bed weighed a ton and effectively restricted free movement. I shuddered and trembled and groaned and gasped. In one thing only was this fiend of a chill defeated: my jaws went through all the movements of chattering without inducing the usual clamour, for my top teeth were under water in the washbasin a few yards away. This was zero hour. I think I was ill that night.

Unfortunately, too, a man and a woman in the next room were engaged in continuous conversation until the small hours. Their voices were pitched in a monotonous key which exasperated me: too loud to be ignored, not loud enough to be listened to. The tone of the man's voice was endearing and persuasive; the woman, speaking less often, was sullen and cross. Several times I heard their bed creak violently, for only the thin wall separated it from mine, and this noise always heralded an earnest attempt on the part of the man to be sick; I think he must have been very drunk. I lay there infuriated, for, until this sordid interlude came to an end, I could not let the girl who hovered in my thoughts approach nearer. And I was in sad need of her company that night.

About two o'clock, however, a hush fell over the house, and with a sigh of thankfulness I yielded to the soft embrace of my comforter and was instantly soothed. Ah, dear girl, this night you were kind and compassionate; your whispered caresses brought new life to my weary body, your clasp was warm, your touch had the power to heal. Why must you come to me only in dreams? Cannot the day hold the joy of the night? You are not a fiction of reverie. You live, as I live. In the hours of darkness I may speak of love and you are always ready to listen, but the day follows and I cannot find you. I glimpse you occasionally across a wide gulf, but you are so distant, so far away that I cannot really be sure you are the one I dream of.

Must you always be out of reach?

Shall I never know?

THE SEVENTH CHAPTER

I AWOKE to find sunshine streaming into the room, making, as it filtered through the curtains, a dancing pattern on the wallpaper. Blessed sunshine! I can greet the most anxious of days with gladness if the sun is shining. It infuses in me a sense of well-being and bodily fitness that make the rough places easy to leap; unscaleable walls dwindle into insignificant hurdles. I cannot feel ill if the sun is in the sky, and I am quite certain that when the time comes for me to pass on the rain will be lashing against the window and clouds will lie heavy over the earth. Sunshine and colour and the love of a woman: these make life worth living. Not success nor wealth. The warmth and brightness of sunshine, the arch of a rainbow, the tenderness of a smile: these are pure gold even when the pockets are empty. To have these with me always I would joyfully forego the most coveted position; I would choose happiness rather than affluence. And I cannot be persuaded that I have a false sense of values.

There had been hot water in plenty on the table last night, but there was none outside my bedroom door when I peeped out furtively this morning, and I decided to postpone my necessary shave. So easy are the first steps down the hill; having broken routine once I never shaved again during the remainder of the holiday, and rapidly assumed a vagrant expression which was, at least, more in keeping with my raiment.

I had a good breakfast, paid up, and departed. Haltwhistle in sunshine is no improvement on Haltwhistle in rain. It is, if anything, worse. Rain is an excuse for depressing conditions, but

sunshine, by its comparison alone, puts the mean and commonplace to shame. As sunshine reveals dust on the furniture in a
room, so here in the streets it revealed dirt and grime that might
otherwise have escaped notice. It made Haltwhistle look shabby
and threadbare. Which it is, precisely.

I hastened along to the bus terminus. Haltwhistle, with its
population of 4,500, is the only town within a radius of fifteen
miles, so that it is the shopping centre for a wide area and, as it was
Saturday morning, the pavements were already busy.

There is no form of excitement quite like that of going into a
shop for your prints. You have been told they will be ready at a
certain hour; you have managed to curb your impatience in the
meantime, but now the hour has struck and you are seething with
anticipation. This is one appointment we never forget. There is a
great thrill when the packet is handed over the counter, although
you receive it with an air of indifference. You get outside, but
cannot go further. You simply cannot wait a moment longer; you
must look at them. You stand looking in the shop window,
ostensibly regarding the display, but feverish fingers under cover of
your coat are tearing the packet open. You have them now in your
hand. In your hand! Look at them, fool! Drop your eyes, look at
them; nobody is watching. See the results of your efforts. You have
paid for them. They are in your hand. Look at them! You need wait
in suspense no longer.

So you glance at them, one after another, quickly, and move
away, conscious of disappointment and the sense that it is all over,
life is empty again. I think we should always have something to
look forward to, no matter what: a promised kiss, a holiday,
marriage, the birth of a child, or even to take this example, a
packet of new snapshots, for life is made tolerable so long as we are
looking ahead into the future with pleasant expectancy. It is when
the prospect offers nothing that inevitably we brood over the
retrospect, and it is bad to think only of the past. The longed for
event, when it finally arrives, may be cruelly disappointing, but if
the foretaste was sweet we shall at least have gained something. It
is better far to rise above the earth now and again and come
crashing down than never to leave it. Half the fun in life is in

counting your chickens while they are yet embryos. If your
schemes end in disappointment, throw your net further; make
new plans for the future. They needn't be practical; I have experienced utter contentment in the contemplation of events I knew
could never happen. I have climbed Everest a hundred times
and planted a hundred Union Jacks on its summit; I have lived
happy hours in a little cottage in Lakeland with a dear lady for
company.

Disappointment never loses its keen edge, but the wounds it
inflicts will heal, not by constant nursing and attention, but by
concentration on some new project make it as wonderful and
exciting and impossible as you please. Disappointments are of
degree, and the risk of disappointment varies according to the
nature of the event. To take my previous examples: my snapshots
are always a blow to me, but this is a minor disappointment;
marriage is a disappointment only if we have chosen badly, and
then it is definitely major; a ruined holiday is a disappointment of
moderate degree. The birth of a child never is a disappointment. I
was never promised a kiss.

Minor disappointments can hurt, however, for a time as much
as the catastrophic blows. A prick can be as painful as a stab. On
this sunny morning, I stood on the pavement with tears in my
eyes. All the time and patience I had devoted to my photography
were proved of no avail. The prints were unbelievably poor. They
had no depth, no detail, no light and shade. Not one of the thirty
merited a second glance. All wasted effort is tragic, but in this
case it was rendered doubly so, because I had set my heart on
having a complete photographic record of this journey. This I had
regarded from the start as being of paramount importance. I had
planned to write a book of my experiences, provided inspiration
came from the right quarter, or consent rather, for the inspiration is always present. And the best feature was to be not the
narrative, but the first-class illustrations. They must be my own
handiwork, this was essential. I had come all the way from Settle
with this end in view, spent hours manoeuvring round suitable
subjects to gain effective camera angles, waited impatiently for
the sun to shine on chosen landscapes.

I went down a quiet byway, out of sight of the people in the
street, and looked at them again. I was heart-broken; the sun
disappeared in a mist. I had expected so much, and got nothing. All
the care and attention I had lavished on the task had been utterly
vain. And, what was infinitely worse, had been made vain by the
negligence of someone else. For I found that neither I nor my
camera was at fault. The negatives had been ruined by careless
handling; they were completely spoilt and could not be used again.
I lifted my face to heaven and called down all manner of odd curses
on girls with vermilion lips behind chemists' counters. What a
pitiful tragedy, to have my hopes frustrated like this! And the
disaster could so easily have been avoided. No special effort was
required; ordinary care would have ensured satisfactory results.

Slip-shod workmanship is a curse; I suppose it is the inevitable
consequence of the evolution from individual craft to mass pro-
duction. The solitary artisan of a century ago was paid according
to the results of his labours; the better his work, the more he
profited, and if quality was lacking he had to improve or starve.
Methods have changed; a man is paid a fixed wage, not for his
output, but for the time he spends on it. He has lost touch with
the ultimate buyer; his contact is only with the crowd he works
with. If he is disposed to slack, or do his work shoddily, only his
mates know. There may be others in the group with the same
attitude to their tasks, muddling through anyhow, simply not
interested, secure in the knowledge that they will not be be-
trayed. Their inefficiency becomes a strain on the conscientious
fellows who have to work all the more industriously to cloak the
defects of the idlers. If ever I have aspired to a position of
responsibility, it has always been when sloppy, inaccurate work
has come to my notice; then, I have thought, how I would like to
fork out the malingerers, roots and all, as one weeds a garden.
The trouble is, of course, that we have not the same pride in our
work that the old craftsmen had. We never dwell lovingly over
the finishing touches; often we haven't the time. We never sit
back and leisurely contemplate the completed task. We do not
love our work the same, nowadays.

Then, all at once, I remembered. Of course, of course. I had forgotten to adjust my camera on the journey north. The photos were ruined because of my own damn carelessness. I was the one guilty of slipshod work. My bitter indictment of others died a sudden death. I was mortified, furious now with myself . . . One of the many advantages of solitary walking is that there is nobody to witness the silly and stupid things you do, and nobody need ever know.

I stood there, sunk in despondency, almost inclined to end my holiday then, and return by train. Without some good pictures to take back, the expedition was robbed of half its purpose.

I knew, however, from experience that the mood would pass, and so I left the unhappy town behind and made my way northwards to the hills. But the feeling of bitter disappointment lingered, and it is noteworthy that although I carried my camera in my hand all the way, I took no pictures that day, and only one in the three days that followed. My plans were wrecked, and after a time I came to blame myself. I left those films in Hexham only because I was consumed with impatience to see how I was faring; my first intention had been to bring all the spools back with me and have them developed and printed by a reliable photographer in my home town. I had a slight measure of consolation: my films of the Wall were safely in my rucksack. But nothing I could do now, short of going back to Settle and starting all over again, would fulfil my original purpose. The disaster was irretrievable. I had to reconcile myself to defeat. And I must lack all true sporting instincts, for defeat rankles long in my breast. I cannot surmount it with a smile; instead, it makes me sullen and resentful. Condolences and sympathy infuriate; I am a dangerous man, and best left alone in my grief. Bruce, in similar circumstances, watched a spider.

I came eventually to the Wall once more. The morning was again brilliantly fine; I had been exceptionally favoured by the weather during the past days. There had been heavy rain in the night, and my path through the grass and bracken was liberally sprinkled with sparkling jewels. The sun was warm, the air still. There was a sweetness rising from the moist earth that refreshed and invigorated. A slight mist veiled the distant scene, adding a touch of mystery to my surroundings as I went along.

As before, the Wall seemed remote and lonely, forgotten by all men except myself; it lay there in the sunlight, tumbled and broken, and a great sadness brooded over it. It is no longer impressive and upstanding, west of the Haltwhistle Burn, but lies grass-grown and neglected, hardly more than a long green mound along the hillside. Where it shoots up to the ridge above Allolee Farm, however, and starts its switchback over the Nicks of Thirlwall, its adventurous course again affords a fine spectacle. These small rough summits of Thirlwall are quite Lakeland in character. There are the same black rocks and fantastic crags; the same suggestion of wildness and desolation, but seen here only in glimpses; the same patchy shagginess of the verdure, vivid in sunshine, dark in shadow.

But try as I would, I could not recapture the enthusiasm of yesterday. It was a perfect autumn morning, but it had started badly, and I needed a night's sleep to re-adjust myself and rid me of the upset that my early disappointment had wrought. I continued to have spasms of vile temper till evening, and this lamentable state of mind itself demonstrates how keen was the sense of frustration of my designs, for as a rule I am most docile and long-suffering.

I rested amongst the bilberry bushes on the highest of the Thirlwall summits, with my back against the ruined Wall, and surveyed a scene that was altogether serene and peaceful. There was not a breath of wind to disturb the long grass which screened my couch. A few shy flowers peeped out of the crannies of the Wall, attracted by the warm sun; tiny stains of colour against the grey stones. Below, in the bracken, sheep were grazing; occasionally they looked up and fixed me with long stares, curious that I should lie there, unmoving. Further below, a herd of young black bullocks was feeding in a pasture, with their heads in the direction of the sun and their shadows behind, as if they were toys set in that position. A well-timbered woodland bordered the lower edge of the field, and beyond that was the valley, robbed of its harshness and given a new, ephemeral loveliness by the indistinct blending of colour and contour, for the haze still hovered over the landscape.

I continued to lie there long after I should have been marching. It was the last day of summer, and for once I was content to idle an hour in the warm sunshine; there would be few opportunities hereafter until the cold winds of winter had blown themselves out, and summer came again. Tonight, I recalled, the clocks had to be moved an hour; backwards or forwards, I wasn't sure, and felt too drowsy to indulge in the intricate reasoning the solution would involve. It was very pleasant to lie there with eyes closed and senses lulled, doing nothing at all. I was engulfed in a silence so profound that the slightest of sounds were greatly magnified. I could hear, occasionally, the movement of sheep in the bracken thirty yards away, and nearer, the murmur of winged insects in flight.

My reverie was disturbed at length by the drone of an aeroplane engine, or so I thought, for when I searched the blue expanse overhead I could see nothing but a bee on an exploratory tour, industrious in its unceasing search for beauty. It disappeared behind me, over the other side of the Wall, and then I could not hear it; suddenly it wheeled back into sight with a loud buzz and came to rest on a cluster of flowers at my elbow. I watched it as it carried out its ruthless mission, its restless movements in marked contrast to my own inactivity. I was proclaimed a shirker by the pulsating life in this tiny black-and-yellow body.

Well, I would count twenty and move on. It was just after twelve o'clock, Saturday noon. The office would be deserted now, save for a diligent few; very soon the crowds would be hurrying to the football match, and I, for once, would be absent from their ranks. I was in temporary exile, out of touch with events, and already estranged from a life which had seemed as if it could never change. Today was the first of October: the date had some significance that I could not recall. It was the day for altering the clocks, yes; but wasn't it set apart for something else, too? I could not think what it was. I had a remote feeling that the day was connected with some event or other, an event which affected me, but it was beyond my power to bring it to mind. It could not be that there was some duty I should do on this day. Silly to think that, for I was free from all obligations, my own master, in allegiance only to a creature of my dreams, and She and I alone peopled the world I was living in. I gave it up after a while: my diary had no information except that there would be a full moon tonight. But I had a feeling that some event much more important and unusual was scheduled to happen; possibly there was to be an eclipse. I banished the vague doubts from my mind and got to my feet.

I bade farewell to the Wall here; a sad farewell, for it had been a most interesting companion. It had led me into strange and beautiful places, brought unexpected romance to my adventure, given me constant delight. It had won my affection and I was loth to part company. I must go now, but I vowed to come back some day when the sun was shining as it was now, and renew acquaintance. And next time we should start from the coast, the Wall and I, and proceed in more leisurely fashion over the hills and across the dales, for it had still many secrets to disclose, hidden joys I could not even suspect.

Ahead, a huge wire barricade stretched across the top of the ridge, forcing me away down through the bracken towards the valley. Here a vast quarry is eating into the hill with great bites, so that the wire barrier which keeps the sheep from the precipice is constantly and remorselessly advancing over pleasant slopes that are soon to be engulfed. Saddest aspect of all, this ugly enterprise is gobbling the Wall; yard by yard it is disappearing for ever after standing so long. Where now its arrogant pride, its majesty?

I turned and looked back once. The Wall lay there, humbled and submissive, a grey line among the green, stretching away into the far distance. I couldn't help feeling very sorry for it. Sympathy on soulless objects is misplaced, I know, and anything more destitute of life than this pitiful wreckage of stones would be hard to find, but over it there is a guardian spirit which reflects on past glories and thinks of the future not at all. And this unseen presence had been very real to me.

So I left the Wall; solitary, lonely, neglected, as I had found it.

I descended into the village of Greenhead where Wade's road comes down from the hills and joins the main artery between Newcastle and Carlisle two miles from the Cumberland border.

I had bread and cheese and a glass of beer in the back room of the inn there, and spread my map on the table before me. Alston, where I planned to spend the night, was fourteen miles away near the head of the long winding valley which bears the South Tyne along to the wide depression of the Vale of Hexham. Alston lay due south, and for the life of me I couldn't help regretting that no more I should face northwards. I must head always for the south now, back to Settle. I was no longer going, but returning; my holiday was drawing to a close. And the concluding days could not possibly hold the delights of the earlier marches. I had attained my objective, and in so doing had drained most of the interest from the venture. Much of my keenness had departed; my enthusiasm I had left at the Wall. The journey back was bound to be a spiritless affair compared with the continuous and growing expectancy which carried me so eagerly to the north.

Yet there was no logical reason why I should not continue to enjoy every moment of every day. The country that lay ahead was all new to me; there still remained the pleasure of making acquaintance with the upper reaches of the South Tyne and the wild hills whence it sprang; Cross Fell, highest of the Pennines, was in my line of march, and possibly I should learn more of the mysterious Helm Wind which besieges its stark summit; there was Appleby and the Vale of Eden, Sedbergh in its frame of mountains, out-of-the-way romantic Dent, and, among limestone again, the lovely waterfalls of Ingleton.

These places flashed through my mind in a series of images, and I tried hard to conjure up a genuine enthusiasm for them. Somehow I couldn't: I was conscious all the time that my holiday was over, now that I had seen what I came to see. The Wall had captured my imagination and affection to an extent that none of the places that belonged to the future could hope to do, indeed it was disloyalty to pretend that they could. No, the Wall was my love, from the moment I saw it, and my devotion should not be shared. I could not be guilty of base betrayal. So it seemed that the miles onward must drag a little, as I confess they did on occasion. Certainly I referred to my maps less often; I made all my plans with a touch of sadness, and often I looked wistfully to the north. I never lost sight of the fact that every step took me further away, increased the gap between me and the lonely hills where I had been happiest. I was destined to see, even yet, scenes of surpassing loveliness before I again walked the streets of Settle, but they were lacking in appeal. I was never in the same appreciative mood on the way back.

I started the retreat from the Wall with a feeling of sorrow, and the same feeling is upon me now as I write. At the time, I was tempted to stay near the Wall for a few days longer and then come home by train. In exactly the same way, I am tempted now to write at greater length about the Wall and then finish the book abruptly, in a few concluding passages. But I stuck to my original intention and finished the walk as I had planned, and I shall finish the book in like manner. Writing this account of my holiday has been like living my holiday over again; by my fireside I have recaptured all the delights and disappointments of the journey, tramped again every mile of the way, and in precisely the same mood. For this reason, since the last five days held least attraction for me, so must the concluding chapters suffer accordingly. I walked the hundred miles south with an indefinable sense of regret that the pleasures that had been mine were fast receding, and if I am to be a faithful scribe, I cannot do other than bring a hint of sadness into the pages that follow. I might summarise the whole return journey in one chapter, and end the book thus, but that would make the narrative lop-sided. So I shall continue as I have so far come. But if reading thus far has been tedium, I implore you to read no further; put the book aside now.

From Greenhead, I followed the road back towards Haltwhistle for a mile, by the side of the railway, until a shady lane on the right gave me an opportunity to start southwards in earnest. I climbed steeply out of the valley to the top of a wide hill which commanded an extensive view. Far ahead, a tumult of rugged moors reared up finely against the sky, diverse in shape and character, alike only in their sombre colourings. Somewhere amongst them, perched on their steep slopes, lay Alston, so effectively hidden that not until I was within a mile of it was I to see it. Out of the heart of the hills came the deep valley I must traverse, a narrow, winding trough which carried throughout its length a writhing silver snake. The hills were gaunt and bare, but the valley they sheltered was beautiful. The expansive parklands of Featherstone Castle choked the entrance, and the trees continued up the slopes on either side. Road, river and railway proceeded side by side through this rich wealth of timber, each under its archway of heavy foliage. Higher up the valley, the scene was less sylvan; the woods gave place to meadows where fat cattle browsed, and a few scattered farmsteads were the only habitations. Here the hills started to crowd in, their rough, uncultivated slopes compressing the fertile ground into a strip of green alongside the river.

At three o'clock, I was standing in moody contemplation of a signpost which told me that I must be prepared to walk twelve more miles if I was to get to Alston. Once more I had bitten off not more than I could chew, but more than I could chew and comfortably digest. I was already tired, for the morning's walk on Thirlwall had been rough and the sun had never ceased to beat down mercilessly. But Alston it would have to be; I could not hope to find accommodation before I got there.

So I set off with a will, and the journey proved to be far more enjoyable than I expected. A Roman road runs through the valley on its way from the fort of Carvoran on the Wall to Appleby and the south, and it is possible in places to follow its original course. This road is, or was, the Maiden Way; a thoroughfare of importance in the days of the Roman occupation, for the Maiden Way and Dere Street were the only approaches to the north and these alone could serve for the transport of all troops and supplies. Dere Street, sometimes called Watling Street, remains to this day a vital link between north and south, because it has been in constant use through the centuries and today is a fine macadam road, but the Maiden Way has fallen into disuse. At its best, the Way is a narrow track amongst reeds and heather; much more often, as across the wastes of Alston Moor, all traces have disappeared. I followed this path where I could. It runs always in a direct line, striking over the shoulders of the fells instead of skirting their bases as the modern road does. A Roman road leads where it is intended to lead in a simple, straightforward fashion which is wholly refreshing in these days when evasion and detour seem to be guiding principles.

It was from the side of a fell where the Maiden Way had led me that I got my last glimpse of the low hills which carry the Wall across the country. Already it seemed I had come far, for all detail was lost; my glance could wander along the ridge from Thirlwall to Housesteads, but it was a featureless view. The many sharp summits were there, like the teeth of a saw; but of the Wall and the camps there was not a sign, of the romance and adventure which awaited those who cared to go, not a hint.

I turned away with a sigh, and pushed on towards Alston. The twelve miles had been reduced to eight; I was by now footsore and hungry, and I began to look out for a place where I could obtain a meal. I was in no way weary of the walk, for the valley holds continuous interest and precludes any possibility of boredom. It owes its charm entirely to the structure of the hills; they encroach so jealously that from no part of the valley can a distant view be seen; instead you are provided with a delightful series of surprise glimpses. It is a valley full of corners; you are always looking forward to the next and are seldom disappointed.

The sun was fast sinking as I passed through the hamlet of Knarsdale, and before I had covered the next mile it had deserted the bottom of the dale, and long shadows were creeping up the opposite slopes. The last village this side of Alston is Slaggyford, and there are five long miles between. I was firm in my resolve to eat in Slaggyford, and when at length I came to it, I was more than ever determined to bide there a while. How the place got its unpleasant name I do not know, but it has triumphed over it. I shall remember Slaggyford for its white cottages and its blue clematis, for its complete tranquillity. There is no inn, and I could find no house of refreshment, so that I was compelled to enter the post office to buy a stamp and institute inquiries.

A very pretty girl behind the counter attended to me. Whether my isolation was causing me to invest all young women with loveliness, I cannot say, but certain it is that the few I came into contact with seemed uncommonly goodlooking. All had a ready smile for me, whether of adulation or amusement I do not know. I could only hazard a reason, and was always left dubious and wondering. Some regarded me roguishly, others honestly; but all of them fearlessly, as they were perfectly justified in doing. Some were ready to talk and laugh and give me flashing glances, others were silent and watched me out of the corners of their eyes. The way of a woman with a man is an absorbing study. Every woman has her own technique, and it is being perfected while the defenceless males of her own age are still kicking tin cans about the streets. The ladies have this advantage, that they step from girlhood to womanhood with one stride, while the men have long years of gawky adolescence to endure.

I was directed to a cottage nearby. A quaint, picturesque dwelling, this, with walls as white as new snow, but most wondrously adorned with great blue and purple stars where the clematis clung. The low doorway carried its own garland of these lovely blooms; they grew in such riotous profusion that it seemed not a doorway at all but an archway of intertwined branches, heavy with foliage and flower, beneath which I had to bend low to knock.

An old lady answered; a frail, delicate figure with white hair and a kindly, sensitive face. She was dressed in black, and wore a narrow black ribbon round her throat. My request for a meal took her aback, but after a moment's reflection, she led me into her best room; a room furnished, surprisingly, in modern style, and quite tastefully ornamented. The old lady was the quietest creature I ever came across; her movements were timid and she was quite delightfully shy. She prepared the table in silence; so softly did she enter and leave the room that I might not have been aware of her presence at all had it not pleased me to watch her above the edge of my map. There was a motherly tenderness in all her actions: I watched her hover round the table, placing every article in position very carefully so that everything would be within my reach, smoothing the folds in the spotlessly clean cover with nervous hands, arranging the cushions on the chair so that I should be comfortable, and when all this was done she stood back, anxiously regarding the table to ensure that she had omitted nothing. Then she looked in my direction for the first time, but I was so obviously intent on my map that she was afraid to disturb me. Instead, she touched everything on the table again, moving them ever so slightly until she was sure they were just right. Then she moved towards the door. I looked up and caught her eye. She smiled at me then, said the one word 'Now', and disappeared, closing the door noiselessly behind her.

I lingered over my tea, for I was tired and very comfortable. The room was quiet and restful, and I heard not a murmur either from the kitchen or from the village outside. There was such an all-pervading air of peace about me, that if by mischance I made a clatter with cup or knife, I was immediately struck with acute self-consciousness, and my meal proceeded therefore in deathly silence. It was a picnic in a graveyard. Most silences are broken by a ticking clock, even in an examination room or a dentist's surgery, but this room had no timepiece to relieve the stillness. From where I sat, I could see through the window, with its frame of flowers, across the quiet road to the fields and the soaring fells beyond. There was not a sign of life.

I finished my meal at last, and got my few things together. I went into the passage and, as my hostess had vanished completely, coughed and shuffled my feet to make obvious to her my impending departure. She did not come. The door was open; the white road lay before me. I stood at the entrance for a minute or two, waiting. Still she did not appear.

I went back inside the house and knocked at a door to attract her attention. Then she came from the kitchen, as quietly as a mouse. 'Now,' I said. She fingered the brooch on her dress nervously, dreading the moment; fancy having to make a stranger pay for a simple kindness done! Quite obviously she was unused to having visitors; the ordeal had been frightful. My hand was in my back pocket, waiting for her to say the word. She could not say it; she looked up at me almost apologetically, and blushed a little in confusion. I fell in love with the dear old lady. She was so small and delicate, so gentle, so alone and helpless. This was an awful moment for her. She really had no idea what to charge; she seemed to have done so little and provided such meagre fare. The stranger may have been disappointed; she might offend or even infuriate. I smiled at her, and she, looking up, fell to smiling also. She asked me then, if I thought a shilling would be too much; she did not look at me as she spoke, but bowed her head and started to smooth her dress industriously. I told her it was not nearly enough for the splendid meal I had had, and with that her anxiety vanished and she laughed. I marvelled at her then. Her eyes were blue, I noticed, and they sparkled like a child's; her face was no longer old and careworn, but fresh and girlish; her smile was lovely. I saw her for a moment as she was forty or fifty years ago, and I admired her as many a young man must have done at that time. I gave her more than she asked, more than the tea was worth, for this old lady, by her frailty alone, inspired me to gallantry, and no knight-errant was ever niggardly.

I went then, though I would fain have stayed and spoken with her, and she followed me to the door and watched my departure until a bend in the road hid me from sight. She was a dear little woman, very like my mother.

The sun had gone, and I pushed on at a good pace in the gathering dusk, eager now for a glimpse of Alston. The narrow valley, always peaceful, acquired a new dignity in the calm of the evening. The bleak fells shed their harshness and assumed a warm, mellow colouring; twilight brought to the river a white haze which spread outwards and diffused the meadows and woodlands with soft light.

After half an hour's walking, I left the road and followed a cart-track down the slope to the river. The ford which, guided by my map, I searched for, proved impassable. The river was at least sixty feet in width, and rushed fiercely over its pebbly bed in open hostility. I saw the cart-track disappear boldly into its waters, and reappear on the far bank, but it was no place for a traveller on foot. I followed the stream south until I came, unexpectedly, to a footbridge, and thus got across dryshod.

Amongst the trees on the other side is a tiny church, built in the corner of a meadow in the shelter of a wood. It stands solitary and quite forlorn, as if it had retired to its corner in a fit of pique, for it is easy to believe that its congregation has deserted it: there are very few dwellings within reach. This church is remarkable for its incredibly slender spire. One cannot help feeling that a ghastly architectural error has been committed. The designer must have regarded it in petrified amazement when the builder took him along to look at the finished job. For it is an unbelievably thin and weedy spire that sprouts out of the roof of the square tower; it has the same proportions as a tightly-rolled umbrella planted upside down, and certainly it could be used as a flag-pole without arousing comment.

I passed by it, and entered the gloom of Kirkside Wood. The lane here passes along a shelf, with high wooded slopes on one hand and the surging river below on the other. It is a magic place in the gloaming; there is romance in the witching shadows, and a melodious refrain from the hidden waters. Dusk is an enchantress. She touches a familiar scene and makes of it a fairyland; she transforms harsh fact into charming fiction. She induces wild, fanciful imaginings into the mind of man, makes of him an adventurer into time and space, sends him voyaging into the highest flights of chimerical fantasy. Worlds have been conquered in the quiet hours of dusk.

As I entered the leafy avenue leading into the wood, the moon came out of a low bank of clouds and, although it was not yet dark, its pale gleam shone weirdly across my path, making of it a patchwork of black shadow and iridescent light.

Kirkside Wood in the daytime I have not seen, but this evening, at least, it was a wonderland of fairy shapes and flitting, fantastic shadows; there was glamour in the still night air. The moon cast a soft radiance over the scene; the trees were bathed in a ghostly luminance, while overhead the dark interlaced branches became, at a touch, a canopy of glittering silver leaves. Dusk and the moon, allied, are irresistible: Kirkside Wood lay under a spell.

I walked quietly: the sound of footsteps was sacrilege.

By and by, I came to a young man and a girl standing by the side of the path. They were embracing: as I approached I saw them kiss. The girl's face was clear in the moonlight; it was the face of one radiantly happy. She chuckled merrily, and her laughing eyes sparkled as she avoided her lover's lips when he would have caressed her again; but she was teasing, for I noticed that she held him all the closer. I kept at a distance as I passed, but really I needn't have done. They wouldn't have seen me. How could they, since there was not a soul in the world but themselves?

I wished I had not seen them; I went on my way sorrowfully. Ah me, that I should witness happiness and it should make me sad!

Dusk and the moon, I have said, are irresistible, and so they are. But add to them a loving woman, and you have allurement complete. The glory of an autumn evening may hold glamour enough for the solitary dreamer; but the kiss of a loved one, the touch of a hand, the warmth and softness of a willing body, the endearing whisper: what after all can nature offer, if these are absent? So it was with me. If, before, I had thought myself perfectly content, I was made now to realise that I had utterly deluded myself. I yearned for someone to walk with, for someone to speak quietly to me in the darkness. I too, wanted to experience the bliss of a lovers' meeting, the thrilling ecstasy of precious moments together and alone, away from all else. But for me it could never happen. I lacked a companion, but one only could bring to me the comfort I hungered for. And she was very far away, as she must always be. . . .

Yet Kirkside Wood will remain in memory a romantic spot. It is a place to recall when the heart is troubled and grieved. A magic wand touched it when I was there, but I think it must ever live in the affection of those who have known it. It is a place, I imagine, where promises are made very easily and, once made, are never quite forgotten.

It was past eight o'clock when finally I saw the lights of Alston ahead of me. There was a great stir and bustle in the main street, such an air of jollity about the townsfolk, and so many voices calling in greeting to each other, that I felt strangely out of place, as if I were an intruder at a festivity. I stood for a time in the darkness of an alleyway, uncertain where to go, idly watching the people hurry past.

The town clings to a hillside so steep that the houses seem to be piled one above another; and an odd assortment they are, of many shapes and sizes, all old, all built of stone. Some confront the thoroughfare, others turn their backs to it. Some abut so far into

the street that there is no room for a pavement, others are recessed
and can be approached only through narrow cobbled alleyways.

I climbed the hill to the corner where the road from Weardale
comes into the town, twisting and staggering down from the
moors as if in the final stages of exhaustion following its long and
arduous traverse of the high Pennines. I was tired now, and cold,
for a cool breeze had blown from the hills since sunset; and my
weary condition was exaggerated by the buoyancy and high spirits
of the thronging crowds. Alston was en fête, for some reason or
other; I was in no mood for jollity and, as a result, felt there was no
welcome for me. Truth to tell, as I plodded up the street, I was
feeling a wee bit depressed, and for the first time wished myself
back at my own fireside. This business of finding a night's lodging
when weary limbs could go no further had for once no appeal for
me; I wished heartily I was in a bed somewhere, with all the
preliminaries dispensed with.

I stood under a lamp and looked round at the uninviting rows of
cottages and ill-lit dingy shops without much hope. I should get
accommodation somewhere; I had never failed yet. But it was such
an effort to get my tired legs in motion again and start my search.
There were groups of people everywhere; young fellows and girls
laughing and joking on the pavements; elderly parties loaded with
parcels, gossiping in a language I could not understand; shouting,
excited children. Not one of these, I told myself as I pushed
between them, had a concern for the night's shelter: I was
friendless and alone.

As events turned out, I could have spared myself these miserable
forebodings. There is a Good Samaritan in Alston, and destiny
directed my faltering steps to her front door. I made my wants
known to her, and reluctantly she had to deny me, for friends of
her daughter were staying there for the weekend. I thanked her,
and went slowly away; slowly, because I could see she was hesitant
and was watching me as I moved away along the street. She called
me back, as I hoped she would; the house was plain and
unprepossessing, but the next might be worse. But again I was
disappointed. She thought hard how she could oblige me, and I
waited silently for her decision. No, she said at length, she was

sorry, very sorry, but she was afraid it was out of the question. Ah well, I replied, and slung my rucksack over my shoulder with a gesture of despair.

I was artful now, and cunning: I could see the woman was in some distress at having to turn me away, and the thought of having to go through all the overtures again at another front door made me all the more determined to get in here somehow. Ah well, I said again, with a sigh which must just have been perceptible to her; I supposed I would get shelter somewhere in the town. I gave her a brave grin, which I hoped she would perceive as forced, and limped away more slowly than ever. She called me back again, told me to come in; she would arrange for the girls to sleep together.

Once inside, and seated by the big fire in the kitchen with my shoes off, I would not have budged even if it meant the whole family sleeping in a row on the rug. My despondency vanished, snatched from me by the roaring flames and whirled up the chimney and out into the inhospitable darkness of the night. It was half-past eight when I entered, feeling ready for bed, but it was long after midnight before I went upstairs. There never was a busier hive of activity than this warm kitchen on this particular evening. I was not left to brood quietly by myself; instead, I sat and witnessed a succession of events, a parade of faces, which bewildered me and made me forget my own troubles.

Tonight, by a coincidence, was the one night in the year for Alston folk. The Annual Show had been held during the day and had been a great success: the weather had been lovely, the exhibits better than ever; visitors had poured in from the surrounding villages and farmsteads, and even come over the fells from Durham and Cumberland. The Show was over now, but the day was far from being spent since a wandering fair occupied the showground. There were fortune-tellers, shooting galleries, games of skill and chance, peep-shows, even roundabouts. The excitement I had sensed outside reached crescendo in this back kitchen; I was in the midst of it. For Richardson, my host, was secretary for the poultry section of the Show, and acted also in a score of other capacities. There were callers every few minutes during the evening, and one and all they came marching boldly into the room without knocking. They had accounts to settle, or maybe they had left their parcels or raincoats here and were calling for them; some were friends from remote places, here for the great day, and perhaps not to be seen again until next year. All were boisterously jolly, inflamed by this rare glimpse of the bright lights, for their own lives are lonely and humdrum and lack opportunities for merrymaking. Aye, it had been a grand day.

I was never sure which was the daughter of the house and which were the guests. When I entered, Mrs Richardson was in the house alone. Then two young women came in, and later a third; they hung about in suspense, without removing hats or coats. They looked at me without surprise, and certainly I was no hindrance to their free chatter. Then they vanished. More people came in, a procession of them, punctuated at intervals by the frequent re-appearances of the three girls. The girls never stayed long, but were off again when the impulse took them. The room was a babel of talk and laughter: when the young women were in, they exchanged confidences, told of their thrilling experiences on the fairground, made their plans quite as though there was not a stranger present. Not that I was ignored; on the contrary, the mother, the girls, and later old Richardson quite took me to their several bosoms, spoke to me as though I had been sitting there for years. I was one of the family.

I began to acquire an intense interest in them, listened sympathetically to their woes, transient though these were on such a night of nights, and found myself sharing in the general agitation. I heard of the carryings-on of Jimmy So-and-so on the fairground with a girl from Haltwhistle, and he engaged to a lass from Garrigill; of the unbelievable antics of Mrs What's-her-name, who was usually so staid and proper; and fancy Jack Who-is-it getting so drunk that he had to be thrown off the premises, for he had never been drunk before! The girls were fine healthy creatures, without a trace of bashfulness or conceit; I was amazed that they could talk so unrestrainedly in front of a stranger, for in reverse circumstances I should have shut up like an oyster, but for me it was a mightily refreshing experience. Once one of them interrupted a conversation to show me a ladder in her stocking, lifting up her dress with a dramatic suddenness that made my eyes pop. I never knew stockings went so high. . . . While women have legs, so long will men pursue.

My host came in after ten o'clock, a little wiry figure bent low under a load of parcels, whereupon his wife surprised me by setting off to the fairground, despite the lateness of the hour; she had been busy all day, she said, but she would not miss the fun for anything. The girls had gone again, restless and excited, eager to make the most of the glorious event. I settled down now to study the apparition which settled, with a sigh, in the big armchair across the fireplace. Mr Richardson proved to be the most entertaining character I happened upon. His appearance was odd. He had, below a thatch of untidy yellow hair, a thin face, pale watery eyes, an enormously long nose which the cold night, maybe, had coloured a fiery crimson, and a drooping, straggling moustache. He was a little man, and sunk deeply in his chair so that I looked down on him and, from this position, the extremity of his nose hung below the confines of his face, so much like a pendulum that I expected it to swing.

But his deficiency in good looks was more than counter-balanced by his vast knowledge of men and affairs. He was, I think, the most learned man I have met, and this despite his rural outlook and broad accent. He was an owl for wisdom, a lynx for perception and shrewdness. I mentioned nothing that he could not expound on at length and, so far as my own limited knowledge could accompany me, he was never guilty of an untrue statement. I got him to talk of his own environment, and of the fells, as I love to do when I am in the company of a countryman. He told me of the shepherd's life; how they lived in huts on the fells, meeting nobody for days, coming into the town only at weekends for a few hours of companionship.

He answered questions that in my ignorance I had often pondered over. He explained how a dog will locate a sheep buried deep in snow, how the sheep is dug out, having during its imprisonment eaten all the grass within reach, leaving a bare circle of ground where it has lain. He told me of the shearing, no longer profitable since the farmer nowadays will get only twopence a pound for the wool, but necessary for the animals' health. He it was who told me what I have already mentioned in airy knowledge, of the black-faced sheep which love the heather and the white-faced sheep which will not eat it. I asked him about the shooting seasons; why did grouse shooting commence on one date, partridge and pheasant shooting on others? Could grouse not be shot in mistake for partridge? Impossible; grouse never came down below the heather line, but partridges were incubated artificially in the valleys and made their homes there. Why did foreigners come to this island to shoot grouse? Because there were none abroad. Then why weren't the birds imported into other countries and bred there? Because there was no heather outside these islands of ours. What's that got to do with it? Well, lad, because grouse are as much a part of heather as the roots of it; they will not live away from it. I tested him then on the geography of his district, for I was on secure ground here, having made a long study of the map. He never faltered; he answered all my questions correctly, without hesitation.

One of the girls came in about eleven o'clock, sat idly for a few minutes, and then jumped up with sudden resolve and said she was going back to the fairground. She gave me a look which told me that I could be popular if I were so minded, but my limbs had stiffened by this time, and the fire had melted me into the shape of my chair. She went alone, and I steeped myself in old Richardson again.

The interruption had disturbed his train of thought. He started to speak now of the Crisis. Crisis! I leaped metaphorically at the word. Crisis! That was it. That was why the date had seemed familiar on Thirlwall. Today a war should have started, a war that would have altered the whole trend of my life. How incredible that I should have forgotten it! The weeks of suspense came to an end only yesterday; already they were out of mind. It was absurd that I could have gone through the day without a thought of the catastrophe which had been so narrowly averted. I had begun to think, these past weeks, that the beginning of war would be the finish of me, and no man can contemplate his own demise with equanimity; yet here I was, forgetting so easily. If the purpose of my holiday had been to rid me of the tense atmosphere of the town, it had succeeded admirably. How were those I had left behind faring? Had they forgotten, too? I was to discover on my return that these days were fearful for them; feverish preparations were made for the disaster that seemed inevitable. I missed all this. Perhaps I ran away from it. But while I was making my way carefree over Cotherstone Moor, my friends were conscripted to issue gas masks; every mile that I moved northwards meant that the trenches for the civilian population, in the park where I played football when a boy, were going deeper into the earth. I had forgotten. I owed an apology to an old man with an umbrella.

Richardson gave a masterly exposition of the international situation. I was astounded at his wide knowledge, and more so at his sagacious comments. His reasonings were always sound, his judgments flawless. He had the knack of discriminating easily between the relevant and the irrelevant, between the vital and the superfluous; he hit the target every time. He did not speak as one having authority, or seek to emphasise his remarks in any way. On the contrary, he continued to sit slumped in his chair with his hands in his pockets, staring in the fire; he spoke quietly and yawned often, for he had had a hard day. I had to coax him to talk at all.

He had been in the front line during the Great War, and his recollections of life in the trenches held me enthralled. He described attack and counter-attack, retreat under fire, advances so rapid that shells from their own guns were falling amongst them as they went forward. He explained the different poison gases that were employed: how they were made, conveyed to the enemy, their effects and the treatment thereof. Certain gases were released and were carried by the wind in vaporous clouds to the opposing trenches; a sudden change of wind brought the murderous stuff seeping back, and caused a retreat in their own ranks; this often occurred. Other gases came in the form of shells. Every soldier learned quickly to distinguish between the sounds made in flight by the different kinds of shells, and they were many: some highly explosive and treacherous, throwing shrapnel over a wide area; others less dangerous and some comparatively harmless.

The ear became so trained to the sound of shells in flight that before long the men came to sense where each one would fall; instinct told them when they were in danger. Raw recruits would fling themselves to the ground at every shriek overhead; hardened campaigners did so only when they sensed that one was coming down in their midst. This natural intuition extended to the aircraft which droned above them constantly; the men never needed to look up to identify an aeroplane. They knew their own, their allies', their enemy's, by the sound of the engines alone. They could tell, also without searching the sky, exactly where an aeroplane was, whether in front or behind, to the left or to the right. Only when an enemy aeroplane was directly overhead did they need to exercise caution.

So he went on, I prompting and questioning him most eagerly, for he was a delightful conversationalist, and I profited greatly from his discourses. This man was wonderful. He never rose above the rank of private in the army; he was nothing in Alston except one of many poultry-keepers, and he attained no greater eminence than that of secretary to one of the sections of the Annual Show; he was small and shabby, quite insignificant-looking. Yet I never enjoyed any man's company more. He was not a man of letters, by any means; it was his downright commonsense that appealed to me, and the manner in which he had learned from experience. He was a thinker, first and foremost, not a reader. His opportunities to ruminate and cogitate were provided by his pastime, for he liked nothing better, he told me, than to put a few sandwiches in his pocket and spend a day fishing in the streams that come down from Cross Fell.

About half-past eleven, his wife returned. The fun on the fairground was at fever-pitch now, she said; money was flowing like water. The roundabouts were full to capacity, and cramming as many turns as possible into the short time that remained before midnight, when business must cease. Where earlier in the evening a ride on the roundabouts cost threepence, now the charge was a shilling, and the rides were becoming shorter and shorter. The crowds up there were inflamed with excitement, throwing money away not merely for a minute's gratification but because they knew the chance of such a glorious carousal would not be repeated for a twelve-month; it was a duty. But if they were happy, what did it matter?

She started to make a supper and, before the table was prepared, the girls came in, flushed, exhausted, happy. They collapsed about the room, throwing off their coats, kicking off their shoes. It was over now, but they had made the day unforgettable, as they had determined to do. Nothing could still their tongues.

I sat at the table between Richardson and one of the girls. Nobody waited on me. Like the rest of them, I helped myself, diving into the big spread as fancy willed. It was a royal feast, a celebration of the success of the Show, with which I was now thoroughly identified. Midnight found me regarding a huge chunk of raw cucumber which had found its way on to my plate. The others all had equally large slices, I noticed; Mrs Richardson had brought a prize exhibit from the pantry and hacked it into six pieces. Raw cucumber in bulk was new to me, but so was the happy camaraderie of the Richardsons' kitchen. I relished this strange fare as much as the rest.

So at last came to an end one of the best evenings I have spent anywhere, with the girls trooping upstairs one after another, Richardson slowly putting the clock forward eleven hours, his wife clearing the table. I felt I should have mentioned how much I had enjoyed their company, for they could not have suspected how refreshingly different was the atmosphere of their little home from anything I was accustomed to. But I refrained. I wished them goodnight, and went to bed.

My room had been vacated in haste by the last tenant. The bedrails were draped with silk stockings, and there were wispy garments which, study them as I willed, I could not see the purpose of, nor what object they were intended to serve. The drawers of the dressing-table were half-open, their contents ransacked; more silk stockings carpeted the floor. Whoever the owner was, she had put all her cards on the table.

I had, of necessity, to play solitaire.

As a result, I slept well that night.

THE EIGHTH CHAPTER

I HAD expected a change in the weather after the coolness of the evening and, when I looked out of my window along the quiet street next morning, I was agreeably surprised to find that not only was it fine, but that there were pools of blue sky amongst the clouds. I had been exceptionally well-favoured as yet, for the wet crossings of Tan Hill and Swinhope Head were the only interruptions in a week of brilliant sunshine, and neither of these drenchings I had minded in the least since they were accompanied by the fascination of mist. Today, particularly, I wanted a fine day, or at least, no rain. I had a heavy programme, for if I was to keep to my itinerary, I must get to Appleby by nightfall, and the county town of Westmorland was twenty-three miles away, across the desolation of Cross Fell.

I went downstairs to find the kitchen still in disorder after the mild brawl of last night, and my hostess tremendously busy sweeping the floor and putting things straight. Her husband was gazing into the fire from the recesses of his armchair, sublimely indifferent to the commotion his wife was making, and quite unaware that magnificent opportunities to assist in the cleaning-up were all around him.

Breakfast would not be ready for some time, so I went out to buy a newspaper. Richardson told me that I wouldn't get one; the shops would be closed all day. There was, however, a man who occasionally sold papers in the street; if I could locate his home I might possibly get one. He told me where it was, in a back alley in the higher part of the town, and I set off in that direction. I was

A PENNINE JOURNEY

143

athirst for yesterday's football results, for I had been unable to get the desired information last night.

The morning air was keen and chilling as I went up the hill past the church. There was a change in the weather, after all. Summer had gone with the sun yesterday; today there was a bite of winter in the cold wind. I pulled my rags closer about me as I walked.

I toiled up to the far end of the town until the houses were behind me and the bleak, rolling moor ahead, with the climbing road like a scar across its breast. Turning, I saw Alston for the first time, falling away from me in a chaotic jumble of rooftops down to the green valley below. It is but a tiny place, with no more than a couple of thousand inhabitants, but it is not without importance, and for those who live there it is the grandest spot on earth. They have a great pride in it, and a stranger will not tarry long before he is reminded that here is the highest market town in England. Roads leave Alston for Penrith, 19 miles; for Middleton-in-Teesdale, 22 miles; for St John's Chapel, 14 miles; for Hexham, 23 miles. Distances are great amongst the lonely hills of the north; the signposts are always interesting. The roads run high across barren uplands where never a habitation nor sign of man's occupation relieve the scene. There is wildness and desolation all around. In country such as this, the lonely outposts of civilisation, those humble dwellings huddled together for warmth at the foot of the passes, assume a great importance for the traveller.

Alston is such a place. Small though it is, it yet forms the biggest collection of houses between the plains of east and west. It is a touch of the urban where all is rural. It is the only town which really lies in the heart of the Pennines, the few others being situated on easier slopes away from the main range. Thus Alston is of some consequence. Most travellers break their journey here; it is a rest between long laps. If you want a meal, a drink, petrol or free air, whatever the latter term may mean, have it now, for you cannot be sure when your next opportunity will come. Free air! Yes, there is free air in and around Alston; it comes with the breeze over vast, trackless wastes; you can fill your lungs with it and feel your stature growing to that of a giant.

But Alston is not seen by parading the main street, old and picturesque though this is. The straggling rows of buildings that flank the street are a mask to the real face of the town. Turn along one of the narrow alleys, follow its twisting course until you are lost in a maze of branching lanes, in a confusion of tottering buildings, set most oddly and bewilderingly at all angles. This is Alston and, when you have delved deep into it, the main thoroughfare becomes, by comparison, a Regent Street.

I did not find the newsvendor's home; it was a hopeless task in the labyrinth in which I found myself, and there was nobody astir to give me direction. I went back to my breakfast, after half an hour's absence, without having met a soul. Alston sleeps late on Sunday morning.

Breakfast was a quiet affair. One of the girls was still abed; the others seemed to have shot their bolt the night before, and ate soberly enough. As for myself, I was sorry to be leaving this hospitable roof, and had very little to say.

I paid, in small part, for what I had had, and shouldered my rucksack, watched silently by the family. I bade them good morning, and they replied in chorus and asked me to call again if I was ever in Alston in the days to come.

I walked away from the house conscious that my departure had a trace of sadness about it, for I had been happy for a while and was turning my back on the house for ever. It was unlikely that I should return, that I should ever see Richardson or his wife or the girls again. A pity. They are fine, honest people.

The weather changed its mood to suit mine, and before I reached the bridge which carries the Penrith road across the river, the cold wind was driving rain into my face. I searched the sky for patches of blue, but they were gone now, blotted out by drifting grey clouds. The aspect was cheerless in the extreme. With the houses behind me, I should have had an unrestricted view across the moors to Cross Fell, but I found the monarch of the Pennines beheaded. Above fifteen hundred feet, the country was obscured in cloud; not the filmy veil of gossamer that touches the ground with ghostly fingers and enchants with its elusiveness, but the heavy, clinging shroud that rests immovable, clasping the earth in a cold clammy embrace.

A glance at the murk ahead was sufficient to convince me that these conditions were here to stay. There was an uncomforting air of permanency about the leaden mass before me; it had settled and taken up residence.

One hope remained: that the high wind, which was gradually increasing in velocity, might dispel the gloom and at least leave my path clear. In this hope, I turned away from the road and followed the lane which leads to Garrigill and the start of the seven-mile climb to the summit of Cross Fell. I was reluctant to pass the mountain without getting to the top, but it became increasingly evident as I trudged along that today I had better not attempt the ascent.

The day became darker, the weather more spiteful. As I came into the little hamlet of Leadgate, a sudden downpour of chilling rain decided me. I accepted defeat with a readiness that was disturbing. Had this been a day on my outward march, I would have gone on in enthusiasm, eager to overcome another obstacle in my way to the finishing post. But it was not. I was on my way home. I had done what I set out to do and, compared with that experience, all that happened now could be no more than mere incident. Compared with the Wall, Cross Fell was trivial. It could so easily have been the other way round: if Cross Fell had been my ultimate goal, the Wall would have had far less significance for me. But I was returning; not once since I left Thirlwall was this fact absent from my mind; at times it would be shelved, as during my stay with the Richardsons, but too often it was the subject of melancholy reflection. It did not detract from my enjoyment of these later days, but the divine spark which could have made them more truly memorable was missing. I was more ready to listen to the voice of reason, faint and unrecognisable though it was.

So on this occasion, the madness of attempting the crossing into Westmorland by way of the fell was apparent. The venture had a hazard about it which appealed strongly, but there was no disputing the vileness of the day. Here in the valley, the storm was already raging; up above, in the clouds, the conditions would be

manifestly worse. Richardson had warned me of the rigours of the
journey, expecting then that there would be neither rain nor mist
nor wind. A spice of danger in a walk is to be welcomed; it is what
apple sauce is to pork. Who prefers to climb Blencathra by Scales
Moor rather than by Sharp Edge? But moments of real peril are
ugly, and do no good. They are pleasant neither to undergo nor to
recall.

I stood in the middle of the lane with my back turned to the
rain, and took out my map. The wind nearly tore it from my grasp.
I saw that if I abandoned the Cross Fell route, the only other way
across the watershed into Westmorland was by the road. Even this
tame alternative was likely to prove arduous, for I should be
heading into the weather all the way, and to start with there was a
five-mile climb to the top of Hartside Cross, at a height of nearly
two thousand feet. Occasional road-walking I do not mind: I do
not belong to those hardy trampers whose prestige would be
damned if they were to walk ten yards on macadam. Or so they
say. I dare bet that every one of them has been reassured at times
by a hard surface underfoot. Every road leads to food and shelter,
but many a mountain track ends in a bog. I know which I prefer
when darkness is falling. And they, too.

I stayed long enough in Leadgate to have a cigarette in the
doorway of a barn, for I should not have another chance of a dry
smoke until I reached one of the villages over the divide. I watched
a little girl dart with a shriek from one cottage to another, a coat
flung over her head to keep the rain off her hair, and followed the
progress of a wretched dog as it padded slowly between the pools
that were already forming in the lane. What a dreary morning! I
wished myself back beside the big fire in the house at Alston. I was
feeling shivery and starved, and this, if I have not already furnished
enough, was another excuse for taking the line of least resistance
into Westmorland. The plain truth was that I set off to the road
feeling a coward, and knowing that I was one. Here was a chance
to tackle a job that called for endurance and ability to overcome
setbacks, and I simply hadn't the heart to attempt it. Cross Fell was
too much for me. I should have been happy if I had conquered the
summit on such a day, but I gave it up and turned miserably away.

As always when we take the less heroic course, I was to suffer pangs of regret: I told myself a hundred times during the day that my action was the only reasonable one, and events proved that it was, for the storm was later to develop into a tempest of malignant fury. Nevertheless, I got no solace from this reflection. My decision to retire caused far more heart-burning than the buffeting I endured on that high-level road across the moor. Yet to this day I believe that if I had gone forward as I planned, I should never have emerged from the mist. I never witnessed a mountain in a blacker mood than Cross Fell on that October Sabbath.

Until I neared the top of the pass, I found walking easier and pleasanter than I had anticipated. I was climbing in the lee of the hills and, although every inch of the way was completely exposed, I was not yet to feel the worst of the gale. It rained continuously, driving across the wild moor in sheets and whipping the wet surface of the road into agitation, but the rain itself I rather enjoyed, for the cape was an adequate protection for my shoulders. My legs were soon soaking, but they didn't matter; they never do matter. My contempt for them, which amounts almost to loathing, has subjected them in their time to all manner of discomforts. Still they carry me along, faithful supporters. If they had eyes they would look at me like a couple of thrashed dogs, reproachfully.

But conditions at Hartside Cross, where Cumberland becomes Westmorland, were relentless. The climb from Alston is gradual; the summit is attained at length, and then, suddenly and surprisingly, the whole moorland collapses at your feet and the road plunges downwards to the plain below. Today, the plain was invisible, and only the steep initial stages of the descent could be seen: out of the void came swirling streamers of cloud, as smoke pours from the crater of a volcano. The rain was heavy, but not worse than it had been during the past hour. It was the wind, a malevolent, howling monster, that made Hartside untenable. It lifted my cape high and dashed it into my face, ballooned it and sent me bounding back in my tracks like a parachutist struggling for a grip on the earth with his feet. If I had worn skirts, as some dear friends think I ought, I should never have crossed the boundary. As it was, I was fain to crawl into the shelter of a disused hut, and rest.

It was useless to wait for an improvement in the weather, and I ventured from my refuge when I had recovered my breath. My movements had all the appearance of a steady gallop, but I made very slow progress against the wind. I was astounded, at the very top of the pass, to see a modern café loom out of the mist. It was a substantial place, with large windows set in white walls, and it offered sandwiches, lunches, teas, hot and cold drinks, and ice cream. It was oddly out of place, there amongst the moorland grass, with sheep bleating in its shelter; it belonged to the pleasure beach of a popular seaside resort. It must be a popular rendezvous for, despite the bleak surroundings, there were motor-cars parked outside. On a clear day, it will command a view across the Eden Valley to the Lake District, and most travellers will halt awhile; but in the depths of winter I fear it must close its doors, for the road by which it stands is silent and deserted.

I went down the hill as quickly as I could, for the wind was merciless and cut through me like a knife. The sooner I was out of it, the better. I was no longer protected by my cape from the rain: it billowed and eddied around my neck, half-choking me, and when it was not flapping noisily about my ears, it was slapping me playfully in the face. And it was very wet. I have once or twice had the mortification of being hit with a wet dishcloth, but I can state quite bluntly that the discomfort caused thereby was not one whit greater than that caused by my present ordeal. Only the pride receives a deeper hurt.

The road zig-zags exasperatingly on its three-mile descent to Melmerby, and when a green lane shot away downwards on my right hand, I was quick to follow it. I was becoming drenched, and my main desire was to get down from the hillside into the comparative calm of the valley. I knew already that I should not get to Appleby that night: I would rest in Melmerby and, unless an unforeseen brightening took place above, stay the night there. This was not defeat; it was a rout, for Melmerby is thirteen miles short of Appleby, and but ten from Alston. As it happened, I did not even get as far as Melmerby.

I splashed along the lane for a mile until it gave place to a narrow byroad. I passed a signpost which pointed to 'Unthank

$\frac{1}{4}$ mile' and, bedraggled though I was, I took out my map there and then to confirm the strange name.

Ten minutes more brought me to the first houses of a long, straggling hamlet known as Gamblesby, a place richly individualistic because of the colour of the stones used in the construction of its buildings. The houses, and the quaint church, have a warm, ruddy shade; an unusual colour, not that of brick, but of sandstone. The effect is uncommon and very pleasing. In other respects, the village is like most villages, and prettier, perhaps, than many. But these observations belong to tomorrow, not to today. For as I turned the corner to come along the road which cuts through the village green, the heavens opened. I struggled onwards, head down against the hurricane that swept in violent gusts, bringing with it a deluge of icy rain.

I was powerless to go further. Every step required the energy of ten. When, through my streaming spectacles, I noticed a low, rambling inn set back a little way from the road, I yielded entirely, and travelled the dozen yards to its open doorway at a commendable speed.

It was twelve-thirty.

I had come nine miles.

I stood in the flagged passage and divested myself of my cape, spraying the walls like a watercart as I pulled it over my head. I entered the parlour with the same trepidation as a suburban gardener enters the house when his shoes are clogged with mud, expecting an angry tirade and a command to get out. Not only was I bespattered with mud, but wherever I halted a pool of water quickly made an island of me.

Instead of protest, I found a welcome. There was a slender girl awaiting my pleasure. Her features were indistinct until I had wiped my glasses, but when this operation was performed, I knew instinctively that I was unlikely to go further that day. The girl was neat. And a neat girl is to me as pleasurable a sight as a cairn of stones on a hilltop.

To a young man seeking a wife, I would say that neatness is the first essential; a trim appearance, a dainty body, a precise outlook. Intelligence is the next virtue to seek, and it is a rare one; it is the

comparative deficiency in intellect that makes woman's claim for
equality with man pathetic. Next in importance is a sense of
humour. But the girl who laughs loudly is to be avoided; look for
one who smiles rather than laughs, whose heartiest guffaw is never
more than a quiet chuckle. Good looks don't matter a great deal,
and don't last, anyway; I have a partiality for blue eyes, to me they
make a face look honest, but I am ready to be convinced that hazel
or brown eyes signify an equally trustworthy nature. For the
further guidance of the young man seeking a wife, let me add the
following counsel; never marry a girl because you are sorry for her,
for sympathy dies swiftly; never marry a girl simply because she is a
good cook, for there are worse ailments than a rebellious stomach;
keep away from the massive women, for they will go worse, and
make you labour like a beast; never marry simply to get away from
a depressing home, for the odds are you will jump from the fire
into the frying-pan, and it is better to roast now than to sizzle for
the rest of your life; beware the girl who is your senior in age and
fawns on you, for you are her last opportunity, perhaps, and
secretly she may be despising you and hating herself. But do not
worry too much about your choice. If you picked blindfold, you
could be pretty sure of getting a wife who would keep the home
tidy, have your meals ready promptly, give you an amazing baby
now and again, and be entirely devoted and faithful. Whether these
qualities are sufficient to make you happy, depends on yourself.

The girl who brought my bread and cheese in the Red Lion at
Gamblesby was not extra-ordinary, but she was in a strange
environment. The village is small and quite away from the beaten
track; it is linked to the world only by a third-class road which is
hardly better than a rural lane. There is no railway within miles, no
bus service, no cinema nearer than half-a-day's journey, no town of
any size within a radius of thirty miles. It is a speck in a vast area of
agricultural country. The place is hidden, remote, lonely.

Into this quiet backwater had come this girl. Manifestly she did
not belong here, yet here she had chosen to live. She was smart,
sophisticated, modern. She dressed beautifully. She had a lovely
walk. She was coiffured, manicured, painted and powdered, but
not by any means obtrusively: her appearance was in keeping with

her general calm demeanour and capable, confident manner. I could not guess her age. At first, I thought she was eighteen; by teatime she was twenty-two, and when I went to bed, twenty-five. Next morning, she was eighteen again. Time marched all ways in the Red Lion.

I had the big room to myself. The girl lit a fire for me immediately, without being asked. She did everything for me without being asked. She seemed able to discern, somehow, that I was a visitor out of the ruck, a sort of gentleman. I was interested in her. I could not help scrutinising her from head to foot every time she came into sight.

She loaded the fire with sticks and twigs, and very soon I had a crackling furnace to cheer me. I crouched over it until I was obscured in the cloud of steam rising from my soaking clothes. It was grand to be beside a big fire again. The rain lashed against the windows; I could hear the wind howling and tearing at the gables. The road outside was deserted, storm-swept, and remained so until the dark shut the scene mercifully from view. Further progress towards Appleby was out of the question. I should be comfortable here. At one o'clock, I was writing in my diary: Stayed at Gamblesby tonight.

I asked if there was accommodation at the inn, and my youthful hostess replied yes, there was. I said if it was still raining in an hour's time, I would stay. I waited in vain for glad surprise to come to her face. She was a wee bit provocative, too. She accepted my conditional decision without a smile. But I noticed she smiled very little at any time.

When next she came in to replenish the fire, she carried a six-month-old baby in her arms. I should have been far less surprised if it had been a doll. I asked if it was hers; unnecessarily, for the cherub was as trim and proper as the mother. I was privileged to dangle it on my knees for some minutes; hitherto they had been rapidly and satisfactorily drying, but now they were to experience a setback. Ah, you little rascal, you are not yet quite like your mother; she wouldn't have done that if I had taken her on my knees, not at least without some apology. But the child was altogether delightful, as of course all babies are. I forget now whether it was a boy or a girl, but it was a jolly companion, and we got along famously until the time came for it to return to the cot. A baby in a home is a great blessing. Those who scoff at harassed parents can surely have no inkling of their joy, of their peace of mind. Life holds no vexation and tribulations when you have an atom of your own flesh to care for, a warm little body to fondle, a tiny creature wrought in your own image to display proudly. How, then, can there possibly be trouble in the world outside to worry and annoy?

The afternoon dragged on to a premature close. There were no other visitors, and again I wondered how these village inns manage to pay for their upkeep. The Red Lion had quite recently been renovated: there were new tile fireplaces, modern furniture even in the taproom, electricity had been installed, the curtains and carpets had not been long in place. Yet I was the only one to see and appreciate them that day.

At three o'clock, when the girl came to fasten the front door, I told her that I would stay the night; and straightway she went into the smaller parlour across the passage, and through the open door I watched her make a fire for me in that room. This done satisfactorily, she retired to the kitchen again.

I think I may be forgiven if I say that I waited for her periodical appearances with interest, for I had absolutely nothing to do to pass the time away. The hours ticked by. I sat over the fire with the poker in my hand, idly prodding the embers, occasionally putting a new piece of coal in place and staring at it until it caught flame, glowed red, and finally disintegrated. . . . A weary business, this of killing time. I am unused to it, and I don't like it. I grieve over a wasted hour as much as over ill-spent money. It makes a man sluggish.

I could think of nothing to while away the afternoon. There were no books in the room. I had my diary and my maps, that was all. My maps I would save until after tea, for the evening would be long, too. My diary I scanned briefly; it was an interesting chronology, but it brought back too vividly the life I had fled from. I held in my hand a few withered souvenirs I took from its page, and gazed at them sadly and reverently for a long long time before

carefully replacing them. Ah me! I poked the fire again, slowly and
with great deliberation. Life is very interesting.

After a while, it occurred to me that I might as well be cleaning
my fingernails, and I did this for twenty minutes. Then I picked up
the poker once more. A wireless set in the kitchen was switched on
to Luxembourg so suddenly that I jumped in the air, and I
welcomed familiar tunes with open arms. Now I could whistle,
softly.

Four o'clock came and went. I thought of all the people I knew,
one after another, thinking longer of some than of others, and I
wondered what each was doing on that Sunday afternoon. How
many of them would wish to be here with me in this remote village
pub, crouching over the fire while the storm raged outside? I could
think of two only, and maybe I flattered myself with this modest
total. How many of them would wish to exchange places with me?
I could think of nobody, not one. Few people seem able to discern
any enjoyment in the situations I find so vastly entertaining. I
reckoned up next how many people I would gladly lay down my
life for. Two were certainties, and neither, I am afraid, would fully
appreciate so noble a gesture; a third I pondered over, but alas,
could come to no decision, though this one is far and away the
most worthy of such a sacrifice.

Just as I was soberly counting on my fingers the girls I might
reasonably have expected to marry me if I had asked them to, a
diversion occurred. And diversions, on this particular afternoon,
were things to be grappled to the bosom. A bugle sounded outside.
I peered through the streaming windows into the gathering dusk.
A motor-van was standing in the lane; the driver was at the rear,
handing out newspapers to the few villagers who scuttled, heavily
shrouded, from their homes like rabbits from a warren, and
returned as rapidly. Newspapers! Football results! I heard the girl
run down the passage and out of the front door. I was after her as
though propelled from a catapult.

It was not now raining so heavily, but the strong wind was so
bitterly cold that my half-minute's absence from the fire chilled me
to the bone. There were fiery streaks of crimson in the western
sky, but they were far distant; Gamblesby lay under black,

scudding clouds. It was a bleak, wintry twilight, and held little promise for the morrow.

I found at last that my favourite football team had been defeated yesterday by four goals to one, and were deposed from the leadership of the league. This was bitter cud to have to chew for the rest of the day; better I had continued in ignorance.

The papers were full of commendation for the Prime Minister; there was a full-page portrait of him, a lengthy biography, a great many references, all kindly and of heartfelt thankfulness for his timely action. I was grateful, too; very grateful. He had saved the country from war, and me from much cowardly reflection on how to keep out of it.

I had tea in the little parlour, a cosy place, beautifully furnished, and with regard for comfort. At the Red Lion I had the best meals I had anywhere. The food was good, all of it, but the service was really excellent. The table was set by an artist. Everything was arranged perfectly: I could start at one end of a semi-circle and work right along to its terminus and yet eat in logical sequence. The cutlery and crockery were of superior quality; a great bowl of flowers adorned me as I ate. There was nothing lacking; I could go ahead leisurely, knowing there would be no disturbances. It is a great tribute to a woman to say that she can even lay a table distinctively, yet this was exactly what my hostess had done, and my admiration for her increased still further.

I have already said, I think, that if I hear music, my thoughts and actions move in tempo with it. This happens quite subconsciously; I think much more keenly and work much harder to a rousing march than to a slow, melancholy dirge. I had further evidence of this phenomenon during my tea. Luxembourg was droning out inconsequential tunes, but all at once began to play Liszt's Hungarian Rhapsody. I was only half-listening, and for a time all was well, but when the preliminary passages were over and the movement became suddenly dramatic, with all instruments vying for supremacy, I found myself cramming food into my mouth so quickly that if I had not realised the danger and put down my tools and sat back till it was finished, I should have choked. I continued, after that, accompanied by Deanna Durbin, bless her, singing 'Ave Maria'.

The evening passed slowly and without incident. Once the table was cleared, I was not disturbed for four hours. I heard nobody enter the house, or leave it. I asked the girl if she had a book for me to read, and she brought me a 'True Story Magazine'. I read it from cover to cover, marvelling that I had gone through life unaware of the trusting innocence of women as it was depicted in these true stories, for every one had shameful betrayal as its theme and they were all written by anonymous females.

After this interlude, I spread my maps out on the carpet and got down on my knees before them; not in reverence, though I might well have done after the unwholesome revelations the cheap magazine had provided.

Gamblesby! There it was, two-thirds of the way down my fourth map, in the same lattitude as Weardale. I had three days left before I was due in Settle, and as a result of today's inactivity, was fourteen miles behind schedule. Settle was seventy miles distant. However bad the weather, I must stick at it henceforward. There must be no more idle hours. I set to and revised my programme. The route I had still to cover divided fairly conveniently into three equal parts. Tomorrow I should rest in Kirkby Stephen, and the following night stay in Dent. This arrangement would ensure arrival in Settle on the third day, and seemed in every way practicable. Each day's march would exceed twenty miles, but my legs were inured to long walks by this time. They were like whipcord, strong and supple; and I had lost so much weight with my exertions that they also had the appearance of it. My feet had been a source of trouble last week, but now they were as hard as iron, and as indifferent to knocks. I could have walked, gingerly, on spikes. And my heart remained stout. So that I feared not for physical disability. Only the weather could prevent me from completing the walk within the time prescribed, and I was not likely to yield again as easily as I had done today.

I had a little supper, a chic and dainty affair, and was led upstairs to bed. The girl preceded me, switched on the light in my room, and stood aside. This was her big moment, the surprise she had been planning. I looked round the room, utterly confounded, too amazed to ejaculate, and back again to her twinkling eyes. 'Will it serve?' she asked. She was very, very pleased with herself. She must have known that I was impressed with the furnishings downstairs, although I had not commented on them; but the guest room was her great coup.

I had never before witnessed such a scene of unparalleled splendour. The bedroom was magnificent. It was three times as large as any in my experience; there had been structural alterations on a vast scale, and the whole front upper floor of the inn had been converted into one spacious apartment. The effect was staggering. The far walls were lost in shadowy distance. In the very middle of the room was the bed, a few minutes' walk from where I stood. The powerful light blazed down on a gorgeous eiderdown, a thing of scintillating colour and great beauty. The room was provided with an ultra-modern suite in walnut, and such was the airy capaciousness of the place that it appeared to be palpably under-furnished; there were expansive areas where the pattern on the thick carpet ran unhindered about the floor, so that the massive wardrobe and dainty dressing-table were oases in a shimmering, colourful desert. Yet, so sure was the touch that designed it, that the room had the cosiness of a boudoir. This, for me! I was unworthy.

The girl had slipped away and closed the door behind her, leaving me alone on the verge of munificence. I walked slowly round the room, touching everything with awe and fingers that filled me with shame. I was filthy; so filthy that I was beginning to itch. A casual ward in a workhouse would have been a fitting abode for me, and there would have been no questions asked. Instead, I had been given a bridal chamber.

I undressed very slowly, and climbed between the clean white sheets. Tonight, I had my final cigarette before turning off the light, for I could not weary of surveying this superb establishment. It was entirely lovely, and we should all look long at loveliness when we chance across it. This room was fit for a king. Hollywood has not conceived its equal.

At length, I slid out of bed and strolled as far as the switch. I plunged the room into darkness; the stately beauty vanished before my eyes. Darkness hides grandeur as surely as it cloaks squalor.

Now, but for the luxurious carpet underfoot, I might have been in a hovel, and my sin did not seem so great.

Back in the soft embrace of the bed, I lay stretched out, with my hands clasped behind my head. Remarkably, I had not thought about the war all day. I was not altogether content. Here was a bridal chamber, and a willing groom, but imagination unleashed could not provide a bride.

I was long in going to sleep. The lady of my dreams, sensing I was fickle, kept at a distance.

THE NINTH CHAPTER

THE STORM had spent itself during the night, and I looked from my window to find the village green bathed in brilliant sunshine. There was evidence in plenty of the heavy rain of yesterday. The grass glittered as though bountifully sprinkled with diamonds; there were streams of rushing water in the gutters, and a continuous dripping from the eaves; the road was still wet. Clouds sailed across the sky, but they were high and not threatening; they were being driven at a great pace. Up above, the wind was still fierce.

Opposite the inn is Gamblesby Church. I had only half-noticed it yesterday. It is an odd structure, undeniably attractive, but not at all what one expects to find in an English village. There is a suggestion of the Orient in its unusual lines; the squat, rounded building is like a mosque, its small spire a minaret.

I had the perfect breakfast and prepared to go. I was asked to sign the visitors' book, and did so. This was the second occasion only that I was requested to comply with this formality, although it is a legal offence for an innkeeper or boarding-house proprietor to fail to keep a complete record of all visitors who stay overnight.

I paid eight shillings for tea, supper, a heavenly bed, and breakfast, and though this was more than I paid elsewhere, I felt that I had had exceptional value for money. If the Red Lion at Gamblesby, or at least its front upper room, could be transported to Blanchland, then there would be the perfect venue for a honeymoon.

The girl asked me if I had been satisfied. She was not anxious, but ever so confident of my reply. She and her husband, she told me, had been there only a few months. I did not see the husband at all; until the baby appeared yesterday afternoon, I had not thought that this slender girl was the proprietress, but a daughter of the house, or a paid servant. I wish them well in their venture, this young couple. I think the man has got a grand wife: she is efficient, and she is house-proud, and both are virtues. I am afraid, though, they have chosen too quiet a spot; there were very few names before mine in the book.

I told her I had been far more comfortable under this roof than any other. A lie, really, for I had enjoyed greater comfort at Alston, only the night before, and at Buckden, though in these cases it was jolly companionship that had made my stay happy. But it was a white lie, and white lies are not only pardonable, but entirely justifiable. It gladdened my old heart to see the girl's face light up when I replied; for the first time she laughed, and it was a joy to see the quiet, thoughtful look dispelled by a happy smile. I fancy she had her own doubts about the ultimate success of their enterprise. And, with all her delightful pretence of maturity, she was very, very young.

I gave her sixpence for the baby, and went out into the sunny road.

I took a photograph of the church, and then stowed my camera away in my rucksack. There would be no time to spend on further pictures that day. It was a quarter to ten, a late start. Appleby was fourteen miles ahead, across level country. I vowed to travel four miles an hour until I got there.

This part of the journey proved to be the least interesting of all. The lanes I followed were long and narrow, with never a rise and fall to quicken the interest. They enabled me to keep at a good pace throughout, but how I longed for a view! I was between high hedgerows for miles; I could neither see my way stretching before me nor the countryside I was traversing. I kept my map in my hand, checking each byway and turning as I came to them, and had I not been working to a timetable, I fear I should have found these few hours rather monotonous.

Shortly after leaving Gamblesby, the sky suddenly clouded, and there was a sharp shower of hail, but the threat quickly passed and very soon the sun was shining serenely again. All the way to

Appleby stretches a chain of villages, very similar in size; some with a church, some with an inn. They are spaced equidistant from each other, so accurately that it seems they must have been plotted geometrically. There is Melmerby, with church and inn; Ousby, with inn; Skirwith, with church and inn; poor Blencarn, with neither; Milburn, with two churches and an inn; Long Marton, with church, inn and railway station; Brampton, with an inn. Melmerby and Skirwith are pretty places; Ousby is awful; the rest are of no account.

Very little happened between Gamblesby and Appleby that remains in memory. Throughout the distance, the long, high skyline of Cross Fell and its satellites was prominent above the hedgerows on my left. The western slopes of the Pennines are quite different in character from those on the east; they fall abruptly here, clean-cut, and at once there is a vast tract of low land; not, as on the other side, a series of high ridges. There are no dales on the west, only a featureless plain.

One compensation was mine. Beyond Milburn, the hedgerows fencing the lane became indeterminate; the thickets that had confined me gave place to grassy verges, and I could look about me without interruption. My gaze wandered to the west, and what I saw there halted me instantly. I saw a long line of hills rising dimly along the far edge of the plain, so far away that they might have been clouds on the horizon. There was a hazy indistinctness about them which contrasted sharply with the clear foreground, as though they had been etched, as an afterthought, on a finished landscape. Distance gave them a touch of unreality: they were purple and blue where all else was green; they were ethereal and misty where all else showed clear, in bold relief, in the brilliant light of the sun; they were poetry where all else was prose. I regarded them at first in disbelief for they had no part in this uninspiring confusion of flat meadows and wide pastures through which I had been threading my way all the morning; they were phantoms off-stage.

I gazed at them long and earnestly. I was not deceived; they were not apparitions. Fairylike they were, but they had substance. There were drifting clouds on their summits, but the hills were immovable. And the miles between could not rob them of their majesty. They appeared lilliputian, but they were giants. They were tiny in the scale of things, dwarfed completely by the massiveness of Cross Fell so close at hand, but they had stateliness and dignity. There were rugged crests, slender peaks, soaring cliffs and rocky pinnacles. And over all, a flimsy veil of translucent blue.

These were mountains. My mountains. There was not a summit within view that had not been mine for a fleeting hour. Throughout the long ridge that confronted me now, there was not a hillside, not a felltop, that I had not tramped, rested upon, and been happy. They were old friends, and as always when old friendships are renewed, memory was deeply stirred. There was gladness in the greeting, but tears were not far. I love these lonely hills of Lakeland with a love that is beyond comprehension. I could not attempt to write of the quiet joy that long days in their company have brought to me, of the peace that lies over my soul when I am amongst them. Others have shared my experiences, and they have wondered, too. No one yet has explained their charm.

I continued more slowly, ever alert for further peeps of them. Glimpses must suffice, this holiday; I could not visit them. They were out of reach; I had forsaken them, made other plans. Now, having seen them, I wanted dearly to go. They were calling me; their voice was the moaning of the wind amid the rocks of chasm and precipice, the rush of cataract and murmur of mountain stream. . . . There are no hills like the hills of Lakeland.

This interruption left me vaguely restless, dissatisfied. It played havoc with my timetable, and sapped away much enthusiasm which I now realised to be false. Why was I trudging through this wilderness of green pasture and meadow? I could have been climbing high on Scafell, or gazing down the valley from Glaramara, or reclining on Blencathra's heights. That was fruitful land; here was desolation. I was tempted, but to desert the path I was pledged to follow was defeat.

I kept on resolutely, to the south.

Somewhere along this lane I passed another gipsy encampment, with men and children huddled over a fire in the ditch, for in spite of the sunshine, there was a cold breeze blowing; the weather had become more wintry. The men called out to me as I passed: 'What time is it?' I told them, and they resumed their broody contemplation of the fire.

A bank of low black clouds which had appeared on the southern horizon after midday, began to draw nearer as I walked the last few miles into Appleby. A dark cloak was spread across the sky, and beneath its creeping shadow the face of the earth grew cold and sullen. Only the north, whence I had come, held warmth and brightness, and there too the change must come soon. I watched the slow advance of a mighty host, marching with inexorable purpose. I saw detachments sent on ahead, forerunners that drifted rapidly above in ragged array and became wisps of smoke where the sun glinted on them. But the main mass was resolute; nothing could stay its approach. Cloud piled upon cloud; the heavens before me were a tumult of writhing shapes, as though the earth were smouldering and sending up great coils of heavy smoke. A powerful force was working within this vast assembly, urging them ever onward, but creating discord and strife so that they came not in harmony but in seething discontent, an angry, quarrelsome, agitated mob. There was an evil portent in their convulsive movements, in their weighty, ponderous appearance, in their colour. They were black where they overhung the countryside, an ominous grey above, where the wind kept them constantly mobile. Only aloft were the white banners displayed.

I raced the rain into Appleby.

I sought temporary refuge in a café, and stayed in its warm shelter for the best part of an hour, writing postcards and a letter, studying my map, looking through the window at the wet streets.

I was not altogether happy. At Appleby, I was halfway home. Across the other side of the map, in the same latitude, was Romaldkirk, which I knew lay midway between Settle and the Wall. Months seemed to have passed since that night in the Kirk Inn. I was not despondent at Romaldkirk, nor at any time during the glorious week I spent foraging ever northwards. Life was at its sweetest then; the sun shone brightly day after day; a wealth of incident kept me perpetually interested in all that was happening around me; there was a succession of lovely views, so that every corner had new appeal; above all, there was the enthusiasm that drove me forward, the thrilling eagerness of attainment, the quieter joy of anticipation. All this was gone: it was incredible that those carefree days could belong to this same holiday. For now, by comparison, life was dull and insipid. Last week I had no doubts, and naught could disturb; now, already, I had turned my back on adventure, and my thoughts were increasingly of home and the office and the old existence, soon to be familiar again. These thoughts crowded in against my will. I was journeying not as an exile returning to his own country, but as an exile leaving his country behind. I was for ever looking back, not forward. The happy days were behind, not ahead.

It was in the café at Appleby that I finally gave up the ghost. I sat there in the big room, amongst dirty pots and stained tablecloths, watching the rain swilling the street below, and I felt suddenly weary. This pretence of enjoyment was ridiculous: if I had not admitted it to myself before, I did now. My plans had been wrong. My walk should have finished at the Wall, in the glorious moment of conquest. I should have made the outward journey longer, or spent more time at the Wall, but certainly not have allotted half my time to the dreary business of coming back. My holiday finished the moment I took the first step south.

So much had enthusiasm done for me. It had made the northward trail a grand adventure, and the ending a fitting climax, but I left it there, 'among the Roman ruins, where the purple flowers grow'. When I tried to recapture the feeling during the days of my return, it eluded me. Last week, my star was in the ascendancy, and I followed it eagerly; enthusiasm was an ever-present companion, urging me forward. Now, my star was dim and lustreless, pale in the growing light of dawn after the night of dreaming. And enthusiasm was a will-o'-the-wisp; I could no more than glimpse it.

I told myself that my mood was silly, as of course it was. My holiday would not be over until I climbed into the train at Settle. I was still as free as the air, still seeing new places, still tramping territory that was hardly less attractive than the Dales and the Northumbrian uplands. My tour was not ill-planned at all; surely

to return by another route was to bring the whole expedition to its
logical conclusion. Had I stopped when I got to the Wall, it would
have been a task half done; I must complete the whole . . . But no, I
could not regard it in this light. I was going back, going back. The
one fact persisted.

It was in this frame of mind that I took pencil and paper and
wrote a letter to a friend at the office, asking for certain
arrangements to be made for my return. Going back, going back! I
thought of Buckden, Tan Hill, Blanchland, Hexham, all behind me;
of the grimy town, the confining walls that cramped the spirit,
where I must live; of the petty jealousies, the bitter disappointments, the old routine and irksome discipline, that awaited me.
Time and distance were lessening; every minute, every step,
brought them nearer. And already they were looming large; I was
becoming reconciled to the dismal outlook. My thoughts were
increasingly of the problems I had fled from; they too were
waiting, knowing I must come back.

I tried to give a happy tone to my letter, but I could not. It
required an effort to scribble down my instructions. They were
minor requests, but I know that whatever I asked would have
attention, for the man to whom I wrote is a faithful fellow. He is
dependable, where many nowadays are not. Reliability seldom gets
its just reward; it has sunk low in the list of necessary attributes to
success, as success is interpreted, and sometimes one wonders if
bluster and cunning are not better thought of. Certainly the ladies,
themselves strangers to dependability, are impressed by the flashy,
clever wastrels with the glib, entertaining tongues. But give me a
rock to lean on, sometimes, and let me have the knowledge that it
is always there.

I had a last cigarette before I set out, and watched the raindrops
racing down the window. I was finding excuses to delay, as one
does in the last few minutes in bed on a cold morning. I had no
heart to get further on my way, but go I must if I was to be in
Settle two days hence. I had nearly sixty miles to travel; what a fool
I was to say it was ended. The one desire that remained to me was
to get back to my starting-point by the appointed time, and only
for the fulfilment of this wish could I scrape together the few

shreds that were left of my departed enthusiasm. I must not fail in this, else I should never afterwards be able to think of this holiday without disfavour.

I left Appleby at three o'clock, following a byroad which, according to my map, would take me over a low fell and into Kirkby Stephen in three hours. I saw little of Appleby: I remember it for its wide bridges and its swirling river, swollen by the rain, flowing swiftly between well-kept banks where public footpaths and gardens had been laid out; for its broad street, with trees fringing the pavements; for glimpses of ancient gateways and castle walls. It is a small town, soon entered and soon left behind.

It was raining steadily, but not too heavily to cause discomfort, when I again came to open country. For a mile I kept to the road which links Appleby with Tebay and Kendal, and here, in a sense, I was on familiar ground, although I recognised it not. This very road featured in an early chapter of a novel I wrote some time ago; my hero travelled the way I was treading, but he, if I remember aright, was conveyed rapidly on wheels, whereas I could only trudge slowly along. It was a bright, sunny afternoon when he came along this road; there was rain for me. What a hero! He was later, if again I am not mistaken, to be adjudged a thorough blackguard; he became a man to be avoided, a leper. . . . My story was never published. It is forgotten. A fitting end to it.

I first became conscious of the wind when I breasted the hill outside the town; the rain did not now descend vertically but was blown in my face in violent gusts. High hedges shielded me to some extent, but I experienced misgivings as to the wisdom of continuing the long walk to Kirkby Stephen. I could be back in Appleby in ten minutes, find comfortable lodgings and perhaps have the cheer of a big fire, go to the cinema after tea. But the thought perished at birth. I must go on. I was not tired. If I went back I should have to idle away seven or eight hours, somehow, and then tomorrow come the same way again, frustrated in my object. I kept at it, left, right, left, right; but there was a particular venom in the dark roof of clouds overhead which I found disturbing.

I came presently to the beginning of the lane which was to take me, without a deviation, to Kirkby Stephen, ten miles away. Once on this byroad, I was committed to follow it: there is not a village, hardly a habitation, until Soulby is reached after eight miles. I needed no map now, for the lane was my guide; all I had to do was to keep it underfoot. I memorised the main features before I stowed the map away out of the rain: a crossroads after a mile and a half, a railway bridge a mile beyond, a bridge across Helm Beck ten minutes further, another crossroads when I had completed six miles.

I set off in earnest, and had not gone far before the rain came down in torrents. There was no escape from it, no hope of shelter. A thicket alongside the road kept the wind at bay, so that I was not hampered and could stride out freely, but I could not fail to hear the agitation in the treetops as the wind tore at the branches, nor its screaming passage overhead.

Although it was still quite early, all brightness had vanished from the face of the earth. The lane ever appeared before me out of a murky gloom, a wet, unending strip of dull grey between sodden banks; a cold, cheerless twilight enveloped the scene. I passed fields that were flooded, with ghostly trees sticking up out of the water as though afloat; in places, the lane itself was awash where the ditches could not carry the downpour.

I passed the first crossroads with a feeling of accomplishment, and began to wonder if the railway bridge I should soon reach crossed the road above or below. My map would have told me in an instant, but I could not consult it in such weather. As it happened, I was to find that the railway line went beneath the road, so that I was denied the moment's respite and dry cigarette I had looked forward to.

The deluge continued, lashing myself and all else into helpless resentment. We bowed before its impact, trees, shrubbery, self. Every drop that fell had its dart of venom; the hands and face were stung with icy barbs, for there was sleet in the air. The surface of the road was transformed into a living thing, so pitiless was the onslaught and so convulsive the recoil.

At Helm Beck, I sought refuge in the field by the side of the bridge. There was scant shelter here, for the stone wall sloped and was itself a streaming watercourse, but I stood close by it and lit a cigarette with wet, trembling fingers. I smoked through it with head bent low to keep the rain from the few shreds of comfort I held in my lips; the position was incongruous, but it served to centre my attention on my shoes, which I found to my horror to be quite surely disintegrating. Soaking lumps and layers of leather protruded in all directions; I could not see from above exactly whence they had come, but without a doubt they were part of my footgear. Curse. They had come well so far; they must hold together two more days.

The beck was in flood; it had the size and force of a river. The one small arch of the bridge could not accommodate the raging torrent; the furious waters hurled and crashed against the ramparts, and in defeat slunk back and spread gradually over the adjoining fields. Only in the middle of the stream was there a smoothly rushing current, and even here the surface of the water was considerably higher than the top of the arch and there was a tremendous struggle for entry into the short tunnel.

Beyond the bridge, the lane climbs a little, and then suddenly shoots out of its friendly hedgerows and strikes across an open, exposed moorland. I stood beneath the last of the trees and looked out at the barren waste I must traverse. No longer now could I escape the wind, if the demoniacal fury which greeted me could be called a wind. I saw sheets of rain flung across the dreary moor with hurricane force; I heard now the voice of the storm, no longer resisted but unrestrained and triumphant. There was moaning from afar, howling as the squally gusts hurled through the tormented sky; the wild shrieking rose to tumultuous crescendo as the gale tore overhead, and fell to a sobbing wail in the far distance. The din of the tempest was deafening; to me it was a roar of mockery. There was a giant madman loose on the moor, and his laughter was horrible.

My apprehension was justified. No sooner was I out of my puny shelter than the unseen monster had me at his mercy. He clutched at me, tore at my cape, hurled me from the comforting road into the muddy morass at the side. I was beaten, battered, more than once brought to my knees. I could not fight this formidable adversary; I could not see him, nor anticipate his blows. He attacked me from the front and the rear, from both sides, from above. I reeled and staggered like a drunken man, being often blown back in my tracks by the force of each squall, only to come struggling and floundering forward into the vacuum created by its retreat. Winds there are so strong that they can be leaned against but this was not such a one. It was fierce, but not of consistent velocity; it raged in wild, sudden gusts, and I could never be certain when the next assault would come, nor from which direction. I could be sure only that each buffeting would bring a deluge of soaking rain, which would pour over me like a breaking wave, and that there would be a deafening bellow in my ear.

The moment I decided I was as wet as I could possibly be, I began to enjoy myself. The tussle became a joyous revel. I was the loser in every skirmish: I could only struggle in vain, with head bent low, my cape flapping round my shoulders and cracking like a machine-gun, my hands holding spectacles in place. But in the brief intervals when my assailant paused for breath, I managed to gather my cape and move forward as stealthily as any Arab with his tent.

I was on the top of the hill, and in the midst of another frolic, when above the rear of the gale I heard a car chugging up the road behind me. Its approach was slow: it offered a broadside to the wind which crashed angrily upon it, and I, with the advantages of stream-lining, was hardly making slower progress. But at length it overtook me and stopped. Through the streaming windows I could see the distorted figure of the driver, saw him motion to the back seat. I shook my head at the invitation, but as he could not comprehend the refusal, I went round to the lee side of the car and opened the door. He was a comfortable-looking fellow, with a cheerful face crowned by a slouch hat. I thanked him, but said I was much too wet, and hadn't far to go, anyway.

I watched him drive forward and disappear into the gloom ahead. He was the only person I saw between Appleby and Soulby, and his was the only car that passed.

When I came to the second crossroads I knew that the worst of the ordeal was over and that my way onward led down a gentle slope into the valley. Beneath the trees in a corner of the field at the crossroads were a few huddled caravans, with wheels already deep in water. There was no sign of life, but the occupants must have noticed my approach for as I passed a screaming enquiry was thrown into the teeth of the wind: 'What time is it?'

I went on briskly down the hill, for now the wind could not retard my progress. It was after five o'clock and almost dark; the light was fast fading over a dreary landscape. The earth was drenched; there was the murmur of running water everywhere. It was raining now harder than ever; the banks of the lane were so saturated that they were crumbling and in places had collapsed and shot muddy soil across the ditch and into the road. Streamlets raced in new channels through the fields, and since my way led along the side of a slope, they burst the hedges and poured on to the lane in cataracts, swept across it and carved out exits amongst the long grass and bushes on the other side. As I came into the low-lying valley, I passed for long distances between flooded fields, as if walking on a low pier thrust far out into a lake.

Soon the road itself disappeared before me. Soulby was ahead; I could see the unmistakable harsh line of buildings amongst the trees, black shadows all against the grey background of western sky where the vile day still lingered. Two walls showed the way to the village, but they enclosed a sheet of water. Had I been anxious for my comfort, the problem would have given me food for thought, for the pastures on either side were also unnavigable, while progress along the top of a wall, though likely to be invigorating, could only prove exceedingly laborious. But I had no such worries, and I marched on without hesitation. My shoes had for miles been squirting jets of water from the laceholes with every movement of my feet; now they could spring fountains.

I splashed along in great glee. At first I was ankle-deep, then the water crept halfway up my shins. It encroached no further, but I would have gone on had it been waist-deep, for I could not have become wetter from my middle downwards than I already was. I enjoyed the experience so much that I halted in the pond, and played awhile at kicking great waves at the dark walls. Canute missed a rare opportunity for some grand fun.

Soulby was laid desolate. The stream which passes through its heart was a furious torrent, hurling itself along with a thunderous roar, lashed into white foam by the bulwarks of the bridge. The open spaces between the scattered houses were sheets of troubled water, writhing in torture, for here the wind again had full play. Branches of trees, torn down by the gale, lay scattered on the village green.

There was no light visible in the Black Bull, but I knocked loudly at the door and waited. It was too dark to go further, and having come within two miles of Kirkby Stephen and done considerably more than twenty during the day, I felt satisfied and was ready to rest. I had brought Settle within fifty miles, and had two days to get there.

I knocked several times before I got a response; then I heard the shuffle of feet in the passage, and the door was opened an inch or two. I asked if I could stay there, and was asked to wait. The door was shut. I had a foreboding that I had chosen badly, and so it was to prove.

The door was opened again, and this time I was asked to enter. I stepped into a black passage, at the further end of which was a lighted room, with the figure of a woman framed in the doorway. The front door, when opened for me, admitted also a fierce blast which rattled every window in the house. I saw the woman shudder and draw a shawl closer about her shoulders. An older woman had let me in and was now struggling to push the door back against a wind reluctant to be shut out. The proprietress, for it could be none other who awaited me at the end of the passage, started to scream at the other in sudden temper, telling her to be quick and get the door shut, for goodness sake. There was a snarl in her voice which made me tremble in anticipation of the effect my appearance would have when I was out of the concealing darkness.

She backed into the room, which served both as kitchen and taproom, and I followed her, with the other woman at my heels. She stood by the table and surveyed me from head to foot with such evident distaste that there was born in that moment a feud between us which lasted as long as my stay. She was about forty

years of age, of medium height, and inclined just a little to
plumpness. With care, she could still have been the handsome
woman she undoubtedly once was; her pale features were regular
and pleasing. Most arresting was her raven-black hair, drawn
tightly from her brow and coiled in the nape of her neck. But she
was untidy, or seemed so by comparison with the girl at
Gamblesby. The room was in disorder, with litter lying on the
table, the floor, the hard bench that ran around the walls, and she
was content all the evening to lounge amongst it and order the
other woman about in uncivil tones. She appeared to be consumed
with bitterness; life had dealt a hard blow at some time, and she
had neither forgotten nor forgiven.

The older woman, the only other occupant of the inn, was about
fifty years old, and the type of person who leaves no impression on
the memory. She was dowdy and self-effacing; when she was not
attending to the men who came in, she sat in a corner industriously
knitting. She was, I think, a relative, here on sufferance, and likely
to remain only while she obeyed (with good grace) the imperious
commands of the landlady.

I stood there, dripping from every protuberance. I was never
wetter in all my life. Icy rivulets were trickling down my neck and
pursuing swift courses along my back and front until they lost
themselves in the general soak which started at my hips. Every
movement I made released a stream of water which made a pool
on the flagged floor.

I asked if they had a dry pair of trousers. The proprietress said
no, instantly, but old Alice, or whatever her name was, timidly
suggested that there was a pair of flannels upstairs: hadn't Jim left
them behind after his stay here? The younger woman, after due
reflection, remembered them: yes, I could have the use of them. I
got a candle and went upstairs to change, pleased at my good
fortune and thinking to myself that Jim must have been in a hell of
a hurry to get away.

Downstairs again, with cap, cape, shoes, stockings and trousers
broiling in the fender, and myself feeling aglow and very fit, I
returned to some degree of respectability; not completely, since
Jim was as short and stout as I am tall and thin and I had to choose

between a low waistline and naked calves, but sufficiently to pass without comment in that odd household. The kitchen was the only room with a fire, and there I had to sit all the evening. There was an outer door to it, used by the men who dropped in for a drink, and the easy familiarity of the men with the two women filled me with disgust. The younger woman, I noticed, could be pleasant when a customer was in the room.

The gale raged outside in a frenzy, growing in intensity with every hour. There was a continuous roar about the house; a shrieking in the chimney and a howling in the eaves, and as a background, the perpetual thunder of the storm, noisy as a sea surging against a cliff. Nor had the rain abated; I could hear it driven on the gables, thrown in sheets on the windows.

On such a night, visitors were not to be expected, but four men called in, singly, between half-past six and seven o'clock, each with a curse for the weather and a demand for drink. Two of them, young men, were bright and cheerful enough, but they were all big, rough fellows from the farms, with whom any sort of conversation was impossible; their presence made me feel thoroughly out of place, and I wished heartily they would be gone and leave me to the fire.

The eldest was Rowley, a farmer of seventy-eight years, as tall and straight and active as anyone in the room. He was very drunk and boisterous when he came in, having had a good day at the Kirkby market, and he proceeded to empty glass after glass with astounding rapidity. He talked in a shouting voice, an ugly, rasping tone that set my nerves on edge, particularly as his dialect was difficult to understand. Now and again his eye would fall on me, sitting quietly without a word, and every time this happened he was most persistent that I should drink at his expense. I refused every time, for I had already had a drink of the Black Bull beer and found it even viler than most. Old Rowley's voice alone drowned the din outside. He was fighting drunk, and threw out challenge after challenge at the younger men. He tried to embrace Alice as she brought yet another drink for him; she evaded him with a laugh and I marvelled that she could contrive to conceal her loathing for him. It was obvious that he was a well-known character; he was boss of Soulby, I was to discover. I detested him, for his loud tongue and his filthy tales, but he was a remarkable old fellow.

Taunted by his insults, the young men accepted the bet that he would beat them both, playing together, at darts. The decks were cleared for action. The young men were good players as far as my inexpert eye could see; at least they hit the board every time and registered a score. But Rowley was marvellous. He had to be placed on the throwing line each time, and stood there rocking on his heels, with dart poised, until the mist cleared before his eyes. Then he would announce the score he was aiming for, and throw. And nine times out of ten his dart came to rest as he predicted. He beat the aggregate scores of his opponents without difficulty. The landlady called him a wonderful fellow; it was an occasion for more drinks. It was not surprising that she liked to have him in the house and pamper him; he was a profitable source of revenue. But she was prepared to sink her self-respect to keep him in a good humour, and thereby I came to despise her.

He told her of an experience he had had with a young woman at Long Preston, and went to some trouble to explain where Long Preston was, between Hellifield and Settle. I alone of the others in the room knew the place he described, but he did it so accurately that I could not disbelieve the rest of his story. He told how he had got the girl into a barn, how she had squealed like a pig. My hair bristled. His tale, recounted in full detail, would have shamed me in a company of men, but here he was, telling it to a woman, and she apparently gloating over it. I could not take my eyes from her face; she smiled in delight, and only at one gross comment did she attempt to dissuade him, and even then with a laugh. I was sickened; my stomach revolted at the beastly story and the sight of that woman's face. Rowley was not content to be merely suggestive; he was most attentive to detail, and at pains to illustrate his remarks. That smiling, amused face haunts me to this day. I have a high opinion of women, because of fortunate acquaintance, and a shaking of my belief comes as a disaster.

I was delivered unexpectedly from a situation which was

rapidly becoming unbearable. Yesterday there had been the harvest services at Soulby Church; tonight there was the harvest festival and the sale of fruit and flowers. The men trooped out shortly before half-past seven for it is every parishioner's duty to be present when efforts are made to augment the funds of the church. Rowley led the way. He was as drunk as a mop, and the others pleaded with him to go home, having regard not so much to his condition as to his age and the vile night. But no, he was adamant. He belonged to the church and had a few shillings in his pocket to aid the event; besides there would be few present, and it was his duty to be there in support. So he went, out into the black night, from inn to church, leaving me to ponder on this new aspect of his character. I learned afterwards that he had spent thirty shillings at the sale, and given all his purchases back to the church to be sold again. That was Rowley, one of the last of the Westmorland statesmen.

Alice busied herself making a supper for me when the men had gone. Rowley and the others would be back in an hour, she said, and I had better have my meal while the house was quiet.

I dined as well as I could expect to in such an atmosphere. Often I found myself gazing at the younger woman's face as she sat, sullen again, staring into the fire. I hated her. Had she really enjoyed Rowley's story, as she appeared to do? Why hadn't she refused to listen? Surely she was not representative of her sex; others were not as she? The incident was disturbing, and gave rise to vague doubts which I found altogether unpalatable.

I retired at eight-thirty; I wanted no more of Rowley and his associates. Alice was out of the room, washing dishes somewhere, and my hostess bestirred herself and found me a candle, and even accompanied me to my room. She bade me goodnight, and hoped I would sleep well, all in so pleasant a voice that I felt a little guilty for my condemnation of her.

The tempest raged throughout the night. My room was at the rear of the inn, sheltered from the full force of the wind by out-buildings, but as I lay there in the darkness I could hear it battering against the gables, and I fancied the walls quaking at each impact.

For an hour or two, there were loud, raucous voices and occasional guffaws of laughter downstairs, and I was glad to be out of it. Then, about eleven, the house grew quiet and settled down to the one task of resisting the forces that laid siege to it.

I had a disturbed night.

THE TENTH CHAPTER

TOWARDS MORNING, the downpour subsided, but it was a dismal scene that I regarded through the window as I was having breakfast. There was no more than a drizzle of rain, but the wind was still blowing at hurricane force, and the wide village street was a playground for its antics. It was a place of fluttering leaves, for the trees had been stripped naked. I watched them dancing in the roadway, saw them whirled high above the houses until they looked like bats silhouetted against the steely sky. In vain they sought to come to rest; they were hounded out of every corner and dashed madly about; they chased each other in circles, were caught up and borne out of sight.

The river, seen across a patch of grass, was in full spate. In the cold light of morning it was a teeming yellow flood, a fearsome, terrible monster carrying out a deadly errand; the swirling torrent raced down from the hills and tore through the village with the speed of an express train. No longer was it confined between narrow banks; it was not five yards wide, but fifty. It encroached far into the fields; trees and hedgerows stood bleakly in the midst of the turbulent waters, not defiantly, but bowed meekly in submission. Clouds of spray enveloped the bridge which alone offered resistance to the invader. The river was evil and malignant. There was murder in its heart this morning.

I ate my breakfast slowly. For the first time I was not eager to be started. My destination that day was Dent. And Dent, studied on a map in Soulby, is half a continent away. I traced out a route without enthusiasm: three miles over Waitby Common to the

junction of the Sedbergh road, a low ridge to cross and twelve more
miles along a twisting valley, another low ridge, and then five miles
of Dentdale. The way was attractive enough, and the Sedbergh hills
had the contours of giants, but my spirit had gone completely. The
bubble had burst. I made the weather the excuse, but I was well and
truly defeated.

After breakfast, I joined the landlady in front of the big fire, the
one cheerful thing in the room, and we gave ourselves over to moody
contemplation. Her sleep had done her good; it had not induced
action into her lazy limbs, for still she huddled in her chair with the
little wrap about her shoulders, but she was more sociable. She
reviled the weather, said it was not fit to turn a dog out. I felt like
asking her to commit the statement to writing, so that I should have
evidence to counter the jeers of my friends when I returned, for I
had three parts made up my mind to catch the first train home.

The clock ticked on. Nine o'clock went by, half-past, quarter to
ten. I should have been off long ago if I was to get to Dent by
nightfall. I cursed myself for a sluggard; silently, since I had no
demands on my companion's self-respect. But the roaring fire was a
magnet, holding to it not steel, nor any semblance of steel, but weary
despondent flesh.

A newspaper came; the headline across the front page was GREAT
GALE SWEEPS BRITAIN; there was a story of disaster by flood and
tempest. Little mention of the Crisis, which by now seemed to be
half-forgotten.

I took a postcard from my pocket to send my last message. Defeat
was mine; it must be acknowledged. But I must couch my words in
dramatic language, make my resignation heroic. I had a reputation as
a sensationalist to maintain. I wrote:

BITTERLY REGRET TO INFORM YOU EXPEDITION
BEEN ABANDONED THIS MORNING ONLY FORTY
MILES FROM BASE CAMP STOP AM RETURNING
IMMEDIATELY BY TRAIN STOP THOROUGHLY
DEMORALISED BY BAD WEATHER AND LACK OF
VITAL RESOURCES STOP THIS IS RETREAT WITH
HONOUR

I addressed the card to the one other fellow whom I might expect to be following my wanderings with a certain amount of interest, another with much the same attitude to life in general as myself, though I fancy he would hotly refute any sort of kinship. A strange thing, but nobody ever said to me: 'I wish I could be like you', nor, now I come to think of it, can I recall anyone regarding me with even mild admiration. Strange, yes, for though I do not profess to have all the virtues I consider myself immeasurably superior to most men; and it seems even stranger now that I come to write of it. Next time I am on a hilltop, I must ponder the problem. But I am grossly misjudged. Not so very long ago, a gentle maiden related to me that she had told her mother I was mad. She spoke ever so quietly, yet quite bluntly; she was so convinced that it did not occur to her that I might be inclined to dispute the assertion; she was stating an obvious fact, not inviting comment. And I am not likely to meet her dear mother. I should like to for a moment, not to defend myself, but just to thank her for the radiant presence of her daughter. Mothers are shy people; they like to remain in the background where they can see without being seen, and we are not half grateful enough to them. If a girl has fine qualities, depend on it the mother has, too. But I am not mad. I like to consider myself a thwarted genius. There is comfort in the thought, and a thwarted genius need not go to the trouble of explaining his conduct to himself.

I took my clothes from the fender. They were so dry that they crackled. I went upstairs and prepared for the fray. I could choose between two railway stations; the nearest was at Crosby Garrett, two miles away. On the other side of Waitby Common was Kirkby Stephen station, remote from the village which gave it its name. This had the advantage of being on the route to Dent, and I decided to go this far and make up my mind, one way or the other, when I got there.

My stay at the Black Bull cost me five shillings, and I paid this amount and went out into the raw morning. It was not raining, but the low black clouds which swept along overhead gave little hope that the respite would be lengthy. As I turned the corner of the inn and made for the bridge the wind spotted me of a sudden, recognised me, whooped, and came to do battle. You again, it screamed. Yes, me again, I muttered; come on, get at me.

I went into the inferno with head held low, using it as a battering-ram. At the bridge I stopped to rest. Fifty yards in five minutes; Kirkby Stephen station became as remote as Dent had seemed earlier. I looked back at the inn, and saw only the big fire I had left behind me. I stood against the parapet and shivered. The broiling river beneath me was itself terrible enough to bring a shudder; it swept along, greedy and lustful in its new-found power, carrying with it a plunder of uprooted timber: fencing, branches, young trees and bushes. It was a foaming, leaping, rushing fury.

I pushed on as well as I was able for a few minutes until a narrow lane turned away from the road, and as I passed into its shelter, between its barricades of thick hedgerows, it was as though a heavy burden had fallen from my shoulders. Here, in this lane, I found relief from the fierce wind and could stride out at a normal pace. So narrow was the way that I could have touched both hedges simultaneously; it afforded an admirable refuge, and though its muddy surface was frequently under water I splashed into Waitby forty minutes after leaving Soulby.

Onwards, then, and upwards, along a grassy road to the shoulder of a low fell, where a fir plantation pointed an array of black spikes to the forbidding sky. The wind was not quite so violent hereabouts, though it still had sufficient energy to stagger me on occasion, but since leaving Waitby a drizzle had descended upon me and seemed likely to continue. I like a drizzle of soft rain; it has no malice, no disposition to hurt: it floats down gently, and its touch is a caress.

But as I came into the dark shadow of the firs, I began to suffer acute discomfort from sharp stabs in my right heel. I limped on for a time, thinking a stone may have jumped into my shoe and hoping that in due course it would slide under the arch of my foot, where it could stay till the cows came home. But no, the pain persisted most cruelly. I decided to count a hundred paces, and if it had not gone then, I would inquire into the trouble. A century of painful strides followed, then off came my shoe. A scrutiny revealed three nails protruding a quarter of an inch from the leather, just where the heel presses hardest. The mischief discovered, it must be remedied. But how? I am an absolute novice at improvisation, and I confess with utter shame to having no ideas at all when a mishap occurs, be it ever so slight. My one impulse is to sit down and weep. I have learnt to replace a broken shoelace with string, but what am I to do when my braces break? When vital buttons come off? I well remember returning from one expedition literally fastened together with pins and bits of string, walking with as little movement as possible so as not to disturb their precarious hold, and even so I could count my scratches weeks afterwards. O for a practical mind! But I may as well wish for the moon. I could not open a tin of sardines or unscrew the lid of a new jar of pickles if my life depended on a successful result. I must have spent months of my life, in the aggregate, wrestling with strange keys in strange locks. Half my life is behind me, and I have never yet lit a fire, or cooked myself a meal. Practice makes perfect, of course, and I have never had the patience to practice. Or had need to; I have been too well looked after, I suppose. To my way of thinking, the supermen are all mechanics.

Well, here were the three little nails sticking up in a row, and me leaning against a wall with a stockinged foot in mid-air, regarding them, and wondering, wondering. They were a comical trio, as alike as three little pigs of the same litter. They blinked when suddenly brought to the light of day, and seemed abashed and half-afraid, as three small boys might be when they have been caught knocking at doors on a dark night and are unexpectedly ushered into a bright parlour for trial by a stern judge. They were in league, must have been, for they had acted simultaneously and in exactly the same manner.

The culprits must be punished, somehow. I regarded them until my leg began to quiver uncontrollably from its unusual posture. Something must be done. A hammer! Ah, blessed inspiration! A hammer was the very thing. I looked across weary miles of soaking pastures. No hammer in sight, now when one was needed. Blast it; no hammer in sight. What atrocious luck. But the idea was sound; a fever of invention seized me. I started to hop about the wet grass, looking for a stone which had the essential features of a hammer.

There wasn't such a stone. I began to claw at the wall, pulling bits off it here and there. This was criminal trespass, an offence in common law, and I felt as guilty as though that humble fence were emblazoned with the specific inscription: 'Don't claw at the wall, man, and use Cooper's Dip'.

I found at length a stone that served admirably: a long narrow pebble with a flat end. It beat down the offending nails beautifully, but now they protruded underneath for a quarter of an inch, the same three, still in a row. It was as plain as a pikestaff that they would come through again when I started to walk on them. I took the stone with me.

I was but a few yards below the top of the hill. As I came over the rise and saw what lay ahead, my enthusiasm returned with a rush. It was a dismal day, and the scene before me held not a suggestion of warmth and brightness. I looked out over a cold, wintry landscape. There was not a glimmer of light in the pall of grey clouds; the earth was running with water; a high wind was driving relentlessly from the south, rippling the long grass, bending low the trees. The drizzling rain was a cloak of mist, a ragged garment that tore easily, leaving gaps through which I could glimpse the further distance. And in the further distance loomed vague, immense shapes, reaching far higher into the sky than the spot whereon I stood; I watched them appear, ever so indistinctly at first so that the eye searched for them where they were not, then more clearly so that I could trace their outline leaping up from earth to heaven; then suddenly they were blotted out and I was left wondering if I had been deceived. For these ghosts were hills.

If I am on a railway journey, I always have my nose flattened against the window; my gaze is ever searching the horizon for a hill until, having found one, I can sit back and watch it slowly changing shape as it falls behind. I climb it a score of times by different routes before it disappears. . . . I came back from London this summer in the company of a man who was born in the shadow of Pendle; a typical Lancashire working-man, crude, honest, rough in speech, sincere; a man who had been exiled in the south and was returning home. At first, I resented his intrusion in my

compartment for I had bought a nudist magazine on the platform
and I was fairly itching to be looking at it. He had therefore to win
me over from surliness, and we had travelled many miles in almost
complete silence, I gloomy and fretting, he willing to talk if only
I would answer. Then he made a remark, and I was not only
appeased but instantly conquered, and almost ready to clasp him in
embrace. He sighed all at once, waved his hand indefinitely at
Buckinghamshire as it sped past, and said, 'I wouldn't live here for
all the money in the world. There isn't a hill anywhere.' Thereafter
we talked hills like old cronies, argued on the merits of hill-paths
we both knew, told of experiences on Pendle, Hambledon,
Boulsworth. The train carried us through Warwickshire, Stafford-
shire, Cheshire, through country as flat as a pancake, with never a
protuberance bigger than a molehill. Then we came through
Warrington, Wigan, Chorley; we spoke less, and gazed more often
through the windows. I shall never forget the supreme moment:
my companion suddenly threw his arm round my shoulder and
pointed with a trembling finger to the moorlands which, at long
last, were slowly growing out of the featureless plain, and said
excitedly; 'Sitha, lad; them's our hills.' Their outline was indistinct,
or my eyes dim, but I saw the square tower of Rivington Pike,
seeming far above us, the huge masses of Winter Hill and
Anglezarke Moor. . . . We parted, this man and I, with a vow to
meet again on Pendle's top.

Oh, this love of the hills is a grand thing. In my case, it was born
in me, for I was climbing hills and beginning my education before I
went to school, but it can as easily be acquired. No man is poor
who has the memory of a thrilling ascent to enrich his idle
moments. No lover of hills ever commits suicide; it is the
uninspired town-dweller who finds life too boring to endure.

So, on this day, when again I saw my way leading into high places,
all despondency vanished. I realised then that all I was suffering from
was a surfeit of the Westmorland plain. That was behind, now, and
behind me too were the hours of depression. I passed the railway
station without glancing at it, and went on into the gloomy mist with
a singing heart. Rain and wind were foregathered there to welcome
me; I went into their stronghold rejoicing.

Rejoicing, yes, but I was also a beast in agony. As I had foreseen, the intruding shoe nails gave me no rest. I was not to be denied the pleasure that awaited me, and I tried all manner of devices to rid myself of the discomfort that attended every stop. I took prodigious strides with my left foot, dragging my right along uselessly, and was able to progress thus fairly well, but now and again there came a stab of pain which made me cry out. Every shout of anguish was a prelude to more industrious cobbling. I can afford to smile now at the recollection: what a picture I must have made as I stood there on one leg in the wet, boggy grass, like a heron in a pond, muttering evil expletives with every blow of the stone, dripping with raindrops. You who know me, imagine it.

After a mile or so, I gave up the idea of keeping them in subjection, and made a shield out of cigarette packets to fit snugly into the heel of my shoe, and for a few minutes was at ease, but soon the nails bored mercilessly through this covering and were once more fitting themselves comfortably into the holes they had torn in my foot. Goodness knows how many times I wrenched off my shoe and regarded their vindictive gleam. I grew so familiar with them that I gave them each a name. They became Wynken, Blynken, and Nod.

I proceeded six more miles in this fashion, limping, halting, pounding. I was hours behind time. At last I could endure the agony no longer, and when I came to a farmhouse by the side of a rushing stream I went across to it, determined to get the nails out of the way even if they had to be pole-axed. But if I was in trouble, the farmer's wife was in far worse straits. The house was flooded, or had been during the night; I entered a kitchen which still held pools of water and was deep in mud and filth. I asked for a meal, not because I was in need of one, but to lead up to a request that she should pull the nails out of my shoe. She looked up from the floor where she was mopping, with tears in her eyes; she was young, not long married, and this disaster had nearly broken her heart. She had not time to make a decent meal, she said, but she would get me a bite of something to eat, and a pot of tea. The kitchen was in absolute disorder; the fireplace was hidden in a welter of stinking, smoking carpets and rugs; the table and sideboard were piled high with sodden wreckage. The dairy was still a foot deep in water. They had never had a flood before, nor known such torrential rain. While she was in the back room cutting bread, I heard her husband come stamping in from the field behind, and ask her roughly to go out on the fell and get the sheep in the pen. She said she couldn't; she had a gentleman in for tea. this brought a snarl from her spouse: 'B—gg—r him! Do as I say.' She refused again, with spirit, and I heard him curse her and slam the door as he went out.

She came in to me then, more tearful than ever, and silently made a hole in the rubbish on the table to accommodate my tea. I asked her if she could take some nails from my shoe; she took it away without a word and I watched her hunt for a pair of pincers in a cupboard, and having found them, proceed to pull out the offenders with easy movements of her strong brown arms.

I could only peck at my tea, and was off again in a few minutes. I was sorry to be the unwitting cause of discord between husband and wife, but I told myself it would be no more than a passing quarrel. There would be peace when the day's work was done, since bed is ever a place of reconciliation for young married folk. I went on, and thought no more about them.

I could walk at ease now, and was more ready to appreciate the beauty of the valley. The grey clouds had gone, and there were intervals when the sun shone glaringly from a clear blue sky and made the whole earth glitter and sparkle with a brilliance that dazzled the eyes. The soaring fells carried a silvery sheen; their steep sides were interlaced with tumbling white cascades; the patches of golden bracken were aflame, glistening as if each curling frond held a fairy light. Down in the valley, the trees still dripped rain, and as I walked beneath them in the bright sunlight I could have filled my hands with falling diamonds.

But it was the river that compelled my gaze. Here was not an ugly, sullen torrent, as at Soulby, but a leaping, foaming beck, rushing onward with gay abandon. The confining walls of the valley were too narrow to permit expansion; it must remain within the gorge that the ages had carved out of the living rock. But at least it could make the gorge a place of joyful music, a place of melodious sounds. Such a display of high spirits as this young river presented could not fail to exhilarate a beholder. It did everything but flow: it jumped and bounded along, throwing up great arcs of white spray. Wherever I saw it, it was playing leapfrog and shouting wild welcome to a hundred tributaries that came hurrying pell-mell down from the hills to join in the fun. There were rivulets and streamlets everywhere, created in a day and night of rain, and already active and vigorous; they had no defined courses, but poured at will down grassy slopes. The river is the Rawthey, which joins the Lune beyond Sedbergh; only here, where it is born, may it indulge in madcap frolic, for the Lune is sedate from the cradle and would frown on childish indulgence.

The sun did not shine continuously; there were times, many times, when a cloud plunged the scene into temporary gloom and the rain and hail came down in torrents. These showers were over in a few minutes, but while they lasted, they came down with an intensity that was startling. They were fierce; they lashed the earth in a frenzy until it moaned at the torture. Then, as suddenly as they came, they were gone, and the valley was smiling again. The wind continued squally. It was so powerful at times that I could not progress against it, but between the cold gusts it was no more than a zephyr, mild and fragrant as a summer breeze.

I was on the second map by this time, and even though I was finding my return route unattractive by comparison with my outward march, yet it was with real sadness that I pushed the fifth, fourth and third maps down into the bottom of my rucksack out of the way. I was nearing home; there were reminders all about me. I was catching glimpses of familiar hills, the rivers were running south-west to the Lancashire coast. I was no longer in a foreign land; the speech of the villagers was becoming more intelligible. The Wall seemed very far away. I was as far south as Swaledale; the evening I spent at Muker was so distant as to belong to a previous existence. The Crisis was remote, too; a memory. Yet it had been real enough, only a few days ago.

So much had happened in the meantime; the hours had been crammed with incident. It is always so on a walking tour. Days do not fly past uneventfully as they do when we are working. Instead, they are disproportionately long. More may happen in the half-hour after breakfast than in a month of routine. Before your day is fairly started, you are in the midst of adventure, and it comes without seeking. It is not elusive, peeping at you from corners of the path; it comes boldly to greet you. Surprises succeed each other so quickly that you are kept perpetually alert, and it is well that the memory can retain their images for the mind is too occupied to dwell long on detail. All you see is brand new, and you see plenty. No two moments are alike. You are constantly moving from one scene to another, and none is before you long enough to become monotonous; you are never jaded. It is always the familiar that bores, and as you swing along your path, nothing is with you sufficiently long to grow familiar; the element of novelty is ever present. Your hardships and discomforts are new too, and they are an essential part of the whole.

A walking tour is the perfect holiday. It is exercise for the body, rest and refreshment for the mind, a sermon for the soul. You experience a lifetime of incident in a week. I could not recall a score of personal events in the twelve months between my holidays, but a hundred perfect cameos of a few days in the hills press insistently to mind. I could cram my diary when I am on holiday; I have not to sit and gaze at a blank page, as on other occasions, and wonder what has happened worthy of record. Many people, most people, do not agree that a walking holiday is the best: they are all people who have never tried it. They prefer to laze in a deckchair on a beach; this is not rest, but stagnation.

You may want a companion on your walking tour. Most walkers are initiated into the joys of walking in the company of others; a few of them, later on, strike into the hills alone. To feel completely free, to enjoy yourself to the uttermost, you must be alone. Solitude brings its responsibilities; dangers are magnified a hundredfold if you have nobody to back you up: you learn to depend on yourself; you have to keep your wits about you. But only alone can you develop your philosophy.

It is good to have a companion on occasion. Choose well, since the one you choose must of necessity be part of every scene, part of every minute of every day. If a man irks in town, he will be intolerable on a hill. If his company pleases you in the town, he may still be intolerable on a hill. Choose only one, never more; three is a crowd anywhere. Make up your mind about one thing: whoever is privileged to accompany you, that man is going to understand you as no man has ever done before, and you too will see him, perhaps for the first time, as he really is. You may nurse a secret at your breast for years in the town; on a hillside, with an understanding, sympathetic companion, it will be disclosed. If your choice has been good, it will continue a secret.

Companionship doesn't mean having someone to talk with; it means having someone at your side. The jolly companion who makes your evenings pleasant after the day's work is by no means the perfect companion for a walking tour. Oddly enough, you must seek for those qualities which seem at variance with the accepted ideas of fraternity. The lively conversationalist, the man who shines at parties and dances, is the last man to choose; leave him where he is; he would not appreciate the strange environment of lonely places.

No; it is the quiet man you want. The best friend is the man who can walk along with you mile after mile and say not a word; in fact, silence is the great test of companionship. I refer not to the stubborn silences which create enmity, but to the understanding silences of comradeship. A look or a smile is always more expressive than the spoken word.

A day on the hills strips a man of all sham and pretence. There are no silly conventions to be observed, no petty restrictions. There are no collars, no silk handkerchiefs. I don't mean that the hills are peopled with clumsy, ill-mannered oafs, I don't mean that at all; but with men who are for a brief spell as they were intended to be, free. Lovers of hills are the truest, the best-tempered, the most genuine fellows you will find anywhere. You can trust them, implicitly. If I were in serious trouble and wanted help, I wouldn't seek on a seaside promenade for a deliverer, but find a man sitting at ease by a mountain cairn. I couldn't pick at random from the pleasant, smiling, well-groomed throng in a ballroom and depend with my life on that man, but of the few who meditate in old clothes on high hills, any would serve. I don't decry the men who like bright lights and synthetic women and gaiety; they are often good companions. But the others are comrades. There are a thousand of the first type to every one of the other. In a crisis, I should turn to the hills for help. Wouldn't you? Would your bright partner of these past evenings be as reliable in a stern test? I give you credit for honesty.

Having spoken of my love for the hills, and having spoken of the fine qualities of those who love the hills, I lay myself wide open to the charge that I am guilty of heinous conceit and self-praise. Nothing of the sort. I am a misfit; it is of the others I speak. I am the exception that proves the rule.

I have digressed so far this time that I must seek your pardon. And if any of my remarks find you in violent disagreement, don't throw the book away because of that. Better an agitated opposition than boredom. Don't blame the book; the book's all right. It's the writer who may be wrong. He is prone to write down impressive pronouncements and weighty judgments because they have a fine ring about them; not always is he as sincere as he should be.

But perhaps, too, you put the book away when I left the Wall, as I suggested you should. In that case, I am on safe ground; I am like a Jew on a desert island cursing Hitler at the top of his voice; my words are without witness. If I could be sure that you are not reading these pages, then I could fill them with blasphemy, pour into them all the evil that is within me, and nobody would ever know. There's a lot of fun in writing a book that no one is to see.

But if you are still with me, let's get on our way.

There is a road through the Rawthey valley, a narrow secondary road, but a good one. Before the road was made, this secluded dale must have been altogether delightful, for the vegetation is luxurious and the flowers profuse; the hills are majestic, having almost the grandeur of mountains. I saw nowhere hills that had the attractiveness of this high group behind Sedbergh. They are not moors: they have a rugged outline, defined ridges, rocks. Cautley Crag and Cautley Spout were amongst the finest natural features I came across; the one a tremendous black precipice, sunless and forbidding; the other a high lace curtain of purest white suspended against the dark green slopes of the hill.

I was almost within sight of Sedbergh when three motor-coaches overtook me and drove me into the ditch. They were loaded with people, sightseers. I was so astounded at this unexpected sight that I gaped after them in wonderment. This was a road for farmers' carts, not for motor-coaches; anyway, there was nothing in this rural retreat, pleasant though it was, for those in a hurry. But here they were, and I sought a reason for their presence. The coaches were from South Shields, which deepened the mystery, for South Shields was very far away, on the other side of the country. It was now five o'clock and the sun was setting; they must have been on the journey since noon. They must have come by way of Hexham, Alston, Appleby. . . . My way; a matter of hours for them, days for me. But whither were they bound? Had the drivers lost direction? I solved the problem eventually. They were heading south-west, and a straight line drawn through the Rawthey valley from South Shields will have Blackpool at the other extremity. Ye gods, Blackpool; the illuminations! What miserable fools they were! They had looked out of the windows in dull boredom as they passed, and no wonder. Five hours on the road and little more than halfway to their destination; sometime during the night they would be coming along this road again, heading for a home that was still five hours away. All this for a couple of hours on a gale-swept promenade. I could imagine them climbing back into the coaches for the long ride through the dark night, in utter wretchedness. Their adventure had a resemblance to mine, but there was a world of difference between them, and surely theirs was the madder and much the less profitable. What a miserable journey home they would have! Or most of them; maybe there were lovers in the party.

Sedbergh I cannot write about. I cut out a sharp angle in my route by entering Dentdale through a maze of narrow, muddy lanes, leaving Sedbergh half a mile to my right. I saw the town across fields; it appears to be a small town set on a level sward, not itself attractive. But the hills that rise sheer behind it are magnificent.

Dentdale runs eastwards from Sedbergh. I had the strong wind at my back now for the first time, and had I been fresh I could fairly have careered along. But I was tired and leg-weary. Wynken's cousins were coming up to avenge the three unfortunates who had so nobly given their all.

Dentdale is ten miles long. For half the distance, to Dent-town, it is straight, but beyond, to the head of the dale where the big railway viaduct leaps across the sky far above the valley, it is shaped like a sickle. Its boundaries are high-topped, monotonous fells; only Whernside, which dominates the scene, has individuality and character. The river Dee threads the floor of the valley, and plays hide and seek with you as you go along; at intervals appearing boldly in the fields below, and often disappearing shyly behind a screen of trees. There are many plantations in Dentdale, and without them the dale would seem as desolate as the moors that enclose it.

It is a lonely valley; not a cul-de-sac, but virtually so, for the roads leading up and out of the remote dalehead are high and exposed and attract little traffic. Yet it is not lonely as Ennerdale is, for in Ennerdale there are no dwellings, while in Dentdale there are many dotted along the road and about the fields; rather, it bears an air of loneliness. It looks forlorn, like a pretty girl who suffers disappointment at a tryst.

I did not see Dentdale at its best this evening. It needs sunshine to dapple the meadows, a blue sky, a warm summer morning; given these, I believe it could preen itself into a very charming picture. But when I was there the cold wind was driving through it, isolated clouds were racing across a darkening sky, violent showers of hail blotted out the distance and made the immediate surroundings sullen.

The five miles to Dent seemed never-ending. It was too wet and gloomy to read my map in comfort, or perhaps I was just too tired to bother with it. I knew that ultimately my road would cross the river, and that the village was a mile beyond the bridge; and often I looked forward hopefully when the river came alongside the road, but always to find that it again swerved away in a wide loop. Dent lay at an elevation on the other bank, and I was constantly straining my eyes through the dusk for a glimpse of clustered rooftops, but I could see only fields and woods stretching onward interminably, till I began to despair of ever getting to Dent at all.

There was one shower of hail which came as a culmination to all the malice and fury shown by the gale in these past few days. It was upon me without warning: a stinging, blinding downpour thrown at me in hatred; the forces of the gale were concentrated for a final attack and suddenly unleashed. I crouched in a prickly hedge until the last shot was fired. In two minutes it was finished, then I went on along a white road between white fields. When I glanced up at the sky I could find no trace of venom in it; over Sedbergh there was a fiery sunset and the few small, scattered clouds overhead were touches of rosy light against the purple dome of heaven.

All things come to an end, and eventually I arrived at the bridge and had the river swirling beneath me. A huge tree, uprooted by the wind, lay from one bank to the other; its branches, plunged deep into the water, threw up clouds of spray.

Five minutes later I came to the junction of the first road leading out of the valley. A signpost stood in the corner, and here it appeared that the wind had played its oddest trick, for the post had been turned round. Its directing arms told me that I had come from Hawes, that Sedbergh lay over the moor to my right, that if I kept on up the valley I should come in due course to Kirkby Lonsdale. Had I not been very sure of my ground, I might well have been baffled. I found later that certain irrepressible spirits among the young men of Dent derive a great deal of wholesome fun from the practice of turning the signposts in the valley. So it is well when in Dentdale to carry a map, and to have confidence in it.

I was impatient for a peep of Dent-town, which was still hidden though no more than ten minutes walk away. One thought weighed heavily: this was my last night. Not again for many months, until the blasts of winter had been and gone, should I be seeking the shelter of a strange roof. Tomorrow I should be home; in a few days back at work. Dent, to which I was now marching and had not yet seen, would then seem very remote, as a dream reviewed in the harsh light of day. My hours of freedom were fast drawing to a close; the curtains were being drawn across the stage. Increasingly my thoughts were of home, of friends left behind so very long ago. Dent was the last link; or rather, the first, since the chains I dreaded were ahead, awaiting me. I was too familiar with their cruel fetters to regard my return to them with indifference. I was a prisoner before, and should be again. My ticket-of-leave was fast expiring.

It was almost dark when I entered Dent, but the concealing shadows of night could not spare me the shock which every visitor must experience. Dent is not of this world. It is a fairy tale, and who believes in fairy tales nowadays? It is a place of cobbles, of jutting gables, overhanging roofs, quaint alleys, wooden galleries and outside staircases. It is so old that you cannot imagine children living there; so decrepit that it seems a strong wind must level it to the ground and scatter its dust about the fells; so apparently tumbledown that if you pulled away a stone the whole town must collapse like a row of dominoes. For Dent is one block of jumbled masonry; one house was built and all the rest fastened on to it; only the church is isolated and independent.

A town it is, since there are many tiny shops, but a field a hundred yards square could accommodate it easily; you could walk from one end to the other in a minute, although you never will. The narrow, twisting streets are all paved with cobbles; there are no pavements. If you meet a cart advancing cumbersomely, you must retreat before it as there is no room to pass; its wheels grace the walls. The town has an infrequent bus service to Sedbergh, but the vehicles do not attempt to enter its streets; they wait outside.

Dent should lie in the shadow of a high castle or, even more appropriately, the Bastille, for one is reminded forcibly of the squalid slums which feature in every film of the Revolution. There should be ragged beggars lying in filthy streets, verminous dogs slinking at your heels, old toothless hags shrieking maledictions after you.

Dent surprises as Blanchland does, but Blanchland is lovelier by far. There is no beauty in Dent's black walls and grotesque lines. Blanchland is medieval, Dent primeval. Blanchland is a dream, Dent a nightmare.

Having wandered in amazement about the town, and being convinced that I was in a haunt of evil witches, it was a shock to enter a house and find there a smiling lady with white hair, wearing prim clothes and a spotlessly clean apron. The home of the

Masons is reached by way of a staircase which rises from the cobbles of the street to a gallery running the length of the house. The unusual approach, however, was forgotten when the front door closed behind me, for I found myself in a comfortable kitchen not in any way odd, but very much like any other.

I sank into a soft chair by the big fire, took off my shoes, and was content. Mrs Mason was extremely pleasant and solicitous; her husband was quiet and taciturn, but had an eye for my welfare, so that I was thoroughly at ease.

I was fed on fish, a welcome change, and gave them their last swim, this time in a pool of H.P. sauce. Nothing appeals to the palate more, at the end of a long day in the country, than sauce. It burns and scorches a throat jaded with too many cigarettes, makes it tingle pleasantly, and sends a glow of warmth to a starved stomach. I search for nothing more eagerly on a table; my desire for it amounts almost to lust. Let there be a bottle of sauce rearing up amongst the dishes, and it becomes the mainstay of the meal; all else, meat, fish, potatoes, being added merely for flavouring. I could eat a mound of scrapings from a stable if there was sauce in plenty to conceal the incongruity of the repast. But on this particular occasion, I had rather too much. There was one interval when I had to turn my head away from the Masons, and let my tongue loll over my chest to cool. And for the rest of the evening I sat with parted lips. But I felt good inside.

Mrs Mason gave me a book on Dentdale to read after supper, and though I had read it before, I found its pages refreshing now that I was actually there. I learned again of the 'terrible knitters of Dent', of the urge to knit which consumes every man and woman in the place, and which every child inherits. Hand-made hosiery is, or was, the chief export of Dent. Knitting parties are still held, but are not so common as formerly. A generation or two ago, it was as customary as breakfast for the husband and wife to leave their home in the evening, equipped with cloaks and lantern, and make their way to the place appointed, a neighbour's house; and there a congregation would sit, telling knitting stories, their bodies swaying in unison, their fingers plying needle and wool incessantly. They worked till past midnight in the glow of a peat fire, and so near to the blaze did they crouch that a necessary part of each one's equipment was a pair of shin cloths, rags that were tied round the shins to prevent them from getting scorched. Shin cloths were as familiar a garb to the men as their braces, and we read how they were often seen going about their tasks at midday wearing them. Later, Dent found a place on the tourists' maps; curiosity and ridicule made the men shy and ashamed, so that now they knit only in secret. But the women's fingers are never idle. I could hear the click of Mrs Mason's needles, as regular as the ticking of the clock, all the time I was reading the book, while her husband's fingers drummed in tune on the edge of his chair.

I had a second supper at ten o'clock, and then went up yet another flight of stairs to my room.

It was my last night, and I could not let it be wasted entirely in sleep. Tomorrow night I should climb soberly into my own bed, my holiday ended, freedom fled. Irksome restrictions and regulations would be all around me the moment I stepped into the train at Settle, and fear would make me again a mild, law-abiding citizen. 'Spitting Prohibited': that would be the first; a £5 fine if I pull the communication cord; this compartment holds six persons; put your luggage on the rack; place your fag-ends in the receptacle provided; you are warned not to put your head out of the window; your ticket is issued subject to by-laws and regulations; and so on. The same on the tram that would take me to the bottom of the road. The same at home. The same, much worse, at work. The same through life. What chance has a man's spirit to expand? Irritating restrictions make me ill. They are like an old saw-edged collar that is rubbing your neck raw, and you can't take it off because you haven't another to put on. They pinch and squeak like new shoes.

My last night! I walked across to the window, opened it, and looked out.

The night was black. I could hear the wind in the trees, now only a moaning whisper, and the murmur of the river, nothing else. There was no moon; a few stars twinkled far above, and since they were all I could see, I regarded them for a long long time. The silence was profound; there would not be another evening so quiet for many a month. There was a stillness in the air, a tranquil hush as the earth slept.

I sang a few verses of that loveliest of tunes, 'Silent Night', very softly, and then closed the window and relit the candle. My last night! I undressed slowly, sadly, cast two jaundiced eyes over the mottoes that decorated the walls, and saw there nothing to rejuvenate my drooping spirits.

I pulled the blankets down. Oh, joy unbounded! Oh, exuberance! Oh, Mrs Mason! My last night was not to be lonely after all; I had been provided with a companion. The hours of darkness would not now be cold and empty; I had a warm bedmate to gather to my breast, to confide in, to put my feet on or to make love to, as I willed. I always think of a hot-water bottle as being of feminine gender, though I could not really say why, and when I saw this one revealed, snug and yet forlorn, I blew out the candle and made haste to join her.

We comforted each other until sleep came. I did not put my feet on her, nor thought of doing, since before many minutes had passed she had assumed familiar shape, developed arms and legs, and become endowed with sweet lips that whispered and caressed and clung. She made my last night happy. There were no reproaches; she knew my mood as a mother her baby. Tonight she was not elusive; she was mine from the moment I took her in my arms. She was all comfort and kindness; the darkness could not hide the tender light in her eyes. Never before had she been so lavish with her kisses; never before had she held me quite so closely. . . .

I had my reward tonight for years of faithful servitude and humble adoration, for years of hopeless yearning. She was mine; she abandoned herself utterly to me. I loved her then, not more, for the cup I offer her has long been overflowing, but in a new and wonderful way. I whispered to her penitently, for she had much to forgive, but her soft lips closed on my words, and I could say no more. She loved me, too. . . . The ecstasy of those precious moments will live forever.

Never before had her embrace been so warm.

Nor, now I come to think of it, had it ever before left a square red patch on my bosom.

THE LAST CHAPTER

THROUGH the curling smoke on a cigarette I watched the grey light of dawn filter into the room.

Day again, another day . . . my last.

A matter of hours now, and I would be in Settle.

This morning I was not peeping early at the sky. The weather no longer concerned me; proof positive that the day held nothing in store for me; nothing, that is, except regret and a vain looking back. The prospect of empty, purposeless days ahead chilled me. Days of noise and bustle they would be, but nevertheless empty and purposeless. I would return to a desk piled with work to be done; my papers would have been disturbed, my drawers ransacked; systems which I had inaugurated and alone could understand would have gone awry in my absence. I should be busy; there would be little time to think of happier days. There would be noise; bells ringing; a drone of conversation always in the background. . . . This morning I could hear birds warbling in a nearby tree; tomorrow there would be factory sirens.

Ah well, discipline and responsibility were good training for the mind. There would be other holidays next year; no use weeping at the graveside of this one. I levered myself out of bed and walked across to the mirror to look at my moustache, now five days old. I studied it from all angles, and came eventually to the conclusion that it was rather pretty. I was not biased in its favour because it was mine; my survey was quite critical. There was a golden sheen about it, as though I had been eating marmalade clumsily; a sort of lustre. Not bad at all. Pity it had to come off, but it certainly must.

This, too, was part of the holiday, part of the freedom. I must leave it here, as I must leave much else of greater worth. Let it clog the drains of Dent; better to be murdered in its prime than to wither and die through ridicule and lack of appreciation. How odd it looked, though, that and my scrubby chin, above a body so smooth and pink! But heavens, look at those miserable legs!

I dressed and got back into bed for another cigarette before going downstairs. My hot-water bottle was no longer feminine, but an icy-cold neuter; I could not touch it now. How typical of everything else it was: the time for dreaming and self-deception was gone; grim reality must be faced. The hour had come for me to abandon my fairyland of delightful imaginings; I must get back to the brutal world I was somehow mixed up with.

I counted my money; I had eleven shillings left, and my night's lodging was not yet paid for. There were other things not paid for, back home; reminders would be awaiting me. There were other things, too, I badly wanted but could not afford: a new suit, new glasses, a good aquarium, a bookcase, a typewriter, a complete set of a new edition of mountaineering books, the house decorating. I hadn't an overcoat for the winter. No underpants. No spare pair of shoes. Not even a decent hat. Now if I'd denied myself this holiday I could have bought some of these things; say, the aquarium and the mountaineering books, and paid a first instalment on a typewriter. And if only I could stop smoking I could quickly get some new clothes. A smart appearance might impress my employer, certainly it would surprise him; it might result in an increase in salary. Think of it: then I could get a model railway, pay for my typewriter, buy some more mountaineering books. I might even be able to have a room of the house decorated, say the dining-room to start off with. Four years amongst the dirty grey plaster of a new house was turning my stomach. Twenty pounds would do the lot. I hadn't the remotest chance of accumulating twenty pounds; I had never at any time had even half that sum saved. . . . Next year Switzerland, icy pinnacles against a blue sky, pine forests, snow, flowery alps. Oh damn the decorations! Stop worrying, man; you've done your best. Go and get your breakfast.

Downstairs, I found Mrs Mason putting the finishing touches to the table with the same meticulous care that an artist bestows on his canvas. Her husband had gone to his work. But before departing, he had patched up my shoes, pulled out more protruding nails. This was a service I appreciated greatly, for he had done it unasked and not waited for my thanks. This is true kindness. It is one thing to perform a service with alacrity when requested; an entirely different thing to espy an opportunity for a kindly act, and to do it quietly and unknown to the one who is to benefit. The one action gives pleasure; the other is inspired by tenderness, and induces tenderness. Acts of true kindness always have an element of surprise; they are unsolicited, unexpected maybe; they speak of genuine affection.

I was away early. Before I set out, I called in the workshop on the ground floor for I found that Mason carried on a wheelwright's business there, underneath his home. I thanked him for repairing my shoes and saw him smile for the first time, a trifle shyly: he wished me a good journey.

The sky was covered with ominous black clouds, save for a patch of blue in the east where the sun shone; it was as though its warmth had melted a hole in the thick roof overhead. As I turned into the narrow street, the brilliant light was blinding, and I went over into the shadow. The glare of the sun was intense, giving an unreal effect against the lowering sky. The church, standing back from the houses, appeared to be floodlit, so white and ghostly was it outlined against the black clouds behind. I got out my camera and took a few snaps; one of the church, one of the street, one of the quaint memorial to Adam Sedgwick, whom I had never heard of before. This memorial is a rough uncut slab of granite standing by the wall at the tiny crossroads in the tiny heart of the tiny town; a hole has been bored through the stone and it serves as a spring of clear water.

Then I said goodbye to Dent and headed for Whernside which, as soon as I left the cottages behind, loomed huge before me. Whernside is higher than either Ingleborough or Penyghent, but it lacks their majesty. Ingleborough is a mountain, wherever you see it from; Penyghent is a noble hill in every view; but Whernside, despite its its greater massiveness, is no more than a long high moor, with only its strange tarns, resting on a shelf below the summit, to lift it out of the ordinary. Yet they make a fine triumvirate, Whernside, Ingleborough, Penyghent, these three, rearing lofty heads above the countryside, watching each other today as they have for countless ages.

I turned along a narrow rutted lane, between scented hedgerows, still enjoying warm sunshine. After the heavy rain the air was fresh and clean, the earth moist and sweet. Before me and above was the sweeping line of the hill, incredibly high; a little cairn on the ridge held my gaze. I climbed steadily, with the green valley ever deepening beneath my feet. Every step now was a trampling upon my sour temper; my spirits soared with my body. Let my toes be pointing upwards and I cannot harbour a churlish thought. Let there be a rough pile of stones before me, above me and perhaps still hidden, and I climb on air. Life is worth living, then. How I wish I could communicate my affection for the hills! But I cannot; with the image of a hill in my mind, my pen becomes inarticulate. . . . I should like to think that when the time comes for me to be judged, I shall be judged by my thoughts and conduct when I have been free on the hills, not when I have been fettered to my desk. On a hill I am alone, and sincere; anywhere else, I am one of a crowd and tinged with mob instincts of selfishness and hypocrisy. Yet it is neither the sight of a hill nor the feel of it beneath me that brings the transformation, for transformation it is; rather it is that in the high places I am very conscious of the nearness of God; so aware of His presence all about me that I could never feel lonely. But if I am in a church in the valley, I am lost: I cannot feel the same, try as I will.

I attained at length a point where I could have my last sight of Dentdale before the slope of the hill hid it from view. The valley far below was bathed in bright sunshine; it presented a sleepy, tranquil picture. I saw it as on a map: road, river, field, farmstead, clearly defined, but without life.

I regarded the scene for a while, wondering when again I should pass that way. Perhaps I was seeing it now for the last time. It may be that never again should I set eyes on lovely Dentdale. It is easy to swear allegiance while one is still half intoxicated with delight;

but loyalty wears away if it gets no further nourishment, enthusiasm has a trick of fading if it is not regularly fed. I was going from an atmosphere of placidity to one of turmoil. Reflection on these past days would be stifled in a babel of noise, I well knew; there would be scant opportunity for quiet meditation. And a reconsecration of my devotion could only truly take place when I was once more on those hills where it was born.

I went on across the watershed and looked down into a new valley. Had I been lost, wandering aimlessly, I should have known, at that moment, that I was nearing home. Before me was limestone country: vivid green slopes, scarred hillsides, white terraces of naked gleaming rock. There is a cleanness about limestone country which one does not find in other districts, as though it has been washed and scrubbed and polished till all stains are erased and the colours show in their virgin purity. The valley before me was Kingsdale, through which runs smoothly the river that is soon to be hurled and tossed on the rocky ledges in the narrow glen above Ingleton.

As I came down to the level strath at Kingsdale House, three young men passed me, loaded with rucksacks, on their way to Dent. This was my eleventh day; these were the first pedestrians I had met. I had been from Yorkshire to the Wall, and back again to Yorkshire, and outside the villages met not a soul out for a walk. On the first day, there had been potholers at Hull Pot and a farmer and his lad on the edge of the moor beyond; nobody at all between Buckden and Muker, nor between Muker and Romaldkirk, save for a gipsy encampment; on the way to Blanchland I had seen a man in a car; the following day there had been women blackberrying in the lane outside Hexham; the Wall had been completely mine; coming through Kirkside Wood into Alston I had seen two people who should really only count as one; I met no one between Alston and Gamblesby, or on the way to Soulby except another friendly fellow in a car; and I was the only walker yesterday on the long march to Dent. Say twenty people at the most, and not one of them walking for the pleasure of it.

I greeted the young men, therefore, in a spirit of affinity, but since my rucksack was a skeleton compared with theirs and I wore flannels where they wore shorts, they could not recognise me as one of them and I got no more than three surly nods as they passed. Three young men out for a walk together; a sorry mistake. They should split up; go alone. Some people fight shy of their own company, and I cannot blame them; these are the people whose minds are not attuned to thought.

But as for myself, I find my own company vastly entertaining; I have never known a moment's boredom. I like to meditate, and if I choose to ponder problems which have no solution, that is my own fault entirely. And if I tire of thinking, I have an inexhaustible imagination to draw upon, and the dearest little lady in the world to introduce into every picture: how then can I find solitude monotonous? I can sing, whistle and shout as I go along, and play the silliest games. One companion, be he ever so well known, imposes restrictions; alone, one is free to do the maddest things. I can be Jekyll in one village, Hyde in another. Nobody knows me. I have no reputation to consider. I remember once going through a village street with both feet turned inward, and a pronounced limp: all pretence, but I got lots of amusement out of the sympathetic stares of the inhabitants. Once I regretted a similar action: I sought a lodging and decided to have a twitching face. I twitched throughout the tea and afterwards, but by eight o'clock my face fairly ached, and rather than continue the horrible game, as I should have to do in the presence of my hostess, I went out and had to wander about dark lanes in pouring rain until bedtime. This is the new form of sanity: anything for a change. We cannot cast off our skins, any more than a leopard can change his spots. But we can change our habits, our thoughts, our mode of life; if we find we can't do this, if we can't get out of the rut when we wish, we are beyond hope.

Kingsdale is by no means attractive. It runs in a perfectly straight line for four miles, as if a great knife had laid it open. Descending into it from Whernside, you can see all there is to see at a glance, so that when later you walk along it, there is very little to hold your attention. The fells on either side are of uniform height and lacking in beauty of outline; their interest is confined to the many caves and potholes they contain. The valley is treeless, if we except the copses around the only two farms. The river is plain, and so straight that it is hard to believe that nature has fashioned it; rather, it seems to have been engineered, like an irrigation ditch or a canal. There is a low ridge barring the exit from the valley at the south end, and as you walk towards it there appears to be no escape for the river unless it runs uphill and over the brink. Actually, it cuts through a very shallow depression which is not apparent from a distance, follows a wide curve, and then, changing character completely, becomes the foaming torrent that hurls itself down the rocky gorge of Swilla Glen. And from this point onward to Ingleton, you must pay sixpence to see it.

Kingsdale was dark and gloomy today, and there were several showers of hail, but when at length I left new country behind and came to familiar ground at Thornton Force, the sun broke through the clouds again. Ingleton Falls are lovely. In flood, they are truly magnificent. I stood on the rocky bluff overlooking the Force and could feel the ground trembling at the thunderous roar of the river as it leaped clear in a boiling cloud of spray. I had not intended to halt here, but I simply had to. Only once before had I been at the Falls, and that on a Sunday afternoon when the paths were thronged and I had perforce to walk in procession. I hated the place that day, and I hated the sweating hordes before and behind me, and most of all myself for being such a fool; while all the time Ingleborough, in splendid isolation, looked down on me in pity and chastised me for being a deserter.

But today was different. I was alone in a world of dazzling splendour. The spectacle of the angry river was superb. From the moment it sprang over the cliff at Thornton Force, propelled far beyond its usual course by the weight of the waters behind, it was pure white; a surging, raging turbulence of sparkling crystals. It was nowhere at rest. The gorge was an inferno. The river was a dynamo of lashing fury; it crashed against the narrow rocky walls, dashed tumultuously in great bounds from fall to fall. It steamed and smoked as if it were white-hot lava pouring from a volcano. Over it lingered white mists of dancing foam, seemingly suspended in mid-air, afraid to rejoin the frenzied waters beneath.

I took advantage of the sunshine at Thornton Force to pose for a couple of photographs. This cost me the best part of an hour, for the operation, as I perform it, is a long and painful one, requiring infinite patience and a gentle touch. I have to place the camera on the edge of a high flat stone and build a cairn of boulders around and over it to hold it firmly in position, at the same time taking care not to obscure the lens. Then I have to fasten a loop of string round the lever, which projects not more than a sixteenth of an inch from the side of the camera, take the loose end with me to the couch I have selected for my portrait, settle down there and look unconcerned, and pull the string. The plan in theory is infallible. But try it: forty times in succession the jerk pulls the string away altogether. Forty times you struggle wearily to your feet and replace the loop on the lever; forty times you go back, trailing the string with you; forty times you sink again in the grass, smooth your hair and tuck your legs away out of sight, look at the camera and jerk the string. At the forty-first attempt the shutter clicks, and by this time the sun has gone and you are so heartily fed up with the experiment that you are no longer capable of looking pleasant. Take care to get in the middle of your picture. Once I got only one ear on a print.

I went on along the path by the side of the racing river. The noise of the surging waters was deafening; there was the continuous roar of a busy railway station. The river was swollen by the heavy rains, and in places rushed along abreast of the path, so that from the opposite bank it must have appeared that I was walking on its surface.

It was an odd experience to have this popular walk to myself. I wasn't at all sure that I wasn't trespassing, that I shouldn't find the gates at the bottom of the glen barred and fastened. I met nobody; away in Ingleton a factory hooter sounded and I could hear an occasional train, but here amongst the trees, the paths and seats and lovers' leaps were deserted. I had a strange feeling, somehow, that I was playing truant, that the world was at work and I was hiding from it, in idleness: the same uneasy feeling that we have when we are unavoidably absent from our place of employment owing to illness, very conscious all the time that our colleagues are there just as usual.

One of the gates near the railway viaduct was open, and in the hut alongside an old man was sitting with a newspaper across his lap. I left a sixpence on the doorstep of the hut as I passed, and the old fellow was so flustered and surprised at my action that I wondered afterwards whether he was in fact the guardian of the Falls or if I had bestowed the toll on someone unauthorised to receive it.

Ingleton lay in the shadow of a particularly venomous cloud, which looked as if it was going to do something very drastic shortly, so I went into a cheap hotel for bread and cheese, and it was fortunate that I did. No sooner was I seated in the cold parlour than the cloud descended on the village in a mass, and the road outside was a whirling flurry of hail and sleet.

The storm passed as quickly as it came, and the sun was again shining brilliantly when I left Ingleton and started on the last lap of my journey. I was quite reconciled by this time to my return and all that my return meant; the fact that I must again take up the threads where I had dropped them had become irrefutable and did not now disturb to the same extent. Having given up the ghost, I could view the future more complacently. My thoughts were more rational, but by comparison they were dull and insipid. Days amongst the hills had given me clearer vision, let me see things in true perspective; back once more in the town, my view would be clouded, my sense of values distorted. I should see selfishness, jealousy, greed, and not recognise them as such. I should witness scheming and intrigue, and alas, be a party to them. I should be in the midst of artfulness and cunning and, being in the midst, find it difficult to discern true merit and true endeavour. To assess and appraise anything, one must stand away from it, be detached. So had I been, these past few days. I had been remote, and all my perplexities and worries had dwindled to very small compass, so that I could regard them lucidly and view them in correct proportion. I had tasted life. Now I must get back to the sorry business of living.

But I was returning also to friends. There were honest faces among the sly, kind glances as well as shrewd. There were warm hearts; there was compassionate regard and sympathy. Not all were concerned with profitable advancement; not all wanted to be first in the race. There were a few solid, dependable fellows content to amble along in the rear and look about them as they went on their way, but they were by no means the less valiant because of that. It takes courage, sometimes, to suffer the thrusts of others as they forge ahead and push you into the background; if you can keep an amiable face and wish them luck before they are gone too far from sight, well then, this is the better success. There aren't many of the type you can rely on to the utmost. And they aren't easy to find. They don't make as much noise as their less worthy brethren; they may be overlooked. If you know of one, value his friendship as a gift to be prized.

I had not, of course, had any word from home or the office during my holiday. Nobody had more than a very approximate idea of my whereabouts. I had flung all my responsibilities to the winds; I could not be reached by letter, telegram, wireless message or police car. A week last Sunday I had put on my cap and disappeared into the void. . . . Now, with return imminent, I began to wonder if I should meet with changes. Were all well at home: son, spouse, Peggy, Paddy, Micky? I had even a thought for the tortoise Andrew which hadn't moved a muscle for the past two months; if he was still torpid when I got back, I would lift a sod in the garden and put him underneath as he must be dead. Had Peter still got his two hairy caterpillars in a matchbox? And at work? Any deaths? Anybody invalided with cancer, appendicitis? Surely affairs couldn't be exactly as I left them ages ago? Ah yes, there is pleasure in homecoming. Fewer people than I could count on the fingers of one hand would be glad to see me, be interested in my story; not many, but quite enough. Better one who understands than a hundred who listen. Better even one who understands and says nothing.

I have little to say of the walk from Ingleton to Settle. I was soon back on my first map. I followed the old byroad that crosses Newby Common, passes by Clapham's lonely station, and then for eight miles skirts the northern fringe of the Bowland country. Gradually I left Ingleborough behind, and Penyghent assumed pride of place in the wide landscape. I have never been greatly attracted to this shallow valley of the Wenning, perhaps because of the ugly main road which runs so purposefully through it, but today it was different. The fields that separated me from the road and the villages were under water; the river was a lake, and mirrored on its placid surface was a charming vista of the rugged slopes beyond. Ingleborough had a solitary cloud resting against its summit all the afternoon; the nearer fells were aglow with warm russet colours, and the distant heights were purple; red rooftops peeped above the trees on the farther shore; the limestone scars glinted white in the sun. It was a day of colour: all about me contributed gaiety to a farewell which must otherwise have been very sad.

These last few miles inevitably held reminiscences for me. I dwelt on past days and past glories as must a man going to the scaffold. I set off again from Settle in the bright sunshine with my shadow before me, going north; crossed the moor from Horton to Foxup, where the rabbit was; saw again in imagination that superb panorama at sunset from the top of Horse Head Pass; came in the black night to Buckden and fell in love with a sweet voice that guided me through the darkness. Where was that girl now, I wondered? Had she already forgotten? She would, of course, when the chocolate box was empty. Bless the dear young lady: she gave renewed conviction to my high conception of her sex.

Make no mistake, whatever I may have written in these pages, I look upon women with wonder and admiration. I think they have got a rotten deal compared with the males: there is so much they may not do, so much restraint in their lives, so much more pain and anxiety. Less disappointment, maybe, since they lack imagination; they are practical, matter-of-fact, endowed plentifully with common sense. There is a phase in every man's life when it seems fashionable to announce himself as a woman-hater; this has not been my lot, for I have never ceased to marvel at their splendid qualities; perhaps it may come later. My admiration is complete; it amounts to worship. Yet I have known few, and not one really well; but in these few, I have been extremely fortunate. I have learned more by observation than by contact, and a spirited imagination has done the rest. Woman is on a pedestal. And, having put her there, any misgivings that arise are very disturbing. The slightest disappointment is a cruel blow which makes not an imperceptible crack in the pedestal but sends the whole edifice tottering. But the next gentle word or pretty smile rights it again.

Disappointments there are: the woman who makes a coarse comment or laughs when she should frown; the girl who professes high principles but is ready to abandon them when it suits her purpose, and here, I think, is the main danger, for they have not the rigid standards of men, nor the same loyalty, and they can see only madness in following a hopeless cause.

Then there is the married woman who goes out to work to gain additional spending money, whom I cannot but regard with contempt; all honour to her if her wage is necessary to keep the home together. And there is the grotesque female who screams for equality with men: give her all the privileges she demands and let her demonstrate her right to be considered an equal, if she can; then at least she may creep quietly back to the kitchen where she belongs. Her protest is not against lack of opportunity: it is man's dominance she resents. Man's dominance is not of mushroom growth; it has been developing through the ages, and his gradual expansion has seen inculcated in him qualities which the ladies might possibly acquire when they have spent as long a time in apprenticeship, not the least of these qualities being a sense of fair play, to which at present they are strangers.

But quite the worst offence is committed by those women, poor darlings, who enter into marriage resolved to have no children. They need a whip across their backs. This is cheating in a way a man cannot understand. A policy of frustration is always deplorable, but when it is directed against God's purpose then surely it is sin. An unmarried girl with a baby is a nobler creature by far than the wife without. How can a husband keep his respect for such a woman? What does she offer him that a prostitute does not? An easy conscience, yes; but a lifetime of bitter regret, too. The man has not been born who does not want a son to follow him.

I am sorry to have to criticise, as sorry as a fond father who can see grievous failings in his children. If I see faults, it does not mean that my faith is wrecked. My conception of women is exactly as high as my regard for the finest girl I know; she sets the standard for all others of her sex. And the standard is very high. I stand with my feet rooted in mud, and marvel that there can be such purity in this same world; but I can look up and wish to attain to her side. And it is no bad thing to have a star to follow, an ideal to strive after. In the same breath as my criticism let me say reverently that most women are little below the standard. They are wonderful beings; in their own sphere, they are so supreme that I cannot understand why they seek to cross into man's territory. The height of any man's ambition is a fireside to call his own, a devoted wife, a few sons and a daughter who is her mother's image, and the respect of his fellows; if it is not, he is on a false trail. A woman is essential to a man's happiness. She has tenderness, sympathy and kindness, and there is especial comfort in her sweet body. We do right to raise our hats to the ladies.

Well, even in brief reminiscence I wander from the path. I recalled the glorious morning when I left Buckden and the grand march over Stake Pass to Askrigg and my coming into Muker in the evening, the sudden, awful threat that hung over the little assembly in the Harkers' kitchen. Next morning, over Tan Hill in the mist, through Sleightholme in the rain, into Bowes in sunshine, the evening walk to Cotherstone and Romaldkirk, the ticking of the clock in the Kirk Inn. On then to Middleton, over the hills and across weeping Weardale to the purple land of enchantment where surprising Blanchland lay, and so at length into Hexham. Then the best day of all, the exhilarating pursuit of a tumbledown Wall; I must go again soon and recapture that mood. The return: south to Alston and the happy Richardsons, the bleak crossing of Hartside to Gamblesby and the girl of the Red Lion, then the least interesting day, which ended miserably at Soulby, followed by new resolve and the long march to Dent.

I summed up. The loveliest scene was upper Wharfedale as I set forth from Buckden to Hubberholme on that warm sunny morning and found the earth delightfully draped in a veil of shimmering haze that hid none of the valley's charms but gave them a fairy touch. Hardly less lovely was Blanchland, and Blanchland has the greater appeal for it not only soothes the eye but stirs the imagination. I prefer Blanchland for its romantic atmosphere; there one can rejoice and sigh and weep and feel sympathy from the very stones of the place. Blanchland is a hidden retreat for lovers, but I was not unwelcome because of that, for lovers, as you well know, are not always to be found in pairs. The truest lover is the man who knows his love is vain, who hopes when there is no hope; not the man whose way to the arms of his cherished one is made smooth and prepared for his approach. . . . So I shall always remember Blanchland with affection. And not only for the air of romance that lies over the valley, but for the purple hills encircling it, the wide sweeping moors where one may wander at will and hear nothing but the wind in the heather and the cry of the birds overhead.

Blanchland's medieval battlemented courtyard was the biggest surprise I had, and second, I think, was queer old Dent, but the bedroom at the Red Lion comes high in the list. Northumberland itself was a great surprise, and I cannot decide whether the Yorkshire Dales can justly claim more loveliness.

My most comfortable lodgings were at Buckden, Alston, Dent and Muker, in that order, and the worst were at Soulby, Haltwhistle and Hexham. I attained to luxury only once, and that at Gamblesby, where I lived like a king. Of the people I stayed with, the Richardsons of Alston, the Falshaws of Buckden and the Harkers of Muker were the most companionable. I saw other people, too, whom I liked: the old lady in the cottage at Slaggyford, the soft-voiced blue-eyed Viking at Housesteads Farm, the lady of the Kirk Inn at Romaldkirk. The man I shall never forget is the drunken Rowley, reeling across the floor at the Black Bull at Soulby, and seeming as he came towards me, with the glow of the fire lighting up his gaunt face, like some horrible Frankenstein.

I recalled, too, moments of exaltation when there were no clouds in the sky and my spirit leaped into space and near to heaven; when, though I was solitary, a dear voice was calling, softly and insistently, and I was eager to obey; moments of exhilaration, moments of complete happiness when I was in the midst of desolation. Moments there had been of sadness and weariness and exhaustion, but already they were slipping beyond recall and would soon be quite forgotten.

The crowning moment was that which set the seal on my success; when I came to the North Gate of Borcovicium and saw the Wall.

Well, it was over, and here before me were the white limestone terraces of Giggleswick Scar; already I could see the green tip of

Castlebergh. Settle was near. It was over, but . . . I could recapture every incident, preserve every thrilling moment, renew every delight, if I were to write the story of my travels in a book. Memory plays tricks as time passes, and oft times we would fain bring to mind thoughts of happier hours, but somehow they elude us. We recall, in snatches, experiences which once filled us with joy, but the fleeting years reduce them to fragments; they have no beginning and no end, and we can never forge the chain of which they are part. The precious moments of life are too rare, too valuable to be forgotten when they have passed; we should hoard them as a miser hoards his gold, and bring them to light and rejoice over them often. We should all of us have a treasury of happy memories to sustain us when life is unbearably cruel, to brighten the gloom a little, to be stars shining through the darkness.

It is a splendid thing to be able to shut out the world and sit quietly at home on a wintry night and spend a few hours in idle recollection, but better still to be able to reach out a hand and take from its secret drawer whenever you wish a journal which will give no less pleasure in contemplation but which in addition will marshal your thoughts in perfect order and ensure that no chapter, no verse, no sentence of your poetry is overlooked. There is much quiet joy in writing: there is exercise for the imagination, escape from the shackled body, solace for the troubled mind. If the story is fiction, then you can dwell in realms long sought and never attained, you can picture your own Utopia and take up abode there and have for your neighbours only those you love best. You can make the impossible come true, if you are writing a novel; you can make happen the things you have badly wanted to happen, and only when your book is finished and put away do they become unreal again. If the story is fact, then it is a part of your autobiography; it is a part of you yourself, and if it is dull reading, that is your own fault; you had better let your life run in new channels henceforward. If the story has appeal, then you have brought into its pages poignant memories, and you have written well.

So with this book I planned. It would mean, not sitting with a pencil in my hand and paper on my knee, but going out again to Settle and starting the journey afresh, tramping once more with the same enthusiasm along every yard of the way, staying a second time with the friends I had met, living anew every incident, every disappointment, every supreme joy. This time, the journey would take not days but months: I could linger where I liked for as long as I liked. I could stay a week in the bright sunshine of Buckden were I so minded, or amongst the Northumbrian heather; and what could it matter then that the December storms were lashing the window as I wrote? Yes, I could transform the cold nights into mellow September evenings, make autumn last until spring.

And perhaps my pen would be able to tell a few of my thoughts and scraps of my philosophy, and even divulge a little of the secret yearnings of my heart. I might, in my own poor fashion, pay a tribute to the girl of my dreams, though I could not hope to tell what she has meant to me in the days that are gone, nor how, through her, I have been privileged to glimpse a happiness that is almost sacred. She is with me yet, as sweet and charitable as ever, and as far out of reach. She is not of my world. To think of her as a human being is to treat her with disrespect. I pray earnestly that she will never leave me, even though I can meet her only in dreams, for without her guiding influence I should stumble in darkness. If my book were to be written, or even started, she must first give encouragement, or at least not frown on the project, for what more natural than that I should wish to discuss it with her every night? But let that consent be given, and my every leisure moment would be devoted to the task; gladly, for then I could pretend that it was to please her that I wrote, and let every word be a dedication of gratitude for all the comfort and blessing she had brought to me.

I walked slowly up the last hill. All around now were familiar scenes, and Settle would be before me when I breasted the slope. Eleven days had elapsed since I left the town behind, and two hundred miles had passed underfoot; I had been far beyond the hills that filled the northern horizon, and had returned.

The sky had been stormy all the way from Ingleton. There were times when sudden squalls swept fiercely from the west and heavy rain drove across the countryside in blinding sheets, so that the distant view was obscured and I could see no more than the

streaming lane ahead; there were intervals when the sun shone
brilliantly from a cloudless sky, and brought something of heaven
to earth. There had been days during the past week when the
weather was unkind; more often it had made my way pleasant, but
its greatest benefaction it saved for the moment I came to the top
of the last hill. Out of the damp vapours that still lingered in the air
after the last shower, was born a rainbow. At first it was indistinct,
and my eyes could not easily trace its course; then, as I watched, it
developed first into a graceful curve of most wonderful tints, and
then gradually became a brilliant array of dazzling colours. Behind,
the sky was black where the clouds were piled up over the
Pennines, and against the dark background the rainbow was
limned so clearly and so vividly that I stood rooted in amazement
at the spectacle. The bow spanned the way before me, having an
end in the fields on either side. The colours were intense, giving a
weird touch of substance to the apparition. As I watched, a second
and larger curve appeared above it, whereupon the mist that hung
over the scene began to dissolve, and through the glorious double
arch I saw the green dome of Giggleswick School chapel appear
out of the gloom, then the square tower of the church, and then,
gradually, the roofs of Settle with majestic Castlebergh reared
behind.

I was conscious of a stillness; there was nobody within sight; the
revelation was for me alone. How strange that I should seek a
rainbow, and find it here at the very end of my journey, spanning
the place whence I had started! I stood in awe at the phenomenon,
thrilled at the beauty that so wondrously illumined the evil sky. I
felt, curiously, that there was clearly a message for me in this
manifestation of God's bountiful goodness but, though I pondered
long after the rainbow was dispelled, I found it not. It may be that I
was being shown the way to the happiness I longed for, if only my
search was assiduous enough; it showed me the way back, to home
and friends. Or it may have been a promise of happy days that
were to be mine when I could again return to the hills. It may have
meant simply farewell. Whatever its meaning, it left me trembling
and vaguely disquieted.

And so I came again to Settle.